SOURCE SELECTION STEP BY STEP

A Guide for Every Member of the Acquisition Team

SOURCE SELECTION STEP BY STEP

A Guide for Every Member of the Acquisition Team

Charles D. Solloway, Jr., CPCM

MANAGEMENTCONCEPTS

MANAGEMENTCONCEPTS

8230 Leesburg Pike, Suite 800
Vienna, VA 22182
(703) 790-9595
Fax: (703) 790-1371
www.managementconcepts.com

Copyright © 2011 by Management Concepts, Inc.

Printed in the United States of America

Library of Congress Cataloging-in-Publication Data

Solloway, Charles D.

   Source selection step by step/Charles D. Solloway Jr.
    p. cm.
   ISBN 978-1-56726-300-8
1. Government contractors—United States. 2. Public contracts—United States. 3. Government purchasing—United States. I. Title.
HD3861.U6S65 2011
352.5'30973—dc22

                       2010046108

10   9   8   7   6   5   4   3   2   1

About the Author

Charles D. Solloway, Jr., CPCM, has more than 40 years of acquisition experience in the government and private sector. As a civilian employee of the U.S. Army, he held positions as buyer, contract specialist, contract negotiator, procurement analyst, contracting officer, director of contracting, and principal assistant responsible for contracting. Solloway twice received the U.S. Army's highest civilian award, the Decoration for Exceptional Civilian Service, for innovations in contracting.

A Certified Professional Contracts Manager (CPCM) and a Fellow of the National Contract Management Association (NCMA), Solloway serves on the NCMA Special Topic Committee on Contract Management Education.

As an educator he has authored a number of textbooks on acquisition topics and has taught thousands of acquisition professionals from both the public and private sectors.

To Jo Ann

Contents

Exhibits

Tables

Preface

Some have called U.S. government acquisition the most complex business arena in the world, and that is not an unwarranted characterization. Thousands of laws and executive orders and innumerable pages of regulations, policy letters, and procedural guidance directly influence the federal acquisition process. And— as anyone connected with federal acquisition knows—changes are nearly constant.

No particular aspect of federal acquisition is more complex and burdened by rules than the source selection process. The laws and regulations that govern the process of selecting a contractor to provide goods and services to the federal government are there primarily to promote social and economic goals, to foster fairness and visibility, and to guard against the inappropriate expenditure of taxpayer dollars. The rules themselves, however, often make it difficult to emulate the kind of efficient and expedient acquisition that often takes place in the private sector.

To function effectively within the parameters of the federal source selection process, acquisition professionals must know the rules. Just as important, they must know how and when to apply those rules in a way that achieves a positive outcome.

The key to a successful source selection is—and always has been—the application of prudent business judgment by knowledgeable and competent professionals who have the ability to function effectively and efficiently within the established constraints of law and regulation.

About This Book

Source Selection Step by Step is more than a listing of the steps in the process. It aims to give the reader insight by examining the evolution of the process and by identifying the issues that must be addressed at each step in the process. In this way, those charged with carrying out the process for the federal government can make better business decisions.

The most daunting challenge in writing this book was to make it meaningful for the neophyte, the "old hand," and everyone in between. For the sake of readability and to promote understanding, the book strives to address a relatively complex subject with maximum clarity, a dose of common sense, and minimum jargon.

Some of the government terms in the text, such as *bundling* or *nondevelopmental item*, may be unfamiliar to the reader. Rather than interfere with the readability of the text by using asterisks and footnotes, we have chosen to identify these and other government-specific terms in a definitions appendix.

To add clarity and to furnish food for thought, the book quotes portions of Comptroller General protest opinions and portions of U.S. Court of Federal Claims opinions. The full text of these opinions generally involves a number of issues, including some that are not germane to the specific issue being addressed. Accordingly, with very few exceptions, we have chosen not to include the full opinions.

In many chapters we have included exhibits showing examples and outlines of government and other forms and formats. These should be considered examples only and not recommendations. If you are a government employee, your agency's own forms and formats may be just as good or better. If they are not, you may want to suggest some changes.

How This Book Is Organized

This book is organized into discrete parts to make it easier for the acquisition professional to access information readily at the workplace.

Part I provides background information to help the reader fully understand the origins of contemporary source selection and the current source selection environment. It explains the two best value source selection methods: lowest-price technically acceptable (LPTA) and tradeoff.

Part II addresses the actions that must take place, and the decisions that must be made, before soliciting proposals from competing contractors. As adequate preparation is key to success in source selection, this part contains a substantial amount of information.

Part III addresses the process of soliciting proposals from competing contractors and preparing for the evaluation of those proposals.

Part IV fully describes the evaluation process, including merit/technical evaluation, past performance evaluation, and price/cost evaluation. It also explains the rules on obtaining any needed clarifications from competing contractors when award is to be made without holding discussions.

Part V explains the process of establishing the competitive range, the dynamic nature of the competitive range, holding communications with competing contractors before establishing the competitive range, and holding meaningful discussions with those in the competitive range. It also addresses the exchanges with contractors that are prohibited by law and regulation.

Part VI addresses proposal revisions, the reevaluation of proposals, and the procedures for making and documenting the source selection decision.

Part VII includes information on the notices to contractors that must be made before or after award, the conduct and sensitivity of debriefings, and the adverse impact of protests filed by disappointed offerors.

Part VIII addresses ways in which the source selection process can be streamlined, including awarding task order contracts and awarding task orders under those contracts.

Part IX describes some of the alternatives to conventional source selection that are permitted under the Federal Acquisition Regulation. These include the advisory multistep procedure, selection of contractors for architect-engineer services, best value selections for simplified acquisitions, source selection for commercial items and services, the combined synopsis/solicitation for commercial items, and broad agency announcements.

Part X is the last, but by no means the least, of the parts. It addresses ethical considerations in source selection, including the protection of source selection information and post-government employment restrictions for source selection officials.

In addition to these ten parts, the book contains four appendices:

Appendix I provides real-life examples of how various military and civilian agencies score or rate proposals.

Appendix II is an example of one agency's request for proposal (RFP) instructions to competing contractors on how to prepare proposals. It also shows how the agency explained to these competing contractors the proposal evaluation factors and subfactors and their relative importance. This appendix also demonstrates the use of sample tasks in awarding a task order contract.

Appendix III presents definitions of key terms used in the source selection process.

Appendix IV lists a number of additional source selection resources available to acquisition team members.

I hope you will find this to be a complete and useful how-to source selection book for every member of the acquisition team. Good luck to you and your team in your source selections.

—Chuck Solloway

January 2011

PART I

THE FOUNDATIONS OF SOURCE SELECTION

This part is essential for the less-experienced professional in understanding the basics of source selection, the current definition of best value, and the advantages and disadvantages of the two primary types of competitive best value acquisitions: lowest-price technically acceptable (LPTA) and tradeoff. It also identifies other sources of guidance and information, both private and governmental, on source selection.

While essential for the new acquisition professional, this part may also prove to be a useful memory jogger for more experienced source selection personnel. It will help all readers, regardless of their experience, by setting the stage for understanding and applying the material presented in the later parts of this book.

CHAPTER 1

BASIC REQUIREMENTS FOR AWARD OF A CONTRACT

Before we tackle the subject of source selection, it is helpful to briefly examine some of the basic requirements for awarding a contract.

Regardless of the manner in which a source is selected, an authorized contracting officer normally cannot make an award to a contractor unless he or she has determined that:

- The contractor is *responsible.* In general terms, this means the contractor has a satisfactory record of perseverance and integrity and that the contractor either has, or has made provision to obtain, the necessary resources to do the job.

  As a part of the responsibility determination, contracting officers must consult the Federal Awardee Performance and Integrity Information System (FAPIIS). This relatively new online system gathers information from various government databases. This includes past performance information from the Past Performance Information Retrieval System (PPIRS) and information on contractor integrity or perseverance from the Excluded Parties List System (EPLS), which contains suspension and debarment information on contractors.

When appropriate, the government may establish special standards of responsibility for any particular acquisition, provided that contractors are so notified when they are solicited for bids, offers, or quotes.

- The proposed contractor (offeror, bidder, or quoter) is responsive. In general terms, this means that the contractor has followed the instructions in the solicitation and has agreed before award to meet all the requirements of the proposed government contract. In negotiated procurements, as described in FAR Part 15, competing contractors that are initially found to have a nonresponsive proposal may be given an opportunity to become responsive through proposal revision if discussions (negotiations) are held and revisions are permitted.

- The price (or cost) has been determined by the contracting officer to be fair and reasonable.

- Money has been appropriated for the purpose of the contract, and the contracting officer has received the proper notification from agency fiscal authorities that the funds are available for use in awarding a contract. This notification of availability is often referred to as *fund certification.*

Only when these requirements have been met (or, in exceedingly rare instances, have been waived) may a contracting officer with the requisite authority execute a contract on behalf of the government. This is true regardless of the source selection process used.

CHAPTER 2

THE SOURCE SELECTION PROCESSES

Source selection is the term used to describe the processes through which the government selects a contractor—a source—to furnish goods or services.

Many acquisition officials consider the selection of a contractor to be the most crucial of all the elements in the acquisition cycle. After all, they point out, it is usually far less difficult and far less expensive to change the terms of a contract than it is to terminate a contractor for default and go through the tedious and expensive process of reprocurement. If an agency selects the wrong contractor, even the most carefully crafted contract will not compensate for the poor source selection.

Government acquisition personnel select contractors in one of two ways:

- They prepare the appropriate justifications, get required approvals, and award a contract on a noncompetitive basis.
- They award a contract on the basis of competition.

When award is made on the basis of competition (either full and open competition or limited competition), contractors are normally selected using one of three selection processes:

- Award to the responsible, responsive offeror or bidder with the lowest price when only a price has been requested and there are no accompanying written or oral proposals.
- Award to the lowest offer among those responsible offerors that, in addition to a price, have submitted a written or oral proposal (or both) that has been found to be acceptable. This method is called lowest-price technically acceptable (LPTA).
- Award to the responsible contractor offering the best value to the government (which may or may not be the lowest price), considering both price/cost factors and those non-price factors identified in the government solicitation and addressed in the contractor's proposal. This is called the tradeoff process.

The tradeoff process was traditionally considered to be the only best value process. However, in 1997 the language defining *best value* in the Federal Acquisition Regulation (FAR), the acquisition bible of the executive agencies, was changed. *Best value* is now defined as an outcome (rather than a process) that may be achieved through LPTA, tradeoff, or some combination of these two processes.

Notwithstanding this change in the FAR, many people in the acquisition community still use *best value* as a synonym for *tradeoff* in their communications with people both within and outside the acquisition community. *Best value* is also frequently used as a synonym for *tradeoff* in articles published in professional magazines and even in some of the protest opinions issued by the Comptroller General or the Court of Federal Claims. It is a longstanding habit that has been hard to break.

The part of the FAR dealing with source selection is FAR Part 15, Contracting by Negotiation. The source selection processes and procedures described in Part 15 deal only with LPTA or tradeoff. Accordingly, we focus on those two processes in this book.

Exhibit 2-1 is an overview of the activities that take place during the source selection process. Exhibits 2-2 and 2-3 are graphic representations of the process, starting with identifying the government requirement and ending at selecting the source. These exhibits may include terms and actions not yet familiar to the reader. If that is the case, it is suggested that the reader examine the exhibits now just to get an overall feel for this complex process. The reader can then refer back to these exhibits, where appropriate, as he or she proceeds through the text. For the benefit of the reader, these exhibits will appear again in Chapter 38.

EXHIBIT 2-1   The Normal Sequence of Events in Source Selection

When award is to be made without holding discussions

1. Identify the requirement.
2. Planning begins; assign responsibilities.
3. Market research begins.*
4. Prepare the acquisition plan (AP) and the source selection plan (SSP).
5. Issue the draft request for proposal (RFP), if any, and conduct other presolicitation exchanges.**
6. Issue a synopsis of the requirement at www.fedbizopps.gov, the government-wide point of entry (GPE). This notifies the public that a solicitation is to be issued and often occurs at the same time as activity 7, preparation of the solicitation.
7. Prepare the solicitation. A request for proposal is used for most source selections other than simplified acquisitions. Simplified acquisitions often are accomplished using a request for quotation (RFQ).
8. Issue the solicitation.
9. Conduct the preproposal conference or site visit, if any.
10. Receive proposals.
11. Evaluate proposals.
12. Obtain clarifications, where appropriate.
13. Select the source, document the rationale, and make the award.***
14. Notify competitors, and offer debriefings.
15. Hold debriefings.

When discussions are to be held

1. Identify the requirement.
2. Planning begins; assign responsibilities.
3. Market research begins.*
4. Prepare the acquisition plan and the source selection plan.
5. Issue the draft RFP, if any, and conduct other presolicitation exchanges.**
6. Issue a synopsis of the requirement at www.fedbizopps.gov, the government-wide point of entry (GPE). This notifies the public that a solicitation is to be issued and often occurs at the same time as activity 7, preparation of the solicitation.
7. Prepare the solicitation. A request for proposal is used for most source selections other than simplified acquisitions. Simplified acquisitions often are accomplished using a request for quotation.
8. Issue the solicitation.
9. Conduct the preproposal conference or site visit, if any.
10. Receive proposals.
11. Evaluate proposals.
12. Conduct communications, where appropriate.
13. Establish the competitive range.
14. Notify those not placed in range; offer debriefings.
15. Hold debriefings at a time determined by the contracting officer. They may be delayed until after award at the request of a competing contractor or if the contracting officer chooses to do so.
16. Hold discussions with those in the competitive range.
17. Receive interim proposal revisions, if permitted or required.
18. Request and receive final proposal revisions.
19. Reevaluate proposals.
20. Select the source, document the rationale, and make the award.***
21. Notify competing contractors of the award, and offer debriefings.
22. Hold debriefings.

---

* Steps 3 through 5 may be concurrent.
** Presolicitation exchanges may be synopsized at the GPE.
*** Advance notifications before award may be given to competing offerors when certain socioeconomic programs are involved, such as set-asides for small businesses.

EXHIBIT 2-2   Flow Chart for Award without Discussions

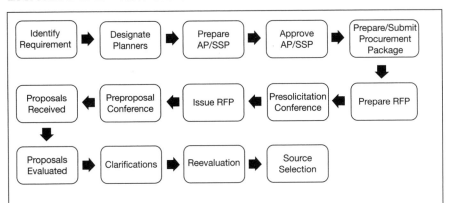

- Requests for information or draft requests for proposal may be issued at any time before the final RFP is prepared.
- Presolicitation conferences may be held before or following preparation of the RFP.
- Clarifications are obtained at the discretion of the contracting officer.
- Synopsis at the governmentwide point of entry (GPE) is normally required before the RFP is issued and again after the contract is awarded.

EXHIBIT 2-3   Flow Chart for Award after Discussions

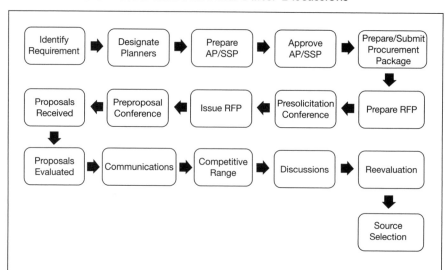

- Requests for information (RFIs) or draft RFPs may be issued at any time before the final RFP is prepared.
- Presolicitation conferences may be held prior to or following preparation of the RFP.
- Communications are conducted as required.
- Synopsis at the governmentwide point of entry (GPE) is normally required before the RFP is issued and again after the contract is awarded.

CHAPTER 3

SOURCES OF GUIDANCE FOR THE ACQUISITION PROFESSIONAL

The acquisition professional looks for official guidance on the source selection process in:

- The Federal Acquisition Regulation (FAR).

- Agency regulations that implement or supplement the FAR. While the FAR applies to most source selections in the federal executive agencies and thus provides for consistency in the process, agency regulations may vary widely in how they implement or supplement the FAR.

- Precedent established by the Comptroller General (Comp Gen), who is head of the Government Accountability Office (GAO), in decisions made in response to preaward or postaward protests from potential or actual offerors. In essence, Comp Gen opinions interpret and, in some instances, supplement the FAR. They are published on the GAO website (http://www.gao.gov/legal/decisions.html).

- Precedent established by the federal courts (most often the Court of Federal Claims) in findings resulting from preaward or postaward protests or other legal action initiated by potential or actual offerors. Like Comp Gen decisions, protest decisions of the Court of Federal Claims also are available online (http://www.uscfc.uscourts.gov/opinions_decisions_general/ Published).

- The *Federal Register,* a government publication that announces proposed acquisition rules and final rules that may affect the source selection process.

The FAR is periodically updated as new laws are passed or executive orders are executed, or when the federal executive agencies themselves otherwise see the need for change. Agency regulations are changed in the same manner. Interim FAR changes are made through issuance of a government publication called the *Federal Acquisition Circular.*

For various reasons, including efficiency and expense, disappointed contractors are more likely to seek redress from the GAO than through the courts. Thus, Comp Gen opinions generally exert more influence on the source selection process. Often precedents that have been established by the Comp Gen or the courts, sometimes referred to as *case law*, are ultimately reflected in changes to the FAR and in agency supplements to the FAR.

Other sources of guidance for the acquisition professional include source selection manuals published by various agencies. One example is the *Army Source Selection Manual,* an unusually detailed agency source selection guide published as an appendix to the *Army Federal Acquisition Regulation Supplement* (AFARS). NASA also has a source selection manual, and the Department of Energy has an acquisition guide that includes source selection information. All are available online and can be accessed through websites such as www.wifcon.com and www.usa.gov.

Some agency source selection manuals tend to emphasize getting organized for source selection, the channels of communication, and various logistical matters, rather than discussing in depth the many choices and business decisions that must be made by acquisition team personnel throughout the process. Nonetheless, all of these government manuals furnish valuable source selection guidance. In particular, they provide forms and formats for myriad source selection documents, and they define the source selection terminology used by the agency.

A number of commercial publications publish and discuss the most recent Comp Gen or federal court cases and the impact they may have on the source selection process. Further, a number of private-sector organizations and some government organizations offer professional and up-to-date training in the source selection process.

Numerous government websites, including the sites of the General Services Administration and the Defense Acquisition University, also offer source selection guidance, as do private websites. For example, the website Where in Federal Contracting? (WIFCON), at www.wifcon.com, includes links to numerous legal opinions and government regulations relevant to source selection. It also has a chat room for acquisition professionals to use to discuss any aspect of government contracting, including source selection.

Another private-sector source of information is the National Contract Management Association (NCMA, www.ncmahq.org). NCMA publishes *Contract Management,* a monthly magazine that often contains articles pertaining to government source selection.

If an offeror formally protests the manner in which a particular source selection is being or has been conducted, it may cost the government substantial amounts of money and cause significant delays, especially if the protest is upheld. Accordingly, it is crucial that government acquisition personnel remain knowledgeable and current regarding changes in regulations and any precedents that have been established by the Comp Gen and the federal courts.

Appendix IV provides a list of additional source selection resources.

CHAPTER 4

DIFFERENCES BETWEEN LPTA AND TRADEOFF SOURCE SELECTIONS

Both lowest-price technically acceptable (LPTA) and tradeoff source selections require that the government evaluate offerors on at least one other factor in addition to price or cost. In fact, the government may use any number of evaluation factors for either type of source selection. These non-cost factors are generally referred to as *merit factors* or *technical factors*. Each factor may have any number of subfactors or may have no subfactors at all.

In an LPTA selection, the proposals must be deemed acceptable on the merit evaluation factor(s) in order to be considered for award. Award is then made to the acceptable contractor with the lowest price or cost, provided that the price or cost has been determined to be fair and reasonable. Some refer to LPTA merit evaluation factors as *go/no go* or *pass/fail* factors. A competing contractor whose proposal is unacceptable (or remains unacceptable after discussions and revisions, if applicable) on even *one* of the evaluation factors is not eligible to receive a contract award.

In a tradeoff procurement, contractors are scored or rated with regard to the merit factors, which are sometimes called *variable factors*. For example, one contractor may be given a rating of "acceptable," while another may be found "outstanding," and yet others could be found "marginal" or "unacceptable." In contrast to LPTA selections, a tradeoff contract award may be made to an offeror other than the one proposing the lowest price or cost if the source selection authority deems the increase in quality, decrease in performance risk, or both to be worth the additional money. Tradeoff procurements are much like the purchasing we do in our private lives. We look at the differences in quality (as we perceive it) in canned soup brands, for example, and then decide if it is worth an extra 30 cents to buy Campbell's® rather than the store brand.

If a source selection combines both go/no-go factors and variable factors, it is considered to be a tradeoff source selection. This is so even if only one of several evaluation factors is variable (comparatively scored).

To better understand how these two source selection approaches differ, consider the following hypothetical situation. A fictional LPTA procurement has three evaluation factors:

1. Contractor technical approach
2. Key personnel
3. Price/cost.

Three contractors, A, B, and C, have submitted proposals. The offer from A has been judged to be unacceptable. Contractor B has a great technical approach and top-of-the-line personnel. Contractor C has an acceptable but less attractive approach, and its personnel just meet government standards. Award will be made without holding discussions.

The offerors propose the following prices:

A. $1 million
B. $2 million
C. $1.98 million.

Contractor A cannot get the award, even though it has offered the lowest price, because its proposal is not acceptable. B cannot get the award because it did not have the lowest price among acceptable proposals. C is given the award.

In a tradeoff procurement, especially one in which the government has made merit factors more important than price, the government could have selected contractor B, which might have been the real best value. Under LPTA, the government must select the lowest price offered among "acceptable" proposals. This is so even if the difference in price is miniscule. In an LPTA procurement, the government must be prepared for a situation in which it may be compelled to award to the "worst acceptable proposal."

Notwithstanding this one significant drawback, the LPTA approach has a number of advantages. When determining which of the two source selection processes to use for a particular procurement, acquisition planners must consider both the advantages and disadvantages that are inherent in each process.

ADVANTAGES OF LPTA

- Evaluation factors must be established, but they are not assigned relative importance. Each factor is equally as important as any other. This makes preparing a source selection plan less complex and less time-consuming than it would be if a tradeoff process were used.

- Evaluating proposals is not normally as difficult as it would be in a tradeoff process because it is not necessary to variably score or rate competing contractors' proposals against the government evaluation criteria. Instead, contractors are simply judged either "acceptable" or "not acceptable" on the evaluation factors. Documentation of the bases for these judgments is made a part of the contract file.

- Because award is made to the lowest price or cost among acceptable proposals, the award is relatively easy to document and relatively easy to defend if a contractor protests the choice made by the government.

- The strong emphasis on low cost or price may encourage competing contractors to "sharpen their pencils" and may well result in prices that are lower than those that would have been obtained in a tradeoff process.

- Of the two source selection processes, LPTA is usually less labor-intensive for the government and usually takes less time.

Considering all the advantages to the government—including lower administrative costs and less consumption of time—government planners could reasonably conclude that using LPTA will result in the overall best value to the government for a specific procurement. This may be especially true when acquisition planners anticipate that there will be minimal quality or risk discriminators between likely competitors.

ADVANTAGES AND DISADVANTAGES OF TRADEOFF

- Tradeoff increases the likelihood of obtaining the true best value among competing proposals because it gives the government (the appointed source selection authority) far more flexibility in applying business judgment.

- The procuring agency must establish evaluation factors and determine their relative importance. This normally consumes more planning time than the LPTA process. It must be carefully done, because the government will have to ultimately make business judgments that are consistent with the evaluation factors and their relative importance as set forth in the government solicitation.

- Proposal evaluators must score or rate each competing contractor on each evaluation factor in the solicitation and must prepare supporting rationale. Again, this is more labor-intensive than LPTA.

- Tradeoff is a relatively subjective process, and the source selection authority is given great latitude in choosing a contractor. The law requires only that he or she make a rational (reasonable) decision that is compatible with the evaluation scheme set forth in the solicitation. He or she is expected to exercise good business judgment and to clearly and persuasively document the rationale for award. The source selection authority thus must assume a great deal of responsibility.

- Because individual business judgment is exercised in the award, and because the evaluation process is more complex, there is more opportunity for error, disagreement, and protest when using tradeoff.

Notwithstanding any disadvantages inherent in the tradeoff process, acquisition officials may reasonably conclude that the amount of money involved, the performance risk, and/or the criticality of a particular procurement warrants using this traditional method of obtaining best value. Tradeoff permits the application of reasoned business judgment, rather than the selection of a source by a calculator.

AGENCY GUIDANCE

Some published agency guidance may encourage the use of one or the other of these processes. For example, the *Army Source Selection Manual* states, "On most acquisitions the tradeoff process will be the most effective and will result in the best value to the government.... In the majority of acquisitions, the LPTA process may not be an appropriate methodology since past performance is not normally considered." (Note that regardless of the source selection process used, past performance is always considered in responsibility determinations.)

Another agency manual, NAVAIR Instruction 4200.39A, says of LPTA, "It is generally not appropriate for the acquisition of design or development effort, software integration, or professional services." These and other agency manuals often use qualifying terms, such as "on most acquisitions" and "normally", so that source selection officials are free to make exceptions to agency preferences.

CHAPTER 5

BASIC ISSUES IN SOURCE SELECTION

Historically, the government obtained best value—sometimes called *greatest value*—using what is now known as the trade-off process. The acquisition regulations that preceded the FAR indicated that, while awarding to the contractor proposing the lowest price was the norm, factors other than price could also be considered for some specific types of procurement actions. The acquisition regulations gave as examples cost-reimbursement contracts and research and development (R&D) contracts.

During this time, the great majority of tradeoff selections, though not all, were for R&D efforts. This was an obvious use of the process since the government was looking for contractors with the best ideas and the talented personnel needed to bring those ideas to fruition. Tradeoff allowed the government to emphasize these qualitative non-cost issues over price or cost.

THE IMPACT OF TOTAL QUALITY MANAGEMENT

In the 1980s and in the early 1990s, U.S. businesses and the U.S. government began embracing the principles of total quality management (TQM) as championed by a number of management gurus. While experts' opinions may have differed on some issues related to TQM, there was near unanimity on one principle: Managers should discontinue the practice of awarding to the low bidder and should instead consider quality issues as well as cost when making an award decision.

As businesses and government began to implement TQM, many government procurements that had been awarded on a low-bid basis in the past were now being conducted as best value (tradeoff) procurements, especially contracts for services. It was reasoned that awarding an engineering service contract (or even a janitorial service contract) to a contractor that could just barely meet the requirements of being a responsible contractor might be false economy. Using a tradeoff method would permit award to an exceptional contractor that could be expected to furnish better service to the customer and perhaps require less oversight.

This new emphasis on tradeoff is reflected in Office of Federal Procurement Policy Letter 93-1, which states that "agencies should ensure that their acquisition strategy will result in the acquisition of services from a quality vendor that constitute the best value considering cost and other relevant factors, and yield the greatest benefit to the government."

Shortly thereafter, in October 1994, President Bill Clinton issued Executive Order 12931, which directed agencies to place more emphasis on past performance and promote best value, rather than simply low cost, in selecting sources for both supplies and services.

In addition to these regulatory changes, the FAR was changed to require consideration of quality as well as cost in making best value awards.

BACKLASH AND CHANGE

There was some backlash against these government TQM efforts. Some agency officials did not want to use tradeoff exclusively to obtain the "best value" that was being required or encouraged by regulation. They believed that LPTA was often a better fit. Others complained that the government appeared to be spending inordinate amounts of money for marginal increases in quality. Still others pointed to the growth in procurement administrative lead time (PALT)—the time it takes to conduct a procurement—and attributed at least part of this growth to the increase in the use of the tradeoff process. And it became obvious to everyone that tradeoff acquisitions were more labor-intensive for the government, at a time when agency contracting personnel were being asked to accomplish more with fewer resources.

In 1997, the FAR was changed to define best value as an outcome rather than a process and to specifically identify both LPTA and tradeoff as source selection processes that could lead to the acquisition of best value. This change was not universally applauded. Some pointed out well-known and oft-quoted warnings against making source selections based on the lowest price. For example, John Ruskin, the British essayist, once said, "The common law of business prohibits paying a little and getting a lot—it cannot be done. If you deal with the lowest bidder, it is well to add something for the risk you run, and if you do that you will have enough to pay for something better."[1] About a century later, quality management advocate W. Edwards Deming reportedly opined, "He that has a rule to give his business to the lowest bidder deserves to get rooked."[2]

Notwithstanding the aversion to a low bid philosophy by TQM proponents, there are, as noted earlier, distinct advantages to using LPTA when conditions indicate an acceptable level of risk in using this more direct and more objective approach.

On the other hand, the government should be permitted—and perhaps even encouraged—to trade off merit factors and price to get the best deal whenever the importance of the requirement, the risk of successful contractor performance, or both warrant the associated additional time and expense. This is, of course, a business judgment that can be subjected to second-guessing and Monday-morning quarterbacking, especially if the procurement is not entirely successful.

THE USE OF GOOD BUSINESS JUDGMENT

Regardless of the source selection process chosen, good business judgment must be exercised in selecting a contractor, and cost must always be an important factor in the source selection authority's decision. Overspending is damaging to the image of government acquisition personnel in the eyes of the public and of Congress and can only lead to further restrictions on the amount of discretion government officials are allowed.

It is also clear that any streamlining techniques that would reduce the lead time and process costs inherent in tradeoff procurement should be encouraged. A number of streamlining techniques are described in Part VIII.

Finally, it should be recognized that knowledgeable, well-trained people are essential to making these source selection processes work. To achieve the best results, acquisition personnel must truly understand the processes and the issues involved, rather than being trained merely to follow directions. The acquisition officials who reportedly paid $300 for a hammer may have done so in accordance with regulatory guidance—but they may not have used good business judgment.

Not only can good business judgment applied by well-trained personnel save money, it can also reduce the likelihood of a successful protest and the consequent adverse impact on the government—including delays in contract performance and the incurrence of significant additional expense.

Notes

1. John Ruskin was a 19th century art critic and social thinker. Although this business balance principle and quotation is universally attributed to him, it has not been linked to a specific essay or other published work. See, for example, Wikipedia, "Common Law of Business Balance," http://en.wikipedia.org/wiki/Common_Law_of_Business_Balance (accessed October 18, 2010).
2. William Edwards Deming, *Out of the Crisis* (Cambridge, MA: The MIT Press, 2000).

PART II

PREPARING FOR SOURCE SELECTION

This part of the book addresses how various agencies organize for source selection and the concerns acquisition planners must address, including creating the source selection plan, choosing non-cost and cost-related evaluation factors, using past performance as an evaluation factor, establishing the relative importance of the evaluation factors, using oral presentations, designing proposal-preparation instructions, and establishing a rating method.

Chapter 6

THE ACQUISITION PLAN AND SOURCE SELECTION PLAN

FAR Part 7 requires that planning take place for all procurements and provides a format for written acquisition plans. Agency regulations, in turn, stipulate the size and character of procurements that require a written acquisition plan. For example, one agency may require written plans for all procurements in excess of $1 million, while another agency may establish only $100,000 as the threshold for a written plan.

The FAR also requires that the head of the agency (or a designee) designate planners for acquisition. As a practical matter, planning normally begins with the identification of a requirement and the assignment of program responsibility to a specific program official. That program official must—in view of the matters that have to be addressed—quickly enlist the participation of a contracting officer.

The acquisition plan format prescribed in FAR 7.105 provides that the acquisition team address a significant number of issues, including some that pertain especially to source selection. For example, one part of the plan is devoted exclusively to source selection procedures, while other parts, such as the treatment of contract cost and the consideration of streamlining techniques, also pertain to source selection matters. An outline of the FAR-prescribed format for the acquisition plan is shown in Exhibit 6-1.

THE ACQUISITION TEAM

Planning for an acquisition is the joint responsibility of all members of the acquisition team and should begin as soon as a requirement (a government need) is identified. FAR 1.102 states that an acquisition team consists of "all participants in Government acquisition[,] including not only representatives of the technical, supply, and procurement communities[,] but also the customers they serve, and the contractors who provide the products and services." In some agencies, the government multidisciplinary team that is established to guide a requirement through the source selection process is known as an integrated product team (IPT).

Note that FAR 1.102 includes contractors as a part of the team. It recognizes that the government should have input from the private sector if it is to be a smart buyer.

FAR Part 1 goes on to state that the role of each acquisition team member is to exercise "personal initiative" and "sound business judgment" in providing the best value to the customer. It further makes it clear at FAR 1.102(d) that acquisition planners have a great deal of discretion by providing that any acquisition strategy that is not prohibited by law (including case law), regulation, or executive order is a permissible exercise of authority. This discretion permits and encourages the use of creative acquisition techniques, including techniques designed to streamline the acquisition process.

The FAR also makes it abundantly clear that contractor participation should not be limited to simply proposal preparation and contract performance. In FAR Part 15—which deals principally with LPTA and tradeoff acquisition—officials are encouraged to "exchange information among all interested parties from the identification of a requirement." Those "interested parties" include potential offerors (contractors), government contracting and program personnel, and end users (FAR 15.201).

THE SOURCE SELECTION STRATEGY

Both FAR and agency regulations require that acquisition planning address the source selection strategy. Most often, agencies create a separate document known as the *source selection plan* (SSP), which formalizes the strategy. The SSP may be referenced in, repeated in, or attached to the acquisition plan. See Exhibit 6-2 for a sample SSP from the Department of the Army Contracting Center for Excellence.

Typically, an SSP will address such matters as:

- The assignment of source selection authority
- The process to be used—LPTA or tradeoff
- Evaluation factors and any significant subfactors
- The relative importance of the factors and subfactors (for tradeoff)
- Socioeconomic considerations, such as the use of small businesses, small disadvantaged businesses, and women-owned businesses
- The source selection organization and the people or types of people who will act as evaluators or advisors
- The information that will be required in proposals and the manner in which the information is to be conveyed by competing contractors
- Any special considerations—for example, whether multiphase selection or streamlining techniques will be used, licenses will be needed, or coordination with other agencies will be required

- Schedules and milestones
- Forms to be used, such as evaluation forms and nondisclosure forms.

Each individual agency establishes internal responsibilities for preparing the plan and specifies plan review procedures and approval levels.

As may be seen in Exhibits 6-1 and 6-2, the written acquisition plan provided for in FAR Part 7 includes information required in the SSP plus a great deal more.

CHANGING THE PLAN

In many agencies, there are various levels for review and approval of both acquisition plans and source selection plans. In some cases, obtaining those reviews and approvals can be an exceptionally tedious, bureaucratic process. Thus, there is a tendency to treat an approved plan as if it were written in stone. However, as time progresses, government planners typically learn more and more about market conditions and capabilities. If there is a benefit to be derived from changing a plan, then it should be changed. Sticking with a game plan that calls for long passes doesn't make much sense when a dense fog has settled over the playing field.

EXHIBIT 6-1   Outline of the Contents of a Written Acquisition Plan (FAR 7.105)

(a) Acquisition background and objectives
1. Statement of need
2. Applicable conditions
3. Cost
(i) Life cycle cost
(ii) Design to cost
(iii) Application of should cost

 4. Required capabilities or performance standards for the supplies or services being acquired; statement of how they are related to the need

 5. Delivery or performance-period requirements

 6. Tradeoffs

 7. Risks

 8. Acquisition streamlining

(b) Plan of action

 1. Sources

 2. Competition

 3. Source selection procedures

 4. Acquisition considerations

 5. Budgeting and funding

 6. Product or service description

 7. Priorities, allocations, and allotments

 8. Contractor vs. government performance

 9. Inherently governmental functions

 10. Management information requirements

 11. Make or buy

 12. Test and evaluation

 13. Logistics considerations

 14. Government-furnished property

 15. Government-furnished information

 16. Environmental and energy conservation objectives

 17. Security considerations

 18. Contract administration

 19. Other considerations

 20. Milestones for the acquisition cycle

 - Additional requirements for major systems
 - Additional requirements for acquisitions involving bundling
 - Additional requirements for telecommuting

EXHIBIT 6-2   Sample Best Value (Tradeoff) Source Selection Plan

Section I: Overview

A. Description of requirement

B. Acquisition approach

Section II: Solicitation provisions

A. Basis for award

B. Factors and subfactors to be evaluated

1. Technical

2. Past performance

3. Small business participation plan

4. Cost or price

C. Evaluation approach

1. Technical evaluation approach

a. Understanding of the requirement

b. Feasibility of approach

c. Flexibility

2. Past performance evaluation approach

3. Price/cost evaluation approach

D. Proposal submission

1. Format

2. File packaging

3. Page count

4. Content requirements

a. Volume I: Technical approach

b. Volume II: Past performance

Section 1: Contract descriptions

Section 2: Performance

Section 3: New corporate entities

Section 4: Past performance questionnaire

c. Volume III: Small business participation plan

d. Volume IV: Price/cost

e. Volume V: Solicitation, offer, and award documents and certifications/representations

Section III: Evaluation organizations and responsibilities

A. Evaluation organizations

    1. Source selection authority (SSA)

    2. Source selection advisory council (SSAC) (Optional)

    3. Source selection evaluation board (SSEB)

    4. Procurement contracting officer (PCO)

B. Responsibilities of the organizational elements

    1. SSA

    2. SSAC

    3. SSEB

    4. PCO

C. Composition of the organizational elements

Section IV: Evaluation procedures

A. Agenda

B. Definitions

C. Rating method

D. Proposal evaluation

E. Source selection

F. Announcement of selection

G. Debriefing of unsuccessful offerors

Section V: Policies, instructions, and standards of conduct

A. General

B. Safeguarding procurement information

C. Evaluation procedures

Appendices

A. Members of and advisors to the source selection evaluation board

B. Source selection participation agreement

C. Summary evaluation form

D. Item for negotiation (IFN) form

E. Item for negotiation evaluation form

Attachments

Past performance questionnaire

CHAPTER 7

ORGANIZING FOR SOURCE SELECTION

In any source selection, there must be a source selection authority, a contracting officer, and one or more evaluators. Sometimes a single person can perform more than one of these roles. The source selection rules and concerns described in this book apply to all competitive negotiated acquisitions, regardless of the size and structure of the organization established for the source selection and the grade levels of those involved.

THE SOURCE SELECTION AUTHORITY

The source selection authority (SSA) is an individual appointed by the agency head to, among other assigned tasks and responsibilities, select the source at the end of the source selection process. If no one else is appointed, the assigned contracting officer is the source selection authority. In other words, to use an IT term the contracting officer is the "default" source selection authority. In some agencies the SSA has traditionally been called the source selection official (SSO).

Who, other than the contracting officer, can be appointed as a source selection authority? There are no governmentwide restrictions, absent any conflicts of interest. Usually the more significant the procurement, the higher on the organization chart agencies will go to appoint the source selection authority.

The source selection authority must be identified early in the acquisition cycle because of the mandatory duties given this individual in FAR 15.303(b). The FAR provides that the source selection authority shall:

- Establish an evaluation team tailored for the particular acquisition
- Approve the source selection strategy or acquisition plan
- Ensure consistency among the various solicitation provisions
- Consider the recommendations of advisory boards or panels (if any)
- Select the best value.

For routine source selections, the contracting officer is most often the source selection authority. He or she will appoint a small group of evaluators to review and evaluate the technical (non-cost) aspects of proposals and assign one or more people to perform a cost or price analysis. Even if the contracting officer is not the source selection authority, he or she always has a key role in the selection process as an advisor to the source selection authority and to others involved in the evaluation process. And, after release of the solicitation, the contracting officer is always the individual who controls any verbal or written contact with competing contractors.

EVALUATORS

The name given to the group of evaluators who rate or score non-cost factors differs from agency to agency and sometimes even within agencies. The agenices use a great number of names. Some of the more common names are:

- Technical evaluation panel (TEP)
- Technical evaluation team (TET)
- Proposal evaluation board (PEB)
- Source selection evaluation board (SSEB).

"FORMAL" AND "OTHER THAN FORMAL" SOURCE SELECTIONS

Governmentwide regulations at one time distinguished between "formal" source selections and "other than formal" source selections. While this is no longer the case, some agency regulations still make this distinction. And some even refer to "other than formal" source selections as "informal," an unfortunate choice of a name for a disciplined process.

The organizational structure for more "formal" source selections (i.e., source selections of higher dollar value or those otherwise determined to be of particular significance) can be relatively complex, as shown in Exhibit 7-1.

In some agencies, a separate group of individuals called a performance risk assessment group (PRAG) may be assigned to evaluate past performance.

ADVISORS

The duties of the source selection advisory council (SSAC), or an equivalent group in other agency organizational structures, are normally to oversee the operations of the source selection evaluation board and advise the source selection authority. Depending on agency regulations or standard agency practices, this advice may or may not include a recommendation as to the contractor(s) to be selected for contract award.

Typically, an SSAC will consist of military personnel, civilians, or both, of relatively high grade and stature. For more formal source selections, agency regulations often recommend or require that SSAC members be at specified grade levels, depending upon the dollar value, complexity, or criticality of the acquisition.

In addition to the SSAC or its equivalent, the SSA may have a number of other advisors, including a business advisor (usually the assigned contracting officer when the SSA is not the contracting officer), a small business advisor, legal counsel, and others.

THE NUMBER OF EVALUATORS AND ADVISORS

The number of evaluators for any given source selection can range from one to more than 100. In fact, some government procuring organizations have assigned as many as 200 people to be evaluators and advisors for a single procurement.

There is no evidence available that links the number of people involved in proposal evaluation with the wisdom of a source selection decision. In fact, some acquisition professionals suspect that too many evaluators and advisors can contribute to communication static and miscommunication between subject matter experts and the source selection authority. Nonetheless, no matter how large or small the crowd, it is important that the proposal evaluators as an entity have the full range of expertise needed to competently address all the evaluation factors in the solicitation.

For more routine source selections, most agencies have established a minimum number of evaluators, either by longstanding practice or regulation. Usually, this is an odd number (3, 5, 7, or 9, for example). Presumably, an odd number of evaluators facilitates voting in the event of a disagreement.

WHERE EVALUATORS AND ADVISORS COME FROM

Technical evaluators, cost evaluators, and advisors are chosen because of their expertise. Most of them are agency employees. But people from other government agencies may be called upon when sufficient expertise is not available in house, when the agency wants to protect itself from charges of organizational bias, or when other agencies will be users of the product or service being procured. (Although it may sound a little cynical, involving the users in the selection process can later reduce the number of complaints about the choices that were made during the evaluation and award phases of the source selection.)

Contractor personnel may also be used as evaluators or advisors. Office of Management and Budget (OMB) guidelines, as described in FAR Subpart 7.5, provide that contractors may participate as "technical advisors to a source selection board" or may participate as a "voting or non-voting member of a source evaluation board." However, common sense tells us that acquisition planners should work closely with legal counsel when contemplating the use of contractor personnel as advisors or evaluators. Issues such as conflicts of interest and protection of source selection and proprietary information must be thoroughly addressed.

The OMB provisions described in the FAR also state that contractors may *not* participate as "a voting member on any source selection board." This is usually not a problem because the FAR provides that the source selection be made by an individual rather than a board.

The use of contractor personnel as evaluators or advisors on a source selection may first require the head of the agency to determine that available government personnel do not have the required expertise. This determination must be made before the contracting officer issues the solicitation. These procedures are fully described in FAR Subpart 37.2, Advisory and Assistance Services.

EVALUATORS' COMPETENCE AND FAIRNESS

Competing contractors have on occasion based protests on the perceived lack of expertise of evaluators or on allegations of evaluator bias. They are rarely successful because protesting contractors have to *show* incompetence or bias, not just proclaim it. For example, they must show how and where the alleged bias occurred, or how and where the alleged incompetence manifested itself in a way that prejudiced the protestor. The following excerpt from a January 2008 opinion is typical of Comptroller General opinions on this matter:

> [W]e have long found that the selection of evaluators is a matter within the discretion of the agency, and, accordingly, we do not review allegations ... concerning the evaluators' qualifications or the composition of evaluation panels absent a showing of possible fraud, conflict of interest, or actual bias on the part of evaluation officials.... (IMLCORP LLC; Wattre Corp., B-310582 et al., January 9, 2008).

This is not to say that there have not been some successful protests related to evaluator expertise or bias. In one instance, an offeror's proposal in a competition that could have resulted in outsourcing work being done by government personnel was found by government evaluators to be unacceptable. However, the offeror pointed out that a number of the evaluators who had found the proposal unacceptable stood to lose their jobs if the proposal had been found to be acceptable. The potential for bias was so obviously great that the agency determined that a new evaluation by other evaluators was necessary.

Agencies should take evaluator competency and potential conflicts of interest seriously. When supervisors are asked to select someone to be an evaluator for an acquisition, they may be tempted to designate the person they can most afford to do without during the time of the source selection process. Source selection authorities and contracting officers should always insist on highly qualified personnel, not just as protection against a protest, but to maximize the likelihood that the real best value source will ultimately be identified and chosen.

Regardless of the size and structure of an organization established for source selection, and regardless of the grade levels of those involved, the source selection rules and issues described in this book remain the same.

EXHIBIT 7-1   Sample Organizational Structure for a "Formal" Source Selection

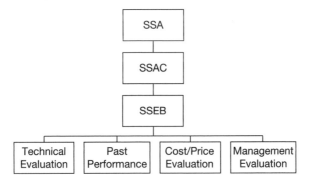

CHAPTER 8

USING MARKET RESEARCH

A relatively new and important addition to the FAR is Part 10, Market Research. Conducting market research is required by law for all planned acquisitions other than simplified acquisitions. While FAR Part 10 outlines the goals of market research and, to some extent, the manner in which it can be conducted, it does not specify the amount of money and time that can or should be spent on market research. Agency officials determine how much market research to conduct based on their own business judgment. Spending $200,000 on market research might be overkill for a relatively straightforward acquisition of modest value, but an expenditure of that amount may not be enough for a complex multimillion-dollar acquisition.

Market research is required whenever:

- A new requirements document is being generated
- Offers are to be solicited for acquisitions for which the estimated value is in excess of the simplified acquisition threshold
- Offers are to be solicited for requirements of a lesser value than the simplified acquisition threshold when circumstances justify the cost of market research
- Offers are to be solicited for acquisitions that could lead to a bundled contract.

One of the major goals of market research is to determine if commercial items, modified commercial items, or nondevelopmental items (NDI) are available to meet government needs, either totally or at component levels. Commercial items and NDI, if available, can help the government avoid the expense of reinventing the wheel.

Other goals are to identify industry practices in the commercial marketplace (when applicable), to ensure maximum use of recovered materials and promote energy conservation and efficiency, to determine whether bundling would be appropriate, and to assess the availability of technology that meets applicable accessibility standards issued by the Architectural and Transportation Barriers Compliance Board.

THE SMART BUYER CONCEPT

The primary goal of market research is to make the government a smart buyer by identifying what is actually available to meet government needs before the government attempts to buy it. Market research efforts should include consideration of socioeconomic issues such as the availability of various categories of small business sources capable of meeting the government requirement. Researchers should also consider the extent to which competition is available in the marketplace or can be developed. Further, as previously stated, it should seek to identify commercial items and NDIs to avoid reinventing the wheel.

Identified market conditions may sometimes result in the government's considering possible cost, quality, and performance tradeoffs in its requirement documents, to accommodate market conditions.

FAR 10.002 identifies the following techniques for conducting market research:

- Contacting knowledgeable individuals in government or industry

- Reviewing the results of previous market research for the same or similar requirements
- Publishing formal requests for information in technical, scientific, or business publications
- Querying governmentwide databases to identify procurement instruments, such as task order contracts, intended for use by multiple agencies
- Participating in interactive, online communications with industry, acquisition personnel, and customers
- Obtaining source lists for similar requirements from government or industry sources
- Reviewing print or online product literature
- Conducting interchange meetings or holding presolicitation conferences to involve potential offerors early in the acquisition process.

Because FAR Part 10 also indicates that market research should be conducted on "an ongoing basis," and because Part 10 clearly applies to both the program and contracting communities, program personnel should work closely with the contracting officer to avoid inadvertently releasing protected procurement information whenever a solicitation has been issued or is imminent. Communications with potential competitors must, by regulation, be controlled by the contracting officer after a solicitation is issued.

DOCUMENTATION OF MARKET RESEARCH

FAR 10.002(e) requires that agencies document the results of market research in an appropriate manner. Agency regulations may require or suggest a particular format. Exhibit 8-1 shows a suggested format used by NASA. The NASA format, which is available online (http://www.hq.nasa.gov/office/procurement/market), has been slightly modified here for general use.

EXHIBIT 8-1   Market Research Report Format

1. Purchase request # _____

2. Title [of the planned contracting requirement]_____

3. Product or service code [e.g., the North American Industry Classification System code]_____

4. Estimated contract value (including options)_____

5. The following market research techniques were used (check all that apply):

____ Personal knowledge in procuring supplies/services of this type.

____ Contact with the requester and/or other knowledgeable people in government and industry regarding the commercial nature of this requirement and standard industry practices in this area of supply/service.

____ Review of recent market research results for similar or identical supplies/services (cite contract or order number).

____ Publication of a formal request for information at the governmentwide point of entry (GPE), www.fedbizopps.gov, and/or in appropriate technical journals.

____ Publication of a formal request for information at the GPE, in review of government, and/or in commercial databases for relevant information.

____ Publication of a formal request for information at the GPE and/or in review of Internet resources.

____ Publication of a formal request for information at the GPE and/or in use of source lists for identical or similar items obtained from government, professional, or industry sources.

____ Publication of a formal request for information at the GPE and/or in view of catalogs and other generally available product literature (online or print).

____ Interchange meetings or presolicitation conferences with potential offerors.

Other: _____

6. Based on the results of the above research, it is determined that this requirement (select one):

____ Can be met by commercial items, commercial items with customary or minor modifications, or nondevelopmental items.

or

____ Cannot be met by commercial items, commercial items with modifications, or nondevelopmental items. Further, a reevaluation has been made in accordance with the FAR, and this requirement cannot be modified to permit fulfillment by any of the above types of items.

or

_____

_____

_____

(Example: Market research may reveal that a combination of commercial/ non commercial items can meet the government's needs.)

Address items 7 through 9 below if the requirement can be met (either in whole or in part) by commercial items, commercial items with modifications, or nondevelopmental items. Continue on additional sheets if necessary.

7. Standard industry terms and conditions (e.g., warranty, maintenance, discounts, buyer financing, freight, delivery, acceptance/rejection) under which commercial sales of the required supplies/services are made:

_____

_____

_____

8. Laws or regulations unique to the required supplies/services:

_____

_____

_____

9. Based on the above information, the basic clauses and provisions prescribed in FAR Part 12:

____ Are sufficient for use in this acquisition and do not require any tailoring to be consistent with industry's commercial practices.

or

____ Require tailoring to be consistent with industry's commercial practices. All such tailoring will be included in the solicitation issued for the required supplies/services.

_____

Contracting Officer   Date

CHAPTER 9

INVOLVING CONTRACTORS IN ACQUISITION PLANNING

The FAR calls any written or oral interaction between the government and contractors that either are competing for or might be competing for a specific contract an *exchange*. Within FAR-restricted limits, exchanges may take place before a solicitation is issued or at various times following the issuance of a solicitation.

FAR 15.201 specifically encourages "exchanges with industry before receipt of proposals." When these preproposal exchanges are conducted before a solicitation is issued, they are known as *presolicitation exchanges*.

As we have noted previously, the FAR encourages contractor participation in acquisition planning. But this raises two questions: (1) Why? (2) What are the limits of contractor participation? The answer to the first is fairly apparent. These exchanges are meant to improve the agency's and potential offerors' understanding of both government requirements and industry capabilities. Potential offerors can then judge whether or how they might satisfy the government's requirements. These exchanges can also help the government be a smart buyer and prevent it from making erroneous assumptions that could result in numerous amendments to solicitations, aborted procurements, or both.

The answer to the second question regarding limits requires a more in-depth discussion. Some elements of the answer might even be surprising.

PRESOLICITATION EXCHANGES

According to FAR 15.201, presolicitation exchanges involving contractors may address concerns regarding:

- The acquisition strategy, including the proposed contract type, terms and conditions, and planning schedules
- The feasibility of the requirement, including performance requirements, statements of work, and data requirements
- The suitability of the contemplated proposal preparation instructions
- Evaluation criteria
- The approach contemplated for assessing past performance information
- Any other industry concerns or questions.

The venues and methods the FAR lists for conducting presolicitation exchanges include:

- Industry or small business conferences
- Public hearings
- Market research
- One-on-one meetings
- Draft requests for proposal
- Requests for information

- Presolicitation conferences
- Site visits, where appropriate.

The potentially surprising aspects of presolicitation exchanges involve one-on-one meetings where the FAR now seems to allow a great deal more latitude than in the recent past. The FAR now permits one-on-one discussions regarding any or all the concerns mentioned previously, including the feasibility of the requirement, proposal preparation instructions, and evaluation criteria. (Chapter 10 discusses one-on-one meetings in more detail.)

Agencies routinely hold conferences and hearings to inform industry of current and planned government acquisitions. These meetings are most fruitful when time is allotted to give potential contractors a chance to voice opinions and ask questions of agency representatives on a one-on-one basis. This is so because contractors are often reluctant to bring some issues up in open forums in front of competitors.

DRAFT RFPS

Draft RFPs allow contractors to consider in depth what the government is considering to include in the final RFP. Thus, they are most valuable when they contain the proposed statement of work, proposal preparation instructions, evaluation factors (and, when appropriate, the relative importance of those factors), data requirements, and the like. Nonetheless, some agencies require special approvals at a level above the contracting officer in order to include contemplated proposal preparation instructions or contemplated evaluation factors in a draft RFP, even though it would seem that the more information exchanged, the better off all parties involved (government and contractor) will be.

Overworked government contracting personnel are sometimes reluctant to issue a draft RFP, apparently feeling that they have barely enough time to issue one RFP, let alone two. Notwithstanding this reluctance, the use of draft RFPs may save time in the long run and certainly leads to better source selections through more competently crafted final RFPs reflecting realistic requirement statements and more meaningful evaluation factors. The challenge for government planners is, of course, to determine which of the comments received from potential contractors are meaningful and which are merely self-serving. Separating the wheat from the chaff is essential.

Requests for information (RFIs) are normally prepared using agency-prescribed formats and usually include a disclaimer that the government will not be obligated in any way for contractor participation. This disclaimer means the government will not be obliged to choose one of the contractors that submits information and that the government will not pay for the information developed and submitted in response to the RFI or otherwise reimburse the contractor in any way.

There is, of course, a line that must not be crossed. While contractors are part of the FAR-defined acquisition team, government planners must avoid both improprieties and the appearance of improprieties. While walking arm in arm with their acquisition partners—contractors—government personnel are still expected to keep the traditional arm's-length relationship.

CHAPTER 10

ONE-ON-ONE PRESOLICITATION MEETINGS

Per FAR 15.201, one-on-one meetings are one method government agencies use to acquire or share information with potential offerors and others involved in the acquisition process. The FAR states that one-on-one preproposal meetings (which would include any presolicitation meetings) that are "substantially involved with *contract* terms and conditions *should* involve the contracting officer." Note the language used here. First, the phrase "contract terms and conditions" presumably excludes matters that would apply to only the solicitation, such as proposal preparation instructions and proposal evaluation criteria.

Second, in FAR parlance, the word "should" normally means that something ought to be done, but it is not mandatory. (The FAR uses the words "shall" or "must" to indicate that something is mandatory.) Thus, the FAR coverage can be interpreted only as an effort to give program personnel more flexibility in acquisition planning, including source selection planning, and to help make sure that they have done all of their homework before committing the government to a strategy.

FAR 15.201(f) does place some limits on one-on-one meetings when it states:

When specific information about a proposed acquisition that would be necessary for the preparation of proposals is disclosed to one or more potential offerors, the information must be made available to the public as soon as practicable but no later than the next general release of information, in order to avoid creating an unfair competitive advantage.

Since the FAR does not place any specific time limits on the "next general release of information," source selection officials must exercise good judgment. Is it all right if the next general release is, for example, six months after the one-on-one meeting when the requirement is to be advertised in the GPE? Until the FAR language is made more specific, or this issue is brought before the Comptroller General or the courts, prudent application of the FAR guidance would be to avoid giving one or more contractors an unfair competitive advantage. Officials must apply sound business judgment.

While the one-on-one meetings "should" under certain circumstances involve the contracting officer, any meeting held after the solicitation is issued "must" involve the contracting officer. FAR 15.201(f) requires that the contracting officer be the focal point of exchanges conducted after the solicitation is issued. And, notwithstanding the increased latitude given program officials under the FAR, the system probably works best when the contracting officer and the program officer work in concert throughout the planning phase of an acquisition.

Individual agencies may have procedural guidance that requires the program office and the contracting officer to work together in source selection matters, from the identification of the requirement until contract award. Along that line, some agencies have in the past required a representative of the contracting office to be invited to all one-on-ones, regardless of where in the process these meetings were taking place. However, this no longer seems to be general practice.

CHAPTER 11

EVALUATION FACTORS OTHER THAN COST

Public law has long mandated that price or cost be a consideration in all government procurements. But in addition to price or cost, procurement laws and regulations have traditionally permitted consideration of non-cost factors, often referred to as *merit factors* or *technical factors*. These non-cost factors may be used in both LPTA and tradeoff procurements.

BASIC FAR REQUIREMENTS

Per FAR 15.304, some specific non-cost factors must be addressed in the source selection processes. These include:

- Quality. The FAR indicates that quality may be addressed through such factors as past performance, technical excellence, personnel, and management capability and experience.
- Past performance. The FAR requires that past performance be used as an evaluation factor for all procurements exceeding the simplified acquisition threshold, but it also provides that this requirement may be waived if the contracting officer documents why an evaluation of past performance would not be appropriate.
- Small business contracting. If the proposed solicitation is to be unrestricted—not set aside for a particular group of

contractors such as small businesses or small disadvantaged businesses—then the proposed use of various categories of small businesses as subcontractors and vendors must be evaluated. This requirement applies to proposed contracts exceeding $650,000 for all but construction contracts. It applies to construction contracts of more than $1.5 million. For Department of Defense (DoD) contracting offices, the plan may also address whether black colleges and universities and minority institutions will be considered as sources.

- Small disadvantaged business subcontracting. For selected industry segments, as identified by the Department of Commerce on an annual basis, tradeoff acquisitions exceeding $650,000 (or exceeding $1.5 million for construction contracts) may also include an evaluation factor for the use of small disadvantaged businesses.

- Other subcontracting considerations. If the contract involves bundling and there are opportunities for subcontracting, the contracting officer must include a factor to evaluate past performance. The past performance evaluation should indicate the extent to which the offeror attained small business subcontracting goals under past contracts.

Additionally, FAR 22.1103 specifies that for service contracts of $650,000 or more that are expected to involve meaningful numbers of professional employees, compensation plans should be reviewed to determine if they are unrealistically low.

FACTORS AND SUBFACTORS

Subfactors may be added under any non-cost evaluation factors. When using the tradeoff method, the relative importance of both factors and subfactors must be determined and later described in the solicitation. In an LPTA source selection there is no relative importance. All factors and subfactors are equally important. Accordingly, if there is a mixture of variable factors and pass/fail factors in the solicitation (a combined tradeoff/LPTA approach), it may be more challenging to communicate the relative importance of the factors and subfactors to potential offerors and to make it clear that only some of the factors are pass/fail. Careful wording would be in order.

Factors and subfactors must:

- Be tailored for the particular acquisition
- Represent the key areas of importance and emphasis upon which the source selection decision will be based
- Be definable and measurable and stated in clearly understood terms
- Support meaningful comparison and discrimination between competing contractors.

CHAPTER 12

SELECTING THE NON-COST FACTORS

Acquisition planners must consider two key areas when establishing non-cost factors. Foremost is the government requirements document, such as a statement of work, a performance work statement, or a statement of objectives. Second, and also of great import, is the information that has been obtained from market research, which includes lessons learned from previous and similar efforts, the names of contractors likely to compete, and knowledge of the state of the art in the particular industry sector involved.

Planners must first ask: What do we need to see in offerors' proposals to assure us that a resultant contract would fully meet the government's needs? For example, if the government is using a performance work statement or statement of objectives, is it desirable to have competing contractors submit technical proposals in which they explain in detail how they plan to do the work? If so, what exactly does the government need to properly judge this aspect of proposals?

The result of contemplating these questions might be an evaluation factor that, in abbreviated form, looks something like this:

Technical Proposal. The offeror shall submit a technical proposal addressing in a work breakdown structure (pursuant to Mil Std ___) how the offeror intends to meet the requirements of the performance work statement in Section C of the solicitation. Each paragraph of the performance work statement must be addressed. Proposals will be evaluated on the bases of completeness, feasibility, and risk. Risk assessment will include cost, schedule, and performance risk.

Presuming that the requirement is expected to result in a cost-reimbursement contract of significant monetary value, the planners may decide that they need to look at how the contractor will control costs while remaining on schedule. If so, they might include a factor that in abbreviated form looks something like this:

Management Plan. The offeror must furnish a management plan that encompasses earned value management techniques and demonstrates how cost and schedule will be monitored and controlled. The management plan must also include the processes that will be put into place to surface and resolve actual or projected deviations from projected costs and schedules. This would include identifying the managerial level of the contractor that will be involved in monitoring progress, participating in problem resolution, and overseeing any corrective actions necessary.

As a separate part of the management plan, the offeror must indicate the proposed compensation plan for professional employees expected to perform under any resultant contract.

The management plan will be evaluated on the bases of feasibility, likelihood of success, and usefulness as a tool in risk management. The compensation portion will be reviewed to determine if compensation is of a level deemed reasonable for attracting and retaining highly qualified professionals.

The planners may also consider the qualifications of the key personnel to be used on the contract to be of great importance. If so, a key personnel evaluation factor could be used. For example, the government could explain the qualifications it is looking for and require offerors to provide a resume in a specified format for each of the key personnel to be used under any resultant contract. Sometimes, to avoid a bait-and-switch situation, the government requires proposed key personnel to submit letters of intent to work under the contract.

THE IMPACT OF FACTORS SELECTED

Similar evaluation factors could be developed for past performance, experience, facilities and equipment, small business subcontracting, or any of a host of other potential evaluation factors. It is important to keep in mind, however, that:

- Each evaluation factor will require both contractors and the government to spend time and money respectively preparing and evaluating proposals.
- The FAR calls for factors that support meaningful comparison of, and discrimination between, competing contractors.
- The greater the number of evaluation factors used, the more likely it is that meaningful differences between contractors will not be readily apparent.

While it is important that the government include those factors essential to obtain the best value under the tradeoff process, or acceptable proposals under the LPTA process, it is clearly foolhardy to ask for too much. If market research indicates that only three potential offerors are expected to submit proposals, and all of those offerors have more than adequate facilities and equipment, then including "facilities and equipment" as an evaluation factor would probably waste everyone's time.

"SAMPLE-ITIS"

It is clear that some organizations suffer from "sample-itis": They prepare new solicitations by copying from previous solicitations rather than tailoring the solicitation to the requirement at hand. All new solicitations in organizations with sample-itis look surprisingly like the organization's other solicitations, even though they address different requirements and different markets and are issued at different points in time. Succumbing to sample-itis violates the FAR requirement that evaluation factors be tailored for the particular acquisition.

GREAT LATITUDE

Comptroller General decisions have given great latitude to agencies in determining what evaluation factors to use. Generally, the Comp Gen will take the position that the agency is in the best position to determine what it needs, and the burden is on the protestor to conclusively demonstrate that an evaluation factor is unreasonable. The Comp Gen has even found for the government when an evaluation factor clearly gave the incumbent a substantial competitive advantage. In Harbor Branch Oceanographic Institution, B-243417, July 17, 1991, the Comp Gen opined, "As a general matter a competitive advantage gained through incumbency is not an unfair advantage that must be eliminated ... rather, such an advantage is improper only where it results from preferential treatment of an offeror or other unfair action by the government."

The choices of non-cost factors that can be used are virtually endless. Different groups of planners could look at the market research and the requirements document and devise different sets of evaluation factors. For example, instead of requiring a detailed technical proposal, as was shown in the previous example, a group of planners might emphasize experience and past performance as non-cost evaluation factors and allow the competent contractor they will choose to determine how to do the job.

Although this is said with some reluctance, there is no doubt that evaluation factors can be skewed to favor or work against a particular contractor—for or against an incumbent contractor, for example. Contracting officers, legal counsel, and the source selection authority are the primary lines of defense in making sure that factors chosen do not unduly or unfairly favor one or more contractors. This does not mean that the project office is not permitted to ask for what it needs even if that has the impact of limiting competition. The Competition in Contracting Act (CICA) allows restrictive requirements, but only to the "extent necessary." And in the Comp Gen opinion cited above, the Comp Gen said, "Where a solicitation includes requirements that restrict the ability of offerors to compete, the agency must have a reasonable basis for imposing the restrictive requirements." Thus, an agency does not have to sacrifice its needs to level the playing field for potential offerors. However, it must be prepared to conclusively demonstrate that the needs are genuine and reasonable.

WHERE TO BEGIN

There are a variety of ways to establish non-cost factors. For example, each individual acquisition planner (or member of the integrated product team) can independently review the government requirement and the information obtained from any market research, as well as any lessons learned from previous similar acquisitions. Then the entire team could meet and brainstorm what should or should not be included as an evaluation factor and whether any factors proposed should instead be subfactors. A consensus opinion reached could then be submitted for approval to the contracting officer and the source selection authority.

Another way to approach the matter is to have the senior planner from the project office propose evaluation factors and subfactors and then obtain team input and recommendations before seeking approval.

Whatever method an agency employs, it can be helpful to keep in mind advice from the Department of Energy's acquisition guide. The guide states, "As a rule of thumb, evaluation criteria should reflect areas *necessary* to determine the merit of a proposal, *pertinent* to the Government's stated requirements and *measurable* to permit qualitative and quantitative assessment against the rating plan." Whatever the procedure used, participants should keep in mind the FAR requirements for factors and subfactors and the other issues that have been raised in this chapter.

CHAPTER 13

SMALL BUSINESS SUBCONTRACTING PLANS

FAR Subpart 19.7 requires that offerors competing for unrestricted negotiated procurements—those not set aside for small business—in excess of $650,000 ($1.5 million for construction contracts) commit to an acceptable small business subcontracting plan in order to receive a contract award. This requirement applies whenever there are "subcontracting opportunities." If the solicitation is set aside for competition only among small businesses, then this subcontracting plan is not required. In unrestricted solicitations, in which both large and small businesses can participate, only large businesses must submit this subcontracting plan.

When a subcontracting plan is to be submitted by competing contractors, acquisition planners must address exactly how this is to be accomplished. The law requires only that the contractor and the contracting officer agree to a satisfactory plan before a contract is awarded. The standard FAR provision at FAR 52.219-9, Small Business Subcontracting Plan (2010), allows the contracting officer to choose between two different subparagraphs when placing the provision in a solicitation. One of the subparagraphs requires a competing contractor to submit a plan "upon the request of the contracting officer." The other requires that all competing large businesses submit such a plan as a part of their proposal. In the first instance, the contracting officer could elect to ask for a plan only from the apparent successful offeror. If a satisfactory plan is not negotiated, then the contractor would not be eligible for award.

The two solicitation provision subparagraphs appear in Exhibit 13-1. While it is presumably the contracting officer's decision which is to be used, agency-published guidance or practice may favor a particular approach.

If the competing contractors are to be required to submit subcontracting plans as a part of their proposals, then acquisition planners, together with the contracting officer and agency small business advisors, must decide whether:

- The plans will be deemed "acceptable"/"not acceptable." This choice is available for both LPTA and tradeoff source selections.
- The plans will be scored or rated, which is done only for tradeoff source selections. The U.S. Army, for example, has a numerical scoring scheme for subcontracting plans with an acceptability goal of 70 percent (Appendix DD to the *Army FAR Supplement*).

Additionally, source selection officials can either:

- Put target goals in the solicitation that competing contractors must meet.
- Allow competing contractors to propose their own goals.

If a competing contractor already has an approved subcontracting plan that covers its government business (company or division plans called either *master plans* or *commercial plans*), it can submit or reference the plan as part of its proposal.

Each agency also has internal guidance on small business subcontracting issues that is either mandatory or advisory. Accordingly, government personnel must review agency guidance before deciding among the choices available. Also, many agencies have prescribed forms or formats that competing contractors must use when submitting a small business subcontracting plan. When appropriate, this information must be included in the proposal submission instructions given to offerors in the solicitation.

SMALL DISADVANTAGED BUSINESS PARTICIPATION PROGRAM

FAR Subpart 19.12 also requires that a Small Disadvantaged Business (SDB) Participation Program provision be placed in solicitations for specific areas of industry that are identified annually by the Department of Commerce. The FAR directs:

> The solicitation shall describe the SDB participation evaluation factor or subfactor. The solicitation shall require offerors to provide, with their offers, targets, expressed as dollars and percentages of total contract value, in each of the applicable, authorized NAICS Industry Subsector[s], and a total target for SDB participation by the contractor, including joint venture partners, and team members, and a total target for SDB participation by subcontractors.

OTHER SOCIOECONOMIC EVALUATION FACTORS

Some agencies, such as some DoD components, may also include in solicitations a Small Business Participation Program requirement. All categories of businesses are asked to identify their subcontracting plans for various categories of small businesses and, where appropriate, historically black colleges and minority institutions. Again, agency instructions should be consulted.

How and when these evaluation factors are used can vary widely among agencies. It is important that the agency small business advisor be a part of the planning team to help navigate through and effectively comply with FAR- and agency-mandated requirements.

EXHIBIT 13-1   FAR Language for the Small Business
Subcontracting Provision

The contracting officer must use one of these two subparagraphs when including the FAR 52.219-9, Small Business Subcontracting Plan (2010), provision in solicitations:

> The offeror, upon request by the Contracting Officer, shall submit and negotiate a subcontracting plan, where applicable, that separately addresses subcontracting with small business, veteran-owned small business, service-disabled veteran-owned small business, HUBZone small business concerns, small disadvantaged business, and women-owned small business concerns. If the offeror is submitting an individual contract plan, the plan must separately address subcontracting with small business, veteran-owned small business, service-disabled veteran-owned small business, HUBZone small business, small disadvantaged business, and women-owned small business concerns, with a separate part for the basic contract and separate parts for each option (if any). The plan shall be included in and made a part of the resultant contract. The subcontracting plan shall be negotiated within the time specified by the Contracting Officer. Failure to submit and negotiate the subcontracting plan shall make the offeror ineligible for award of a contract.

or

> Proposals submitted in response to this solicitation shall include a subcontracting plan that separately addresses subcontracting with small business, veteran-owned small business, service-disabled veteran-owned small business, HUBZone small business, small disadvantaged business, and women-owned small business concerns. If the offeror is submitting an individual contract plan, the plan must separately address subcontracting with small business, veteran-owned small business, service-disabled veteran-owned small business, HUBZone small business, small disadvantaged business, and women-owned small business concerns, with a separate part for the basic contract and separate parts for each option (if any). The plan shall be included in and made a part of the resultant contract. The subcontracting plan shall be negotiated within the time specified by the Contracting Officer. Failure to submit and negotiate a subcontracting plan shall make the offeror ineligible for award of a contract.

CHAPTER 14

ESTABLISHING EVALUATION SUBFACTORS

FAR Part 15 requires that proposals be evaluated solely on the basis of the evaluation factors and significant subfactors that have been tailored for the specific acquisition and identified in the solicitation. It neither defines what subfactors should be nor requires their use.

Subfactors are normally used when government acquisition personnel want to break out an evaluation factor into separate components to better ensure that offerors understand the evaluation factor, to better ensure that important components of the evaluation factor are specifically addressed in proposal preparation and proposal evaluation, and/or to establish the relative importance of the various components within an evaluation factor.

To demonstrate how this might be done, let's break out some of the components of the Management Plan factor mentioned in Chapter 12. In an abbreviated fashion, such a breakdown might look something like this:

Management Plan

    a. Earned value management

    b. Key personnel

    c. Employee compensation plan

    d. Involvement of contractor management.

Note that in the above example we have taken "key personnel," which could be a standalone evaluation factor, and made it a subfactor. This further demonstrates the broad flexibility that acquisition planners have in establishing factors and subfactors.

There is no governmentwide template for determining factors and subfactors. The choices are almost limitless. Planners can establish any number of factors and subfactors, and two different groups of planners could look at a particular situation and come to widely different conclusions about what factors and subfactors (if any) should be used.

As discussed in the next chapter, the government must convey to offerors the relative importance of factors and subfactors when using the tradeoff process. Each factor and subfactor must then be addressed by competing contractors in proposals and addressed by the government in the evaluation of those proposals.

If a contractor challenges (protests) factors or subfactors used in a solicitation, the government must demonstrate a reasonable basis for the choices made. If a reasonable basis is shown, the Comp Gen and the courts usually will not substitute their judgment for the judgment of agency officials.

CHAPTER 15

ESTABLISHING THE RELATIVE IMPORTANCE OF EVALUATION FACTORS AND SUBFACTORS

FAR 15.304 requires that evaluation factors and subfactors that will affect contract award, and their relative importance, be clearly stated in the solicitation. There are sound reasons for this requirement. It helps the government get the types of proposals it seeks, and it helps contractors in preparing their proposals by indicating the areas they should emphasize. Further, evaluation factors and subfactors and their relative importance can help contractors determine whether to submit a proposal at all. If, for example, past performance is significantly more important than all other non-cost factors, a contractor with a marginal past performance record may decide that it would be a waste of time and money to prepare a proposal because the chances of receiving an award would be minimal.

RELATIVE IMPORTANCE IS IRRELEVANT IN LPTA

When LPTA is to be used, there is no need to identify relative importance. If a contractor is acceptable on all factors, it will receive the award if it has the lowest price or cost. If a contractor is rated "not acceptable" on just one factor, even following discussions and proposal revision, it cannot receive the award. Accordingly, the coverage in this chapter applies only to tradeoff selections.

DISCRETION OF PLANNERS

As they do when establishing evaluation factors, acquisition officials have broad discretion in determining relative importance and, once again, two separate groups of acquisition officials could come to two different conclusions. This has been vividly demonstrated hundreds of times in classroom settings, where experienced student professionals are divided into separate groups and given the same scenario. The groups are asked to develop evaluation factors and subfactors and to determine their relative importance. Invariably, no two groups come to the same conclusions—in fact, their results often vary widely.

It should be abundantly clear by now that best value source selection using tradeoff is very subjective and requires the exercise of business judgment throughout the process.

DESCRIBING RELATIVE IMPORTANCE

How relative importance will be reflected in the solicitation is also a matter of choice. In the past, it was common practice to use numerical scoring. Although there was no requirement that they do so, maximum scores almost always added up to 100 or some multiple of 100 (such as 500 or 1,000). Table 15-1 shows a possible scheme for the numerical scoring of evaluation factors, weighted by relative importance.

TABLE 15-1 A Numerical Scoring Scheme

Factors and Subfactors	Maximum Points
Factor 1. Technical Approach	50 points
a. *Feasibility (25)*	
b. *Completeness (25)*	
Factor 2. Key Personnel	25 points
Factor 3. Management Plan	25 points
a. *Cost control (15)*	
b. *Schedule control (10)*	

Over the years, describing relative importance in the solicitation by using numbers fell out of favor with most agencies. It implied a degree of precision that just is not inherent in the very subjective source tradeoff process. Using the scoring scheme in Table 15-1, for example, it's debatable whether a competitor should actually receive 20 points for the feasibility subfactor. Why not 22 or 18?

The FAR does not require the use of numbers, nor does it prohibit their use. Some agencies still use numbers, but today it is far more common to use broader characterizations of relative importance. For example, instead of using numbers to describe relative importance, a solicitation might read:

> Technical Approach is most important and is significantly more important than Key Personnel. Key Personnel is equal in importance to Management Plan. Subfactors A and B under Technical Approach are equal in importance. Of the subfactors under Management Plan, Subfactor A is more important than Subfactor B.

This meets the FAR requirement for disclosing relative importance. However, this approach does have a downside, especially as far as contractors are concerned. Imagine that a solicitation contains ten or twenty or more evaluation factors and dozens of subfactors. Explaining the relative importance of each of these factors and subfactors can result in a solicitation provision that is convoluted and difficult to understand. It is not without justification that some contractors call this part of the solicitation "the riddle." If the planning team is going to pose a riddle, it is to everyone's advantage to make it a riddle that is easy to solve.

Part M.3 in Appendix II gives an example of a riddle that is relatively easy to solve because the planners did not elect to include a large number of evaluation factors and subfactors in the solicitation.

DESCENDING ORDER OF IMPORTANCE

Some agencies routinely describe the relative importance of factors and subfactors by simply saying that they are listed in descending order of importance. This can be effective when there are more or less uniform gradients between the factors and subfactors—or, to put it another way, when factors and subfactors reflect "a reasonable downward progression." The Comptroller General has held in a number of protest opinions that without a relatively uniform downward progression of factors, simply using "descending order of importance" without further clarification as to relative importance was not enough.

In Table 15-1 there are no uniform gradients between factors, nor is there a reasonable downward progression of the factors. In fact, one factor is twice as important as either of the others, which are equal in importance. In situations such as this, the government solicitation should not merely indicate that factors and subfactors are given in descending order of importance. Instead the government should give further clarification in the solicitation to provide competing contractors with a reasonable understanding of the relative importance of the factors and subfactors.

Based on observation, improper use of "descending order of importance" in solicitations is a relatively common occurrence. And most often, competing contractors do not complain. However, if the acquisition team wishes to remove an opportunity for protest based on the failure of the government to adequately communicate the relative importance of the factors and subfactors, care should be taken to make sure that "descending order of importance" is used in the proper manner.

FAILURE TO IDENTIFY ANY RELATIVE IMPORTANCE

The Comptroller General has also opined on a number of occasions where the government did not state the relative importance of the factors or subfactors that competing contractors had a right to assume they were equal in importance, and the government was required to act accordingly when making the source selection decision.

THE IMPACT OF RELATIVE IMPORTANCE

Once relative importance is established in the solicitation, the government is bound to make decisions consistent with the promises made. It cannot, for example, indicate that past performance will be the most significant factor in a source selection and then make a selection in which differences in evaluated past performance played little or no role.

WHAT IF?

When establishing evaluation factors and their relative importance, it may be helpful to go through some mental gymnastics known as *what if*. For example, if the government intends to make technical approach far more important than key personnel and past performance, government planners could ask themselves, "What if we get an attractively priced proposal with some really great technical ideas from a competing contractor with undistinguished key personnel and a so-so performance rating? Is that what we really want?" As in so many other aspects of source selection, establishing relative importance requires the exercise of sound judgment by those involved in planning for and executing the source selection.

CHAPTER 16

SELECTING A RATING METHOD

Typically, when proposals are evaluated for tradeoff, they receive a score or rating of some sort, to help the contracting officer, source selection authority, or both determine the competitive range (if discussions are to be held) and select the successful contractor(s). It's important to note, however, that the scores themselves are not binding on the contracting officer or other source selection authority but are looked upon as guides for these individuals and other source selection officials. The FAR does not refer to "scoring" per se, but instead calls the scoring process a "rating method."

FAR 15.305(a) permits any rating method or combination of methods, including:
- Numerical weights
- Color ratings
- Adjectival ratings.

DISCLOSURE OF THE RATING METHOD IN THE RFP

At one time, the rating method was disclosed in all solicitations. The FAR no longer requires that the planned rating method be shown, so many agency solicitations do not include this information, except as might be necessary to comply with FAR direction on evaluating past performance (see Chapter 17).

USING NUMBERS

In the past, it was common to use numerical ratings or scores. However, this procedure sometimes made it difficult to make a true best value decision when using tradeoff. This was especially true when cost was scored. Let's return to the hypothetical weighting given to the factors and subfactors discussed in Chapter 15 (see Table 16-1).

TABLE 16-1   A Numerical Scoring Scheme

Factors and Subfactors	Maximum Points
Factor 1. Technical Approach	50 points
a. Feasibility (25)	
b. Completeness (25)	
Factor 2. Key Personnel	25 points
Factor 3. Management Plan	25 points
a. Cost control (15)	
b. Schedule control (10)	

Now let us assume that we have decided to give cost or price a maximum of 50 points. Table 16-2 shows the three remaining competitors' total scores on non-cost factors. Their proposed costs are also shown.

TABLE 16-2   Three Competing Contractors' Scores and Proposed Costs

Contractor	Score for Non-Cost Factors	Cost
A	90 points	$1,875,000
B	87 points	$1,687,500
C	80 points	$1,500,000

Because the cost proposed by offeror A is 25 percent higher than the lowest cost, proposed by offeror C, A's cost score will be reduced by 25 percent. It will receive 37.5 of the maximum 50 points. Since B's offer is 12.5 percent higher than C's, its cost score is reduced by 12.5 percent to 43.75 points. C, offering the lowest cost, receives all 50 points.

Thus the final scores were as follows:

- A. 90 + 37.5 = 127.50
- B. 87 + 43.75 = 130.75
- C. 80 + 50.00 = 130.00.

Using this method, which applies no business judgment to the final decision, the offeror with the highest total score would get the award.

This method led to some poor source selection decisions, and the practice of scoring costs fell into disfavor. (Costs have been scored using other methods, as well. For example, some agencies used sophisticated algebraic equations to perform a "best buy analysis," wherein the winner was chosen by a price analyst or some other knowledgeable person who could understand the equation.)

Even though most agencies, but not all, drifted away from the practice of scoring costs, the practice of using numbers to score non-cost factors continued in many agencies. This too led to some untenable situations. Consider a situation in which two competing contractors have the final scores and proposed costs shown in Table 16-3.

TABLE 16-3   Two Competing Contractors' Scores and Proposed Costs

Contractor	Score for Non-Cost Factors	Cost
Contractor A	90 points	$900,000
Contractor B	86 points	$1,000,000

The source selection authority and his or her advisors have noted that contractor B is planning to use the top scientist in the country as the principal investigator, so they would really prefer to give the award to B. However, awarding to the lowest-rated contractor at the highest cost might be a very difficult (but not impossible) decision to defend. Perhaps if they had weighted key personnel more heavily, the scores would have come out differently. But they did not, so they have to live with the consequences.

USING ADJECTIVES OR COLORS

In an effort to avoid similar tough situations, agencies began to embrace rating methods that characterized proposals in a less specific fashion than do numbers. For example, offerors could receive a rating of "outstanding," "highly acceptable," "acceptable," or "not acceptable" instead of receiving a numerical rating or score on evaluation factors. In the example shown in Table 16-3, both contractors would probably be rated "highly acceptable," and the source selection authority could more readily pick contractor B merely by explaining in the source selection decision that the exceptional expertise to be gained was worth the additional cost.

Some agencies use colors instead of adjectives, but the impact is essentially the same. The color ratings reflect broad ranges of suitability rather than a precise number. Table 16-4 shows a simplified example of a color rating scheme.

TABLE 16-4   Sample Color Rating Scheme

Blue	Surpasses government minimum requirements
Green	Meets government requirements
Yellow	Not acceptable, but susceptible to being made acceptable through discussions
Red	Not acceptable, and not reasonably susceptible to being made acceptable through discussions

VARIATIONS ON COMMON RATING METHODS

In addition to the rating methods identified in the FAR, agencies have used symbols (such as plus signs and minus signs), narrative descriptions, and various combinations of the approaches we have discussed. Some apply both qualitative ratings (e.g., "outstanding," "marginal") and risk ratings (e.g., "high risk," "low risk") to the evaluation factors.

Others have used numbers to score technical proposals and adjusted these numbers using the notion of expected value based on an adjudged confidence level after evaluation of past performance. As shown in Table 16-5, contractor A has received 90 merit points and has a superb past performance rating (confidence level) of 100 percent. Contractor B has received 95 merit points, but its past performance rating is only 80 percent, so its overall rating is lower than contractor A's.

TABLE 16-5 Combining Technical Scores and Confidence Assessments

Contractor	Proposal Score		Confidence Assessment Score	Rating
A	90	*	100%	90
B	95	*	80%	76

Agency officials—unless restricted by agency regulations—have broad discretion. The selection of a rating scheme should be a key consideration in the what-if exercises we discussed earlier.

CONSISTENCY OF APPLICATION

Regardless of the method of scoring or rating chosen, it is important that the meanings of the various adjectives, colors, or whatever be carefully and uniformly defined for evaluators so that there can be consistency among the evaluators in how the rating method is applied.

EXAMPLES OF RATING METHODS

Appendix I includes a relatively wide range of scoring/rating methods used by various federal agencies. It should be noted that achieving the highest merit rating may sometimes require a proposal that "exceeds requirements" or offers "innovations." This can sometimes lead competing contractors astray. They may increase estimated cost or price in order to give the government something extra that it does not want or does not need. Accordingly, it behooves the government to identify during discussions any excesses in proposals that could keep a contractor from being a viable competitor.

It should also be noted that some government agencies' rating systems further distinguish between proposals that have been found to be unacceptable. A proposal may be unacceptable but "susceptible to being made acceptable through discussions," or it may be unacceptable and "not susceptible to being made acceptable through discussions." This characterization could apply to proposals for LPTA selections as well as tradeoff selections.

CHAPTER 17

PAST PERFORMANCE AS AN EVALUATION FACTOR

One non-cost factor worthy of special consideration is past performance. Contractor past performance has been considered a factor in source selection for many, many years, but it was usually not a variable or comparative factor. Instead, it was part of the determination of whether an offeror was a responsible contractor with the ability to perform and the demonstrated will to perform. Accordingly, a contractor with outstanding past performance had no competitive advantage over a contractor with adequate past performance as far as the government was concerned.

Past performance as a non-cost evaluation factor differs somewhat from experience. Basically, experience addresses *what* work the contractor has done, while past performance addresses how *well* the contractor performed. However, the government normally looks not just at past performance but also at the relevancy of that past performance—in other words, the type of experience—when making source selection decisions.

In various attempts to make government source selection more like contractor selection in the private sector (which was generally assumed to be more efficient), one aspect of the government acquisition process was a particularly hard nut to crack. Most private-sector buyers carefully select beforehand the sources from which they will solicit proposals. They also strive to establish long-term business relationships with dependable suppliers, which is a basic tenet of total quality management. The government, on the other hand, is required by the Competition in Contracting Act, with some limited exceptions, to solicit offers from every Tom, Dick, and Harriet who wishes to compete for a government requirement. Further, with respect to long-term relationships, the government may not "favor" one contractor over another.

These constraints add time and expense to the process, as some of the private-sector firms that wish to participate may not be viable competitors for the requirement involved. If they are allowed to participate, the government must evaluate the proposals of, and perhaps hold exchanges with, contractors that have little or no opportunity of receiving a contract award. And, of course, the contractor has the expense of preparing a proposal.

Beginning in the late 1980s, the government undertook a process-improvement initiative to emphasize past performance in the selection process by making past performance a significant non-cost evaluation factor. In fact, the Office of Federal Procurement Policy now opines in its *Best Practices for Collecting and Using Current and Past Performance Information* (May 2000) that no other non-cost factor should be considered more important. There is considerable merit in this opinion. If there is such a thing as a successful horse-racing bettor, then it is likely to be someone who looks closely at past performance before he or she puts money on the line. Long shots occasionally rise to the occasion, but you can't depend on them.

Making past performance a significant non-cost evaluation factor can achieve two goals:

- It may discourage contractors with poor or marginal performance records from participating.
- It could serve as a powerful motivator for contractors to do well on their current contracts.

ADDRESSING CONCERNS ABOUT THE USE OF PAST PERFORMANCE

Seldom has a change in the source selection process caused as much widespread concern as the emphasis on past performance. Most of these concerns were alleviated by the following government actions:

- Providing a mechanism wherein contractors could appeal government past performance reports at a level higher than the contracting officer. This addressed contractors' concerns that a single unfair performance report could severely impact their continuing competitive status.

- Considering the currency and relevancy of past performance information obtained when evaluating contractors. This addressed contractors' concerns that past performance from many years ago would come back to haunt them even though they had taken corrective action and improved their performance.

- Development of PPIRS—the Past Performance Information Retrieval System—a governmentwide past performance database. This addressed some government acquisition officials' concerns about the difficulty of collecting and using reliable, consistent, and relevant data.

- Addressing in the FAR and in case law how competing contractors with no relevant past performance will be rated (a situation that is further addressed in Chapter 28). Some likened this situation to the difficulty that young job seekers face when they cannot get a job without experience, but they cannot get experience without a job.

- Providing in the FAR that past performance need not be evaluated if the contracting officer documents the reason past performance is not an appropriate factor for the acquisition. This addressed government acquisition officials' concerns about being compelled to use an evaluation factor that might not be appropriate for a specific acquisition.

LPTA AND PAST PERFORMANCE

There is one very substantive difference in how past performance is used as an evaluation factor in LPTA versus how it is used in tradeoff. In LPTA, contractors are rated either "acceptable" or "unacceptable" on the evaluation factors. Thus, a contractor that is deemed "not acceptable" under an LPTA past performance factor is, in effect, being found to be "not responsible" and is therefore not eligible to receive a contract award.

When a small business is found to be "not responsible" in an LPTA selection, it may appeal to the Small Business Administration (SBA) for a Certificate of Competency (COC) pursuant to FAR Subpart 19.6 and still have an opportunity to receive a contract award. But in a tradeoff selection, small businesses do not have this particular right of appeal simply because they were rated lower than other contractors on a past performance evaluation factor. In that case, the government would not be making a determination of responsibility; it would merely be rating the quality of the past performance of competing contractors and, in so doing, happen to score one contractor lower than another.

CONCERNS TO BE ADDRESSED BY PLANNERS

The matters related to evaluating past performance that the planning team will have to address, subject to the approval of the contracting officer and source selection authority, include:

- Whether to include past performance as an evaluation factor
- The relative weight to be given to past performance (if it is a tradeoff selection)
- The rating method to be used
- Whether a separate group, such as a performance risk assessment group (PRAG), will evaluate past performance
- The instructions that will be given in the solicitation to guide offerors in submitting past performance information
- Instructions given to evaluators and the forms, such as past performance questionnaires, to be furnished for evaluator use.

FAR GUIDANCE

Unlike other non-cost factors, FAR 15.305 offers relatively detailed guidance on the use of past performance as an evaluation factor. This guidance includes:

(2)(ii) The solicitation shall describe the approach for evaluating past performance, including evaluating offerors with no relevant performance history, and shall provide offerors an opportunity to identify past or current contracts (including Federal, State, and local government and private) for efforts similar to the Government requirement. The solicitation shall also authorize offerors to provide information on problems encountered on the identified contracts and the offeror's corrective actions. The Government shall consider this information, as well as information obtained from any other sources, when evaluating the offeror's past performance. The source selection authority shall determine the relevance of similar past performance information....

(v) The evaluation should include the past performance of offerors in complying with subcontracting plan goals for small disadvantaged business (SDB) concerns....

REQUESTING PAST PERFORMANCE INFORMATION—AN EXAMPLE

Section L in Appendix II illustrates how one contracting center requested past performance information in a solicitation. Note that the center asked offerors to provide past performance data from the last five years and required information not only on prime contracts but also on those contracts on which the offeror was a "major subcontractor."

Chapter 18

PRICE OR COST AS AN EVALUATION FACTOR

Acquisition planners must decide whether they will use either price analysis or cost analysis to distinguish between proposals. The basic purposes of these analyses are to give the contracting officer the information he or she needs to determine if the price is fair and reasonable and to identify any price or cost issues that must be addressed before a source selection decision can be made.

PRICE ANALYSIS

Under price analysis, the government does not address the individual elements of a contractor's proposed price or cost and profit. Instead, the offered price is compared with available information to determine if it is indeed fair and reasonable. A proposed price could be compared with any or all the following data:

- Other prices received in response to the solicitation
- Previous prices offered or paid for the same or similar requirements
- Prices being paid as determined by parametric estimating techniques such as dollars per pound or cost per square foot
- Catalog prices in competitive markets

- Independent government cost estimates
- Any other rational and reasonable basis for comparison.

COST ANALYSIS

Cost analysis, as defined in FAR 15.404-1, is the review and evaluation of the separate cost elements in an offeror's cost proposal to determine how well the proposed costs represent what the cost of the contract should be, assuming reasonable economy and efficiency. For example, the government could examine a contractor's proposed labor costs, material costs, overhead and profit.

WHICH METHOD TO USE?

The solicitation must tell competing contractors what price information or cost information the government wants them to include in their proposals. While price analysis is the preferred method of determining reasonableness, it obviously cannot fit every situation. For example, in a research and development procurement, the technical approaches may vary widely, and merely comparing prices would not provide definitive evidence that a given price is fair and reasonable for the technical approach proposed.

The government may also use other techniques as a part of the price or cost analysis. For example, value analysis can be used to determine the value of a product or service. Value may include factors other than just the proposed cost or price, such as life cycle cost, which could include the cost of acquisition, the cost of using and maintaining the product being procured, and the cost of disposal.

COST REALISM AND PROBABLE COST

If the government is contemplating a cost-reimbursement contract, then the government "shall" perform a cost realism analysis of each proposal to "determine the *probable cost* of performance for each offeror" (FAR 15.404-1(d)(2)). Probable cost is determined by adjusting the cost and fees proposed by an offeror to reflect any additions or reductions in individual cost elements that the government believes are necessary to reflect a realistic amount for the proposed effort.

The government performs cost realism analysis for cost-reimbursement contracts because contractors working under such contracts assume relatively little cost risk. They will, in most cases, be reimbursed for all authorized costs that were reasonably incurred. Accordingly, contractors may be overly optimistic about costs when preparing proposals, and the pressure of competition may encourage them to submit their most optimistic proposed costs rather than their most realistic proposed costs. Because the government will ultimately have to pay the bill, the government compares the probable costs of proposals rather than the proposed costs when making the source selection decision.

Cost realism analysis may also be used for contract types other than cost-reimbursement to help the government determine if the contractor truly understands the government requirement. It may be used in similar performance or cost risk assessments as well, such as in making responsibility determinations and/or assessing the potential for schedule slippage.

Section M in Appendix II shows how one contracting center addressed cost realism and probable cost for cost-reimbursement evaluation tasks (sample tasks).

CHAPTER 19

DETERMINING THE RELATIVE IMPORTANCE OF COST OR PRICE

In the past, it was common practice for some agencies to include cost as an integrated factor in tradeoff procurements. For example, evaluation factors might be ranked in order of importance as follows:

1. Technical approach

2. Key personnel

3. Cost

4. Management plan

5. Facilities.

Some people in the procurement community took exception to this practice. In an article in *Contract Management Magazine*, this integrated-factor practice was compared to selecting a brand of beef stew at the supermarket.[1] It would make little sense to integrate cost into the buyer's assessment of the beef stew ingredients. That would create an order of importance somewhat like the following:

1. Beef

2. Potatoes

3. Cost

4. Gravy

5. Carrots and peas.

One cannot buy beef and potatoes from one can (brand) of stew and get gravy from a different can. One has to buy the entire can or nothing. Thus, to determine the best value, it is necessary to consider all the ingredients of a can and then measure the perceived value of those combined ingredients against the cost of that can. Similarly, the government cannot take a technical approach from one proposal and key personnel from another. It has to "buy" a whole proposal or nothing.

FAR GUIDANCE

Ultimately, the FAR was changed. FAR 15.304(e) now requires that, at a minimum, a solicitation state whether all evaluation factors other than cost or price when combined are:

- Significantly more important than cost or price
- Approximately equal to cost or price
- Significantly less important than cost or price.

Accordingly, acquisition planners have to decide the relative importance of cost or price. In tradeoff procurements, agencies often opt for "significantly more important than cost or price." This gives a great deal of flexibility to the source selection authority since, notwithstanding the emphasis on cost or price, the selection authority may choose a lower-priced proposal if he or she does not think that any increase in proposal merit is worth the corresponding increase in price.

Some agencies have a practice of informing offerors that as merit scores tend to equalize, cost may become a more significant factor. While this may not be necessary, these kinds of commonsense qualifying statements probably do no harm and may help competing contractors to better understand the process.

Although the FAR clearly indicates that cost or price should be compared to all non-cost factors combined, some agencies have continued to consider past performance as a third factor, following merit and cost. In these cases, it seems to be used more as a tiebreaker, rather than as an integrated factor. Remember, however, that you cannot get merit from one proposal and past performance from another. You have to buy the whole enchilada or nothing.

THE CONTINUUM

FAR 15.101 describes a continuum on which the relative importance of cost or price may vary. It states, as an example, that "in acquisitions where the requirement is clearly definable and the risk of successful contractor performance is minimal, cost or price may play a dominant role in source selection. The less definitive the requirement, the more development work required, or the greater the performance risk, the more technical or past performance may play a dominant role." The FAR offers this information only as an "example," so presumably the desire or need for "quality" could also be a factor in determining the relative importance of price or cost.

Note

1. Charles D. Solloway, "A Beef Stew Approach to Source Selection," *Contract Management Magazine* (January 1989).

CHAPTER 20

DESIGNING PROPOSAL PREPARATION INSTRUCTIONS

Each solicitation must include instructions to offerors identifying the required format to be used in preparing proposals, and it must list the matters that offerors have to address in their proposals. There are virtually no limiting ground rules—except that the instructions should not conflict with any of the other content in the solicitation. Thus, planners have a wide range of choices in specifying content, format, and media.

Typically, competing contractors are asked to submit proposals in two parts:

1. The technical/merit proposal

2. The cost proposal.

Usually, one group of people evaluates the technical (or merit) proposal, and another group (or one individual) evaluates the cost or price proposal. However, there is no FAR requirement that merit and cost proposals be separated.

If different groups are to be assigned to evaluate discrete aspects of the non-cost factors, competing contractors are often required to submit proposals in more than two discrete parts (usually referred to as *volumes*). For example, in an Air Force acquisition involving the environmental remediation of 14 Air Force bases, contractors were asked to submit the following volumes:

- Volume I – Executive summary
- Volume II – Technical proposal
- Volume III – Management proposal
- Volume IV – Site-specific information
- Volume V – Past performance
- Volume VI – Administrative proposal
- Volume VII – Cost proposal.

Competing contractors were permitted to submit offers for just one site, all sites, or any number in between. And, of course, the Air Force provided specific instructions about what was to be included in each volume. Obviously, the Air Force planned to have separate groups concurrently evaluate separate volumes.

In the sample solicitation in Appendix II, a contracting center requested proposal information in four volumes:

- Technical
- Management and related corporate experience
- Past performance
- Cost/price.

Section L of the sample solicitation describes for the competing contractors what must be included in each volume.

Agencies can require that proposals, or parts of proposals, be submitted on paper, on disc or tape, or as an oral presentation. They may specify requirements for font size, paper size, margins, or length, and they may also impose any other restrictions or offer any other additional guidance. The instructions almost always include the topics that offerors must address and the order in which they are to be addressed.

In training courses given on proposal preparation, contractor personnel are sometimes told that they should not give the government anything it did not ask for in the solicitation. On the government side, it is good advice to:

- Ask for only what is needed.
- Make sure that what is asked for includes *everything* that is needed.
- Get contractor feedback in the planning stage through draft RFPs or other presolicitation exchanges.

ISSUES TO CONSIDER

Planners must consider a number of issues when designing solicitation instructions. Foremost, the instructions have to be compatible with the requirements document and with the evaluation factors. The government has to have the information it needs to evaluate proposals in the manner it has promised in the solicitation, and it has to have the information needed to ultimately determine which proposal offers the best value.

Secondly, the instructions should be designed to permit an efficient evaluation process. For example, it is useful for planners to specify the order in which offerors are to present information so that there will be uniformity among proposals and so that evaluators will not have to search through the proposals for specific required information. Limits on size and content can facilitate evaluation since evaluators will not have to wade through trade puffery of questionable value in order to ferret out meaningful content. Specific instructions can also level the playing field by limiting the size and content of proposals. Competing contractors will not have to guess what the government wants or strive to outspend one another to make a favorable impression.

BEWARE OF SAMPLE-ITIS

A number of protests regarding proposal preparation instructions that were not compatible with the requirements document, the evaluation factors, or both have been upheld. Ensuring compatibility should be taken seriously. Don't fall victim to sample-itis—copying from previous solicitations rather than tailoring the solicitation (see Chapter 12).

CONSIDER THE PREPARATION COST

The cost to competing contractors should always be a consideration in devising proposal preparation instructions. If competition is to be limited to small businesses, including small disadvantaged businesses, extra care should be taken to limit the cost of competing by designing cost-effective proposal preparation instructions. The idea is to help these small businesses, not to bankrupt them.

USING MARKET RESEARCH IN DESIGNING INSTRUCTIONS

Market research should play a part in the design of the proposal preparation instructions just as it does in establishing evaluation criteria. In one highly publicized acquisition, a government agency indicated in its proposal instructions that all offerors would be given an opportunity to give an oral presentation after written proposals were received and that the oral presentations would be evaluated. The agency apparently expected a modest number of written proposals when it designed these instructions, but it actually received more than 200 written proposals. Giving hundreds of offerors an opportunity to deliver an evaluated oral presentation would have consumed an onerous amount of time. Consequently, the agency did not give all offerors an opportunity to give an oral presentation, but instead devised a modified evaluation scheme wherein only selected offerors had that opportunity. The agency did this without amending the RFP to revise the evaluation criteria and the proposal preparation instructions. Not surprisingly, this provoked protests.

The Comp Gen upheld the protests and recommended that the agency either afford all offerors an opportunity for an oral presentation or amend the RFP and allow offerors to revise their proposals (Kathpal Technologies, Inc.; Computer & Hi-Tech Management, Inc., B-283137.3, December 30, 1999). The outcome for the agency was the loss of a considerable amount of time, energy, and money. Perhaps more extensive market research that included contacting the private sector through RFIs or draft RFPs would have disclosed the high degree of interest in the acquisition and spurred government planners to rewrite the proposal preparation instructions. Or perhaps some "what-if" gymnastics would have been in order during the planning phase. Planners could have asked themselves, "What if we receive a large number of proposals?"

CHAPTER 21

USING ORAL PRESENTATIONS

In the previous chapter, we briefly addressed the use of oral presentations. However, the potential value and the complexity of this component of source selection requires more in-depth coverage.

Oral presentations, sometimes called oral proposals, began to be used in earnest in the late 1980s and early 1990s during a period of great change and experimentation in the source selection process. This experimentation was intended to both improve the effectiveness of source selections and streamline the source selection process. Most of those streamlining efforts were aimed at reducing the expense associated with source selections and the amount of time the process consumed.

Initially, acquisition reformers believed that the process could be streamlined by *substituting* oral presentations for written material. However, during the experimentation phase, many contracting officers found oral presentations to be most valuable when they *augmented* written material. They felt that oral presentations gave them far greater insight into the written material and allowed for more accurate proposal evaluations and better source selections. Ironically, however, oral presentations used in this manner usually added time and expense to the process. For example, instead of just submitting a written proposal, a contractor would also be required to prepare a slide show and fly to Paducah to present it to the government. Government evaluators were also impacted since they had to spend more time on the evaluation process.

FAR GUIDANCE

In a relatively rare occurrence of regulation following practice, oral presentations were widely used throughout federal executive agencies before they were covered in the FAR. Ultimately, the FAR was changed to address oral presentations. The FAR allows for oral presentations to be used either to substitute for or to augment written material (see Exhibit 21-1 for the relevant FAR guidance). The FAR coverage also provides that oral presentations may be given at any time during the acquisition process. As a practical matter, this means that:

- If award is to be made without holding discussions, oral presentations may be held on or after the initial due date for submission of proposals and before award. The presentations may not provide an opportunity for a contractor to revise the proposal. To put it another way, dialogue at oral presentations may not constitute discussions because discussions are held for the purpose of permitting proposal revisions.

- If a competitive range is to be established and discussions are to be held, oral presentations may be held before the competitive range is established and/or at any time thereafter prior to final proposal revisions. Oral presentation dialogue after the competitive range determination may involve discussions, provided that meaningful discussions have been held with all offerors still in the competitive range before final proposal revisions are requested and received. (The requirement for *meaningful* discussions is examined in Chapter 33.)

Acquisition planners should consider these alternatives and craft the proposal preparation instructions accordingly.

As the FAR makes it clear that oral presentations provide an opportunity for *dialogue* between the government and competing contractors, videotape or disc presentations are not considered oral presentations. There is no prohibition against having information conveyed to the government in this manner, if allowed by or required by the solicitation; it is just that these formats are not considered oral presentations.

When oral presentations are to be used in lieu of written material, planners have a great deal of flexibility. The FAR mandates only that required *representations and certifications* (see Appendix III for the definition of this term) and a signed offer sheet be in writing. Most acquisition officials seem to interpret a "signed offer sheet" as the signed price/cost offer.

As may be seen in subparagraph (c) of Exhibit 21-1, planners should consider a number of issues before determining how—or if—oral presentations will be used, including the need to incorporate any information that must be reflected in the resultant contract. A government contract may not simply reference oral discussions. Anything that is to be incorporated into the contract must be reduced to writing. Subparagraph (d) of Exhibit 21-1 identifies a number of issues that should be addressed in the solicitation, including the scope and content of exchanges.

WHO SHOULD GIVE THE PRESENTATION?

The government most often requires that oral presentations be given by one or more of the key people who would work on the contract, such as the offeror's project officer or senior scientist. Consequently, some government program officials refer to an oral presentation as a job interview. This is because the oral presentation gives attending government program officials a chance to judge the competence and demeanor of the individuals with whom they may be working in the months or years ahead.

THE POP QUIZ

Some agencies use a pop quiz technique during oral presentations, wherein presenters are asked questions about the general subject area of the contract. For example, if the contract requirement is for environmental remediation, the presenter or presenters might be asked questions about hazardous waste disposal or some other important aspect of environmental remediation. The point of quizzing the presenters is, of course, to find out if they know what they are talking about. If presenters are to be evaluated on the basis of a pop quiz, the solicitation must indicate this.

When the government was just beginning to use oral presentations in source selection, some people in the acquisition community championed them as a sorely needed device for making better source selections. They argued that the reliance on written proposals was turning source selection into an essay-writing contest. But others were concerned that the charisma and presentation skills of presenters could just as easily unduly influence evaluators. The pop quiz technique may be one way to guard against that happening. An Army contracting officer told this author of an instance in which two competing contractors had high marks on their written proposals, and both were given an opportunity to deliver oral presentations. Contractor A's key personnel were clearly the best presenters, and their PowerPoint presentation was superb. Contractor B's key personnel were not skilled presenters, and their presentation media, while satisfactory, was nothing to write home about. However, it was the pop quiz that made the difference. Contractor B's key personnel were clearly the more knowledgeable and competent. Contractor B was awarded the contract.

PLANNING CONSIDERATIONS

Issues to be considered when planning for oral presentations include:

- *Location.* If presentations are to be given at a government location, planners should select a location that is readily accessible to contractors, that will be available when needed, and where disruptions are unlikely.

- *Equipment.* If presentations are to be given at a government location, the solicitation should identify the equipment available for contractor use in giving the presentation, and someone on the government side should make sure the necessary equipment is actually available at the promised time and is suitable for use. It may be wise to have standby equipment available.

- *Number of attendees.* The solicitation should address the number of contractor personnel that will be permitted to attend the oral presentation in addition to the presenters.

- *Order of presentations.* Most competing contractors want to present their material either first or last, since behavioral research indicates that material presented first or last in any presentation makes a stronger impression than material presented in the middle. To be fair, most agencies determine the order of presentations through a lottery procedure (such as drawing names out of a hat), and contractors are normally informed in the solicitation that this will be the case.

- *Time.* There are no regulatory prescribed time limits for oral presentations. In the examples shown in Exhibit 21-2, for instance, presentations ranged from 90 minutes to a day and a half in duration. The ability of evaluators to maintain an effective level of concentration over time should be considered when determining the duration of presentations. In this regard, shorter may be better.

- *Recording of presentations.* As Exhibit 21-1 shows, the contracting officer must maintain a record of oral presentations. The recording method and level and detail of the information documented are at the discretion of the source selection authority. If presentations are to be electronically recorded, it is suggested that two recording instruments be used in case one fails. (In at least one instance, a government agency has had to bring a contractor back to redo an oral presentation because of a faulty video camera.) It is also suggested that the government not rely on briefing slides alone as the required record. Few things are more ambiguous than the bullet points on a briefing slide when there is no one there to explain them.

- *Time of evaluation.* Planners will have to decide how and when evaluators will assess the presentations. Generally, evaluations will be more accurate if they are done immediately after each presentation. If evaluations are not to be done until all presentations have been given, then it is suggested that presentations be electronically recorded so that evaluators can refresh their memories before evaluating individual presentations.

- *Rescheduling.* Planners will have to decide whether to permit any rescheduling. If rescheduling is allowed, planners will have to address the circumstances under which it will be considered and the procedures competing contractors will use to request it.

Obviously, planners must address a significant number of issues when considering the use of oral presentations. This should not deter planners from using this valuable tool when it can contribute to an effective source selection.

DIALOGUE AND DISCUSSIONS

Exhibit 21-2 which comes from the Office of Federal Procurement Policy's *Guide for Oral Presentations,* is a compilation of excerpts from solicitations issued by various agencies, in which they inform offerors about the ground rules for oral presentations. As you will see, some agencies seem to have a great deal of concern about dialogue becoming discussions.

While oral presentations offer a valuable opportunity for dialogue, care should be taken in how this dialogue is conducted, especially when the government does not intend to hold discussions. This does not mean that dialogue must be eliminated or be so severely restricted as to be of little value. Certainly a contracting officer should be able to control the dialogue when award without discussions is planned and make sure that contractors are not given an opportunity to revise their proposals. (The opportunity for proposal revision is normally the acid test for determining if discussions have taken place.) Simply prohibiting dialogue in presentations, as some have done in our examples, seems a draconian solution to avoiding discussions and diminishes the value of oral presentations.

Some in the acquisition world believe that offerors can address their past performance and experience in dialogue until the cows come home, and that still would not constitute discussions because a competing contractor obviously cannot change its past performance or experience. It can only influence the government's perception of the facts.

If oral presentations take place under solicitations in which discussions are to be permitted, then the only problem would seem to be ensuring that meaningful discussions have taken place at some time before final proposal revisions. If all meaningful discussion issues are not addressed during oral presentations, they can be addressed later through written or oral exchanges with the contractors before the final proposal revision is requested.

The Comp Gen issued the following opinion on a situation in which oral presentation exchanges went past dialogue and became meaningful discussions:

> The FAR generally anticipates "dialogue among the parties" in the course of an oral presentation, FAR § 15.102(a), and we see nothing improper in agency personnel expressing their view about vendors' quotations or proposals, in addition to listening to the vendors' presentations, during those sessions. Once the agency personnel begin speaking, rather than merely listening, in those sessions, however, that dialogue may constitute discussions. As we have long held, the acid test for deciding whether an agency has engaged in discussions is whether the agency has provided an opportunity for quotations or proposals to be revised or modified. See, e.g., TDS, Inc., B-292674, Nov. 12, 2003, 2003 CPD __[*sic*] at 6; Priority One Servs., Inc., B-288836, B-288836.2, Dec. 17, 2001, 2002 CPD 79 at 5. Accordingly, where agency personnel comment on, or raise substantive questions or concerns about, vendors' quotations or proposals in the course of an oral presentation, and either simultaneously or subsequently afford the vendors an opportunity to make revisions in light of the agency personnel's comments and concerns, discussions have occurred. TDS, Inc., *supra*, at 6; see FAR § 15.102(g) (Sierra Military Health Services Inc; Aetna Government Health Plans, B-292780; B-292780.2; B-292780.3; B-292780.4; B-292780.5; B-292780.6, December 5, 2003).

Holding discussions during an oral presentation, even if unintended, is not a fatal error if it is recognized before final proposal revision and selection of a source. If discussions are held with one offeror in the competitive range, then discussions have to be held with all offerors in the competitive range, and they must be meaningful discussions. Thus, if an agency intended to make award without discussions, but it inadvertently held discussions with one competing contractor, the contracting officer can then establish a competitive range and hold meaningful discussions with all the contractors in the competitive range.

The apprehension that some acquisition officials feel with regard to oral presentations was made very evident when a private-sector instructor recently taught a source selection class at a government location where the agency training officials asked that oral presentations not be addressed at all during the class. The agency apparently had a bad experience with oral presentations and had decided to throw this tool out of the toolbox. It is likely that the problem may not have been with the tool but with the manner in which it was used. If oral presentations did not work well for the agency, then perhaps a more productive reaction would have been to learn from the experience and make the adjustments needed to use oral presentations in a more effective manner.

EXHIBIT 21-1   FAR Guidance on Oral Presentations (FAR 15.102)

(a) Oral presentations by offerors as requested by the Government may substitute for, or augment, written information. Use of oral presentations as a substitute for portions of a proposal can be effective in streamlining the source selection process. Oral presentations may occur at any time in the acquisition process, and are subject to the same restrictions as written information, regarding timing (see 15.208) and content (see 15.306). Oral presentations provide an opportunity for dialogue among the parties. Pre-recorded videotaped presentations that lack real-time interactive dialogue are not considered oral presentations for the purposes of this section, although they may be included in offeror submissions, when appropriate.

(b) The solicitation may require each offeror to submit part of its proposal through oral presentations. However, representations and certifications shall be submitted as required in the FAR provisions at 52.204-8(d) or 52.212-352.2(b), and a signed offer sheet (including any exceptions to the Government's terms and conditions) shall be submitted in writing.

(c) Information pertaining to areas such as an offeror's capability, past performance, work plans or approaches, staffing resources, transition plans, or sample tasks (or other types of tests) may be suitable for oral presentations. In deciding what information to obtain through an oral presentation, consider the following:

(1) The Government's ability to adequately evaluate the information;

(2) The need to incorporate any information into the resultant contract;

(3) The impact on the efficiency of the acquisition; and

(4) The impact (including cost) on small businesses. In considering the costs of oral presentations, contracting officers should also consider alternatives to on-site oral presentations (*e.g.*, teleconferencing, video teleconferencing).

(d) When oral presentations are required, the solicitation shall provide offerors with sufficient information to prepare them. Accordingly, the solicitation may describe—

(1) The types of information to be presented orally and the associated evaluation factors that will be used;

(2) The qualifications for personnel that will be required to provide the oral presentation(s);

(3) The requirements for, and any limitations and/or prohibitions on, the use of written material or other media to supplement the oral presentations;

(4) The location, date, and time for the oral presentations;

(5) The restrictions governing the time permitted for each oral presentation; and

(6) The scope and content of exchanges that may occur between the Government's participants and the offeror's representatives as part of the oral presentations, including whether or not discussions (see 15.306(d)) will be permitted during oral presentations.

(e) The contracting officer shall maintain a record of oral presentations to document what the Government relied upon in making the source selection decision. The method and level of detail of the record (*e.g.*, videotaping, audio tape recording, written record, Government notes, copies of offeror briefing slides or presentation notes) shall be at the discretion of the source selection authority. A copy of the record placed in the file may be provided to the offeror.

(f) When an oral presentation includes information that the parties intend to include in the contract as material terms or conditions, the information shall be put in writing. Incorporation by reference of oral statements is not permitted.

(g) If, during an oral presentation, the Government conducts discussions (see 15.306(d)), the Government must comply with 15.306 and 15.307.

EXHIBIT 21-2   Excerpts from Agencies' Oral Presentation Solicitation Instructions

Nuclear Regulatory Commission

"Total presentation time shall be no longer than 2 hours.… During oral presentations NRC technical representatives will not ask the offeror to elaborate on ideas or otherwise request information. Clarification requests will be limited to asking the offeror to repeat statements that were not heard clearly. The NRC will not inform an offeror of [its] strengths, deficiencies, or weaknesses during the presentation, and the NRC will not engage in discussions during the presentation."

Bureau of Engraving and Printing

"The presentation will not exceed a two hour time limit for the oral presentation. The Government may ask questions at the conclusion of the presentation but it will not count against the time limit. The question and answer period will not exceed one hour."

Department of Energy

"Offerors shall be scheduled for presentation of the oral proposals by lottery. It is expected that no more than one and one-half days will be allowed for each offeror to present its [o]ral [p]roposal.… The oral proposal shall be presented by the proposed management personnel with each manager presenting the portion of the proposal for which he/she would be responsible.… After completion of the oral presentation, the Government may request clarification.… [I]nterchange between the offeror and the Government will be for clarification only, and will not constitute discussions.…"

NASA

"Total briefing time will be limited to 90 minutes. The Government will ask questions at the conclusion of the briefing which will not count against the time limit."

Health and Human Services

"In addition to the Sample Tasks provided for the video tape presentation, the Government will provide two 'pop quiz' question[s] at the video taping for response by the offeror's proposed contract manager. The answers to the 'pop quiz' will be numerically scored as part of the technical evaluation...."

Internal Revenue Service

"Requests from offerors to reschedule their presentations will not be entertained...."

PART III

SOLICITING PROPOSALS AND PREPARING FOR EVALUATIONS

This part of the book examines the rules for publicizing the planned issuance of a solicitation, the actual preparation and issuance of the solicitation, use of the uniform contract format, suggestions on holding preproposal conferences, and preparing evaluators and advisors for the task ahead.

CHAPTER 22

SYNOPSIZING A PLANNED ACQUISITION

The FAR and public law require that proposed contract actions of $25,000 or more be publicized on a government website, Federal Business Opportunities (www.fedbizopps.gov), the governmentwide point of entry (GPE). Agencies publicize such contract actions by issuing a synopsis (a brief description of the proposed action) that can readily be accessed by contractors. FAR 5.207 gives very specific guidance on the content required. Exhibit 22-1 is an an example of a rather straightforward synopsis. It explains what work is required, when the work is to be performed, and where it is to be performed.

FAR 5.203(a) requires that a synopsis for planned procurements be published at least 15 days prior to issuance of the solicitation, but less time may be allowed for a commercial item acquisition. FAR 12.603 permits a combined synopsis/solicitation for commercial items (see Chapter 47 for more details).

WHY ARE SYNOPSES IMPORTANT?

The goals of the synopsis requirement are to increase competition, broaden industry participation in government requirements, and aid certain socioeconomic categories of contractors (including small businesses, veteran-owned businesses, small disadvantaged businesses, women-owned businesses, and HUBZone small businesses) in obtaining contracts and subcontracts.

When a contractor reviews a synopsis and determines that it has a reasonable potential for submitting a winning proposal, it may request an opportunity to participate in the procurement. Accordingly, synopses should be carefully worded to attract offerors that could feasibly furnish the product or service and not unfairly encourage proposals from those that would have little or no chance of receiving a contract award.

EXCEPTIONS TO THE SYNOPSIS REQUIREMENT

There are 15 exceptions to the synopsis requirement. In brief, they are:

1. National security issues

2. Unusual urgency

3. Certain procurements on behalf of foreign governments or pursuant to international agreements

4. Procurements authorized or required by statute to be made through another government agency

5. Utility services (other than telecommunications) where only one source is available

6. Orders placed under indefinite delivery contracts

7. Actions under the Small Business Development Act of 1982

8. Procurements resulting from unsolicited proposals under which a synopsis would improperly disclose original, innovative, or proprietary information

9. Certain actions for perishable subsistence supplies

10. Certain brand-name items intended for resale

11. Certain actions under contracts previously synopsized

12. Defense agency contracts performed outside the United States and its outlying areas and for which only local sources will be solicited

13. Certain simplified acquisitions to which the public may respond electronically

14. Certain expert services involving litigation or dispute

15. An agency head has made a written determination that advance notice is not appropriate or reasonable (requires consultation with the administrator of the Office of Federal Procurement Policy and the administrator of the Small Business Administration).

OTHER SITUATIONS IN WHICH SYNOPSES ARE PERMITTED OR REQUIRED

Issuing synopses is permitted or required for procurement actions other than proposed contract actions of at least $25,000. These include:

- R&D Sources Sought notices, which may be synopsized when market research does not identify a sufficient number of potential contractors to obtain adequate competition
- Establishing or changing the mission of a federally funded research center
- Issuing special notices of events related to procurement, such as business fairs, long-range procurement planning meetings, and proposal conferences
- Certain architect-engineer service acquisitions
- Private-public competitions under OMB Circular A-76

- Small disadvantaged business competitive acquisitions under Section 8 (a) of the Small Business Act
- Notices of draft RFPs or RFIs.

EXHIBIT 22-1   Sample Synopsis: Veterans Administration Health Services Procurement

---

Solicitation Number:
VA25710RP0201

Notice Type:
Solicitation

Synopsis:
VA North Texas Health Care System has a requirement for Home Health Care Services. Contractor shall provide in-Home Health Care to Veteran beneficiaries located within the following Texas & Oklahoma counties:

Cooke, Delta, Fannin, Grayson, Hopkins, Hunt, Lamar, Red River counties; and Bryan and Choctaw counties. (Bryan and Choctaw are located in Oklahoma.)

Levels of care shall include Skilled Nursing, Homemaker Services, Home Health Aide, Physical Therapy, Speech Therapy and Occupational Therapy.

The contract shall be effective for a base period beginning on award date and continuing through 06/30/2011, with two one-year option periods available.

The NAICS code for this requirement is 621610, and the SBA size standard is $13,500,000.

Anticipated solicitation issued date will be on or about 06/02/2010 with the closing date of 06/23/2010 and will be issued as a commercial item requirement. Interested parties may obtain a copy of this solicitation number VA-257-10-RP-0201 at the following URL: http://www.fedbizopps.gov.

CHAPTER 23

PREPARING THE SOLICITATION

Now that all the planning has been accomplished and the many solicitation content choices have been made, it is time to prepare the solicitation. The Uniform Contract Format (UCF) shown in Exhibit 23-1 is the format used for most conventional source selections using RFPs. While other formats are used for specific purposes, such as the solicitation/contract format for commercial items, all the formats have these common elements crucial to the source selection:

- They define the requirement.
- They give proposal preparation instructions, as appropriate.
- They inform offerors of any evaluation factors and any subfactors and, if it is a tradeoff acquisition, the relative importance of these factors and subfactors.

FAR 15.303(b) specifically requires that the source selection authority shall "ensure consistency among the solicitation requirements, notices to offerors, proposal preparation instructions, evaluation factors and subfactors, solicitation provisions or contract clauses, and data requirements." In other words, it is critical that all key elements of the solicitation be compatible. The government cannot evaluate a competing contractor's technical approach unless it first asks the contractor to furnish a technical approach as part of the proposal. And the government would not consider a technical approach at all if the requirements document specifies that the successful contractor must use a government-directed technical approach. Although this all sounds like common sense, these issues have caused a great deal of problems in the past—probably due to sample-itis and a lack of thought.

THE FAR PROVISION ON INSTRUCTIONS TO OFFERORS

A solicitation must also include the clauses and provisions that are required by FAR and agency regulations. This is done by either including the clauses and provisions *en toto* or by referencing the particular FAR part or other citation where the clause or provision can be found. One of these standard provisions, Instructions to Offerors—Competitive Acquisitions, is especially important in the source selection process. A copy of the current version of this provision appears in Exhibit 23-2. Subparagraph (f)(4) of the standard provision informs competing contractors that the government intends to make an award without establishing a competitive range and without holding discussions. However, that subparagraph also gives the government the right to hold discussions if the contracting officer later decides that discussions are necessary.

Exhibit 23-2 also contains an alternate subparagraph (f)(4). This subparagraph informs competing contractors that the government intends to establish a competitive range and hold discussions.

The contracting officer and the source selection authority will have to determine which of these subparagraphs to use. It appears that the basic clause is used most of the time, and the alternate clause is used primarily for acquisitions of major systems or other complex acquisitions.

Other matters covered in the provision in Exhibit 23-2 include information/rules regarding late proposals, withdrawal of proposals, marking of proprietary/protected data, alternate proposals, and debriefing information.

COMPATIBILITY AND CLARITY

It is essential that the solicitation be carefully prepared and that all source selection provisions be clearly written. Section L and Section M of the example shown in Appendix II give some indication of how specific proposal-related information ought to be.

Since acquisition planners will have already done the lion's share of determining what goes in Sections L and M of the UCF when they reach the point of preparing the solicitation, the only major task remaining is to include the information in the solicitation in a way that ensures clarity and compatibility. This can be especially challenging if different authors have written different sections, if section content has been designed by committee, or if the contracting organization has a practice of cutting and pasting material from past solicitations.

SPECIAL STANDARDS

The example shown in Appendix II also contains another noteworthy feature: Competing contractors must meet certain security requirements in order to be considered responsible contractors. FAR 9.104-2 provides:

> When it is necessary for a particular acquisition or class of acquisitions, the contracting officer shall develop, with the assistance of appropriate specialists, special standards of responsibility. Special standards may be particularly desirable

when experience has demonstrated that unusual expertise or specialized facilities are needed for adequate contract performance. The special standards shall be set forth in the solicitation (and so identified) and shall apply to all offerors.

When the acquisition planning team develops special standards, it is a good idea to put them in Section M. Potential contractors especially look at the evaluation factors in Section M to help them determine whether to compete. Of course, they also look at Section C to see if they can do the work required at a profit and at Section L to judge the cost of competing.

CAREFUL PREPARATION AND PROOFREADING

Under normal circumstances, much of the content of the solicitation becomes the contract. In fact, when using the UCF, only sections L and M are peculiar to the solicitation. It is critical that the entire solicitation be carefully prepared and that it be as unambiguous as the government can make it. The solicitation should be read multiple times by different people to ferret out any ambiguous language. Remember that both parties have to live with the solicitation promises made to, and instructions given to, competing contractors during the source selection process, and the parties will be legally bound by the resultant contract.

MAKING THE SOLICITATION AVAILABLE

The solicitation is made available to all contractors on an agency source list, when one is used, and to all contractors that have properly responded to the synopsis. Often, the agency furnishes hard copies. In other cases, the solicitation is made available on the Internet at a site specified by the contracting officer.

EXHIBIT 23-1   The Uniform Contract Format

Part I: The Schedule

  A Solicitation/contract form
  B Supplies or services and price/costs
  C Description/specifications/statement of work
  D Packaging and marking
  E Inspection and acceptance
  F Deliveries or performance
  G Contract administration data
  H Special contract requirements

Part II: Contract Clauses

  I Contract clauses

Part III: List of Documents, Exhibits, other Attachments

  J List of attachments

Part IV: Representations and Instructions

  K Representations, certifications, and other statements of offerors or respondents
  L Instructions, conditions, and notices to offerors or respondents
  M Evaluation factors for award

EXHIBIT 23-2   Instructions to Offerors—Competitive
                          Acquisition (FAR 52.215-1)

(a) Definitions. As used in this provision—
    "Discussions" are negotiations that occur after establishment of the competitive range that may, at the Contracting Officer's discretion, result in the offeror being allowed to revise its proposal.

    "In writing," "writing," or "written" means any worded or numbered expression that can be read, reproduced, and later communicated, and includes electronically transmitted and stored information.

    "Proposal modification" is a change made to a proposal before the solicitation's closing date and time, or made in response to an amendment, or made to correct a mistake at any time before award.

"Proposal revision" is a change to a proposal made after the solicitation closing date, at the request of or as allowed by a Contracting Officer as the result of negotiations.

"Time," if stated as a number of days, is calculated using calendar days, unless otherwise specified, and will include Saturdays, Sundays, and legal holidays. However, if the last day falls on a Saturday, Sunday, or legal holiday, then the period shall include the next working day.

(b) Amendments to solicitations. If this solicitation is amended, all terms and conditions that are not amended remain unchanged. Offerors shall acknowledge receipt of any amendment to this solicitation by the date and time specified in the amendment(s).

(c) Submission, modification, revision, and withdrawal of proposals.
(1) Unless other methods (e.g., electronic commerce or facsimile) are permitted in the solicitation, proposals and modifications to proposals shall be submitted in paper media in sealed envelopes or packages (i) addressed to the office specified in the solicitation, and (ii) showing the time and date specified for receipt, the solicitation number, and the name and address of the offeror. Offerors using commercial carriers should ensure that the proposal is marked on the outermost wrapper with the information in paragraphs (c)(1)(i) and (c)(1)(ii) of this provision.

(2) The first page of the proposal must show—

(i) The solicitation number;

(ii) The name, address, and telephone and facsimile numbers of the offeror (and electronic address if available);

(iii) A statement specifying the extent of agreement with all terms, conditions, and provisions included in the solicitation and agreement to furnish any or all items upon which prices are offered at the price set opposite each item;

(iv) Names, titles, and telephone and facsimile numbers (and electronic addresses if available) of persons authorized to negotiate on the offeror's behalf with the Government in connection with this solicitation; and

(v) Name, title, and signature of person authorized to sign the proposal. Proposals signed by an agent shall be accompanied by evidence of that agent's authority, unless that evidence has been previously furnished to the issuing office.

(3) Submission, modification, revision, and withdrawal of proposals.

(i) Offerors are responsible for submitting proposals, and any modifications or revisions, so as to reach the Government office designated in the solicitation by the time specified in the solicitation. If no time is specified in the solicitation, the time for receipt is 4:30 p.m., local time, for the designated Government office on the date that proposal or revision is due.

(ii)(A)Any proposal, modification, or revision received at the Government office designated in the solicitation after the exact time specified for receipt of offers is "late" and will not be considered unless it is received before award is made, the Contracting Officer determines that accepting the late offer would not unduly delay the acquisition; and—

(1) If it was transmitted through an electronic commerce method authorized by the solicitation, it was received at the initial point of entry to the Government infrastructure not later than 5:00 p.m. one working day prior to the date specified for receipt of proposals; or

(2) There is acceptable evidence to establish that it was received at the Government installation designated for receipt of offers and was under the Government's control prior to the time set for receipt of offers; or

(3) It is the only proposal received.

(ii)(B)However, a late modification of an otherwise successful proposal that makes its terms more favorable to the Government, will be considered at any time it is received and may be accepted.

(iii) Acceptable evidence to establish the time of receipt at the Government installation includes the time/date stamp of that installation on the proposal wrapper, other documentary evidence of receipt maintained by the installation, or oral testimony or statements of Government personnel.

(iv) If an emergency or unanticipated event interrupts normal Government processes so that proposals cannot be received at the office designated for receipt of proposals by the exact time specified in the solicitation, and urgent Government requirements preclude amendment of the solicitation, the time specified for receipt of proposals will be deemed to be extended to the same time of day specified in the solicitation on the first work day on which normal Government processes resume.

(v) Proposals may be withdrawn by written notice received at any time before award. Oral proposals in response to oral solicitations may be withdrawn orally. If the solicitation authorizes facsimile proposals, proposals may be withdrawn via facsimile received at any time before award, subject to the conditions specified in the provision at 52.215-5 Facsimile Proposals. Proposals may be withdrawn in person by an offeror or an authorized representative, if the identity of the person requesting withdrawal is established and the person signs a receipt for the proposal before award.

(4) Unless otherwise specified in the solicitation, the offeror may propose to provide any item or combination of items.

(5) Offerors shall submit proposals in response to this solicitation in English, unless otherwise permitted by the solicitation, and in U.S. dollars, unless

the provision at FAR 52.225-17 Evaluation of Foreign Currency Offers, is included in the solicitation.

(6) Offerors may submit modifications to their proposals at any time before the solicitation closing date and time, and may submit modifications in response to an amendment, or to correct a mistake at any time before award.

(7) Offerors may submit revised proposals only if requested or allowed by the Contracting Officer.

(8) Proposals may be withdrawn at any time before award. Withdrawals are effective upon receipt of notice by the Contracting Officer.

(d) Offer expiration date. Proposals in response to this solicitation will be valid for the number of days specified on the solicitation cover sheet (unless a different period is proposed by the offeror).

(e) Restriction on disclosure and use of data. Offerors that include in their proposals data that they do not want disclosed to the public for any purpose, or used by the Government except for evaluation purposes, shall—

(1) Mark the title page with the following legend:

This proposal includes data that shall not be disclosed outside the Government and shall not be duplicated, used, or disclosed—in whole or in part—for any purpose other than to evaluate this proposal. If, however, a contract is awarded to this offeror as a result of—or in connection with—the submission of this data, the Government shall have the right to duplicate, use, or disclose the data to the extent provided in the resulting contract. This restriction does not limit the Government's right to use information contained in this data if it is obtained from another source without restriction. The data subject to this restriction are contained in sheets [insert numbers or other identification of sheets]; and

(2) Mark each sheet of data it wishes to restrict with the following legend:

Use or disclosure of data contained on this sheet is subject to the restriction on the title page of this proposal.

(f) Contract award.

(1) The Government intends to award a contract or contracts resulting from this solicitation to the responsible offeror(s) whose proposal(s) represents the best value after evaluation in accordance with the factors and subfactors in the solicitation.

(2) The Government may reject any or all proposals if such action is in the Government's interest.

(3) The Government may waive informalities and minor irregularities in proposals received.

(4) The Government intends to evaluate proposals and award a contract without discussions with offerors (except clarifications as described in FAR 15.306(a)). Therefore, the offeror's initial proposal should contain the offeror's best terms

from a cost or price and technical standpoint. The Government reserves the right to conduct discussions if the Contracting Officer later determines them to be necessary. If the Contracting Officer determines that the number of proposals that would otherwise be in the competitive range exceeds the number at which an efficient competition can be conducted, the Contracting Officer may limit the number of proposals in the competitive range to the greatest number that will permit an efficient competition among the most highly rated proposals.

(5) The Government reserves the right to make an award on any item for a quantity less than the quantity offered, at the unit cost or prices offered, unless the offeror specifies otherwise in the proposal.

(6) The Government reserves the right to make multiple awards if, after considering the additional administrative costs, it is in the Government's best interest to do so.

(7) Exchanges with offerors after receipt of a proposal do not constitute a rejection or counteroffer by the Government.

(8) The Government may determine that a proposal is unacceptable if the prices proposed are materially unbalanced between line items or subline items. Unbalanced pricing exists when, despite an acceptable total evaluated price, the price of one or more contract line items is significantly overstated or understated as indicated by the application of cost or price analysis techniques. A proposal may be rejected if the Contracting Officer determines that the lack of balance poses an unacceptable risk to the Government.

(9) If a cost realism analysis is performed, cost realism may be considered by the source selection authority in evaluating performance or schedule risk.

(10) A written award or acceptance of proposal mailed or otherwise furnished to the successful offeror within the time specified in the proposal shall result in a binding contract without further action by either party.

(11) If a post-award debriefing is given to requesting offerors, the Government shall disclose the following information, if applicable:

(i) The agency's evaluation of the significant weak or deficient factors in the debriefed offeror's offer.

(ii) The overall evaluated cost or price and technical rating of the successful and the debriefed offeror and past performance information on the debriefed offeror.

(iii) The overall ranking of all offerors, when any ranking was developed by the agency during source selection.

(iv) A summary of the rationale for award.

(v) For acquisitions of commercial items, the make and model of the item to be delivered by the successful offeror.

(vi) Reasonable responses to relevant questions posed by the debriefed offeror as to whether source-selection procedures set forth in the solicitation, applicable regulations, and other applicable authorities were followed by the agency.

(End of provision)

Alternate I (Oct 1997). As prescribed in 15.209(a)(1), substitute the following paragraph (f)(4) for paragraph (f)(4) of the basic provision:

(f)(4) The Government intends to evaluate proposals and award a contract after conducting discussions with offerors whose proposals have been determined to be within the competitive range. If the Contracting Officer determines that the number of proposals that would otherwise be in the competitive range exceeds the number at which an efficient competition can be conducted, the Contracting Officer may limit the number of proposals in the competitive range to the greatest number that will permit an efficient competition among the most highly rated proposals. Therefore, the offeror's initial proposal should contain the offeror's best terms from a price and technical standpoint.

Alternate II (Oct 1997). As prescribed in 15.209 (a)(2), add a paragraph (c)(9) substantially the same as the following to the basic clause:

(c)(9) Offerors may submit proposals that depart from stated requirements. Such proposals shall clearly identify why the acceptance of the proposal would be advantageous to the Government. Any deviations from the terms and conditions of the solicitation, as well as the comparative advantage to the Government, shall be clearly identified and explicitly defined. The Government reserves the right to amend the solicitation to allow all offerors an opportunity to submit revised proposals based on the revised requirements.

CHAPTER 24

HOLDING A PREPROPOSAL CONFERENCE

A preproposal conference may be held if a solicitation provides for one, or if it later becomes clear that one is needed and the solicitation recipients are so notified. Preproposal conferences give potential offerors and the government an opportunity to jointly review the requirements in the solicitation and further ensure that everyone understands the requirements in the same way. While the term *preproposal conference* has traditionally been used for conferences held after the solicitation has been issued, some agencies (such as NASA) also use the term to describe meetings held after a draft RFP is issued but before the actual RFP is issued.

Preproposal conferences can provide one last chance for surfacing misunderstandings that could have significant negative impact if they are not discovered until later in the source selection process or after award. Information on planned preproposal conferences for competing contractors can be included in the solicitation, included as an amendment to the solicitation, or be sent by letter to everyone who received a copy of the solicitation. It can also be posted at the GPE.

Often the government follows up a preproposal conference by issuing a solicitation amendment that sets forth all the questions asked and answers given at the conference. When the work to be required under the contract will include work done at a government facility, it is typical to invite potential offerors to visit the work site. The site visit can be considered a preproposal conference whenever questions are asked and answers given. Sometimes, but not always, the government makes such site visits mandatory.

The FAR once had more detailed coverage on the conduct of preproposal meetings but now only mentions them briefly at 15.201 under the general heading of "Exchanges with industry before receipt of proposals." The more detailed coverage offered sound advice. For that reason, it is quoted here:

Preproposal Conferences

(a) A preproposal conference may be held to brief prospective offerors after a solicitation has been issued but before offers are submitted. Generally, the Government uses these conferences in complex negotiated acquisitions to explain or clarify complicated specifications and requirements.

(b) The contracting officer shall decide if a preproposal conference is required and make the necessary arrangements, including the following:

   (1)   If notice was not in the solicitation, give all prospective offerors who received the solicitation adequate notice of the time, place, nature, and scope of the conference.

   (2)   If time allows, request prospective offerors to submit written questions in advance. Prepared answers can then be delivered during the conference.

   (3)   Arrange for technical and legal personnel to attend the conference, if appropriate.

(c) The contracting officer or a designated representative shall conduct the preproposal conference, furnish all prospective offerors identical information concerning the proposed acquisition, make a complete record of the conference, and promptly furnish a copy of that record to all prospective offerors. Conferees shall be advised that—

(1)   Remarks and explanations at the conference shall not qualify the terms of the solicitation; and

(2)   Terms of the solicitation and specifications remain unchanged unless the solicitation is amended in writing.

Some agencies have their own have written procedures and policies specifically addressing preproposal conferences, while others do not. Exhibit 24-1 shows a National Institute of Allergy and Infectious Disease (NIAID) checklist for preproposal conferences.[1] It identifies administrative and other details that should be addressed before, during, and after the conference. The bulk of responsibility rests on the contract specialist, but he or she must frequently coordinate with project officers.

EXHIBIT 24-1   Preproposal Conference Checklist

General Guidelines

- Work with project officers to determine whether to limit the number of people from each company.
- Work with project officers to determine whether to allow personal recording devices, cameras, or video equipment.
- Work with project officers to decide whether to create a reading room where offerors can review documentation.
- Post the date, time, and location to give offerors enough time to read the RFP, prepare for the conference, and make travel arrangements.
- Notify offerors they will need a picture identification to enter the facility.
- Post the following disclaimer when inviting offerors or read it at the conference.

"A preproposal conference is for informational purposes only. It may answer some offeror questions; NIAID posts all questions at_____. Statements or representations made during the conference are not legally binding. Changes resulting from the conference are official only if issued through an amendment to the RFP."

Attendance Requests

- If reservations are needed due to anticipated size of the meeting, create a cut-off date for attendance requests.
- Send offerors an email address or fax number to submit their requests.
- Determine whether to post the attendance list or otherwise make it available to potential offerors.
- Notify offerors if releasing their name or company.

Preparation

- Reserve a meeting room large enough for group and accessible to handicapped persons.
- Work with project officers to identify conference presenters.
- Work with project officers to identify needed technical resources.
- Work with project officers to prepare an agenda.
- Prepare extra copies of the RFP and amendments for the conference. Make sure all materials are posted for the general population; see FAR 15.201.
- Ensure the conference is recorded or a transcript is made.
- Prepare a registration sign-up sheet.

Conducting a Preproposal Conference

- Initiate the recording by noting the date, time, RFP number, and project title.
- Welcome participants and introduce key people.
- Remind participants they must sign the registration sheet.
- Explain the purpose of the conference and how it will be conducted.
- Ask attendees to state their name and organization before asking questions, for recording purposes.
- Reread the disclaimer stated above.
- Work through the prepared agenda.

After a Preproposal Conference

- Review the transcript or recording of the conference to determine if an amendment to the RFP is required.
- Post all questions and answers.
- Post a register of attendees.

Note

1. National Institute of Allergy and Infectious Diseases. Online at www.funding.niaid.nih.gov (accessed June 2010).

CHAPTER 25

BRIEFING EVALUATORS AND ADVISORS

Before the government receives proposals, everyone who will be involved in the evaluation process is briefed. This briefing is controlled by the source selection authority and is usually given by the contracting officer or his or her representative, such as a contract specialist. Legal counsel and senior program officials may also participate in the briefing.

A thorough briefing helps put everyone on the same page and gives added protection against potentially grievous errors. A briefing should include:

- Reiteration of the rules for protecting sensitive procurement information, including a discussion of the Procurement Integrity Act
- A reminder that any contact with competing contractors must be authorized or directed by the contracting officer
- Discussion of conflict of interest rules and considerations, including offers of employment
- Examination and discussion of the requirements document
- Examination and discussion of the proposal preparation instructions

- Examination and discussion of the evaluation factors
- An explanation of the evaluation process to be used, including examination of the rating methodology and the scoring/rating categories to be used
- Discussion of the lines of communication in the source selection organization structure
- Informing evaluators that their job is to evaluate the proposals against the criteria in the solicitation, not against each other
- Explanation of the FAR requirement that the relative strengths, deficiencies, significant weaknesses, and risks supporting proposal evaluation be documented in the contract file
- Definition of *strengths, deficiencies, significant weaknesses, weaknesses, risk, clarifications, communications, and meaningful discussions*
- A review of individual evaluation forms (A sample form for a tradeoff procurement appears in Exhibit 25-1.)
- A review of summary evaluation forms
- If an SSAC or other advisors are to be used, discussion of the role these advisors will play in the process
- If nongovernment personnel are to be used as evaluators or advisors, discussion of the role they will play in the process and an explanation of limits on the material/information to which they will have access
- A review of established milestones for the remainder of the source selection process
- Questions and answers.

Some agencies prepare briefing materials, including booklets, CDs, or DVDs for use by the contracting officer to supplement or enhance the briefing.

EXHIBIT 25-1　Sample Proposal Evaluation Form[*]

Proposal _____

Evaluation factor _____

Evaluator _____

Score/rating _____

Note: Evaluator should attach continuation sheets as needed.

Strengths/benefits

_____

_____

_____

Clarifications/explanations needed

_____

_____

Deficiencies

_____

_____

_____

Significant weaknesses

_____

_____

_____

Weaknesses

_____

_____

_____

Comments/rationale

_____

_____

_____

Signed _____ Date _____

*Reprinted with permission from Scitech Services, Inc., Edgewood, Maryland.

PART IV

EVALUATING PROPOSALS AND CONDUCTING LIMITED EXCHANGES

This part addresses the evaluation of proposals, including merit/technical factors, past performance, and cost or price. We explain the use of probable cost in lieu of proposed cost and examine in detail the manner in which past performance is handled when a contractor has no relevant past performance.

This part also looks at the rules pertaining to adherence to the planned rating methodology. It explains the exchange known as clarifications and the flexibility afforded the contracting officer regarding clarifications.

CHAPTER 26

EVALUATION OF MERIT/ TECHNICAL FACTORS

In some acquisitions, a single team, often called a technical evaluation team (TET) or some other similar name, evaluates all non-cost factors. In others, there may be individual teams for the various evaluation factors. For example, there may be one team to evaluate technical approach, another for management considerations, another for past performance, and so on. The steps described in this chapter apply to both of those approaches.

The evaluation of proposals begins after the closing date for receipt of proposals. At that time, the contracting officer distributes copies of the proposals to the chair of the evaluation team or teams. This distribution may take place after contracting personnel do an initial screening to determine if contractors have followed the government's instructions regarding media, content, format, and length. Noncompliant proposals are identified for the contracting officer so that he or she can take appropriate action. He or she may, for example, determine that the offeror is not responsive (and is thus not eligible for award, unless discussions are held and proposal revisions are allowed).

Following distribution of proposals, a typical evaluation process might go as follows:

1. The chairperson of the evaluation team convenes a meeting and distributes the relevant written portions of the proposal and pertinent evaluation forms to team members. This meeting may also include a review of earlier briefings given on the duties and responsibilities of evaluators.

2. If offerors are to give oral presentations, the schedule for the presentations and pertinent evaluation forms are distributed.

3. The evaluation methodology is reviewed in detail so that all evaluators have a common understanding of the characteristics that a proposal must have to earn a specific rating for an evaluation factor or subfactor. (If it is an LPTA acquisition, the only ratings are "acceptable" or "not acceptable.")

4. Each team member evaluates the relevant portions of the written proposals and prepares an evaluation form. Typically, the evaluator will read the proposal through first, then reread and rate the proposal. This helps prevent evaluators from jumping to erroneous conclusions before considering the contents of the entire document.

5. In the case of oral presentations, evaluators normally perform any evaluations immediately after the presentation. In other cases, evaluators wait until all presentations are complete before assigning ratings. When this latter method is chosen, evaluators should review electronic recordings or written records of the presentations rather than just relying on memory and notes.

6. If it is an LPTA acquisition, the evaluation form must indicate whether the proposal was acceptable or not acceptable for each factor being evaluated. Evaluators must also provide supporting rationale for their findings on the evaluation form. This supporting rationale must clearly identify the deficiencies, significant weaknesses, or both that resulted in a finding of "unacceptable." It is not necessary to address the strengths of the proposal, except perhaps to justify a finding

of acceptability, because the relative strengths of acceptable proposals are not a factor in an LPTA selection.

7. In a tradeoff acquisition, the evaluator gives a rating or score for each evaluation factor on the evaluation forms for that factor, along with supporting rationale. FAR 15.305 specifically requires at a minimum "an assessment of each offeror's ability to accomplish the technical requirements." Unlike in LPTA acquisitions, "proposals may be evaluated to distinguish their relative quality by considering the degree to which they exceed the minimum requirements or will better satisfy the agency's needs" (ViroMed Laboratories Inc., B-310747.4, January 22, 2009).

8. If it is planned to make award without discussions, the evaluators must identify any areas of a proposal for which clarifications may be needed or desired before a finding regarding acceptability is made or a tradeoff score is assigned. The exchange that the FAR calls clarifications applies *only* to situations in which award is to be made without discussions.

9. The team meets at the call of the chairperson and attempts to reach a consensus on scores or findings so that a summary report can be sent to the contracting officer and source selection authority. In more complex procurements, this report is submitted to the source selection authority through a source selection evaluation board (SSEB) chairperson (who oversees the functioning of the individual evaluation teams), a source selection advisory council (SSAC), or other advisory persons or groups.

10. In the event a consensus opinion cannot be reached, some agencies forward a majority report and a minority report, while others use some sort of averaging method or go with the majority vote. Or they may rely on the chairperson to make a final decision. It is recommended that minority

opinions be given a voice in the summary report. It is a dangerous practice to hide disagreements from the contracting officer and SSA by taking an averaging or majority-rules approach.

11. When award is to be made without discussions, the summary report or advisory reports submitted to the source selection authority identify the strengths and shortcomings of proposals and may contain a recommendation for award. Some agencies require such a recommendation, others prohibit it, and still others leave the matter to the wishes of the particular contracting officer or source selection authority. No recommendation for award is necessary for LPTA acquisitions since the award will go to the lowest price among acceptable proposals.

12. When a competitive range is to be established, the report indicates whether, in the view of evaluators, there is any need for communications before the competitive range is established. (The exchange called communications is used only when a competitive range is to be established and discussions are to be held.) Some agencies require or request recommendations in the summary report as to which contractors should be included in the competitive range, while others do not.

13. If communications or clarifications occur, proposals are reevaluated, and changes may be made to the summary report as appropriate. (Note that in some situations, the contracting officer is notified of the need for communications or clarifications with contractors before the summary report is prepared. In that case, only a single summary report is prepared, after communications or clarifications are held.)

14. When a competitive range has been established, evaluators may be asked to help prepare for discussions. If written

discussions are planned, they may be asked to participate in preparing the letters to the competing contractors that have been placed in the competitive range. If oral discussions are to take place, evaluators may be asked to help prepare the negotiation plan, participate in the discussions, or both. Some agencies have an approval process for negotiation plans and use a "business clearance memorandum" to obtain the required approval.

15. Following completion of discussions and receipt of final proposal revisions, evaluators reevaluate the proposals still in the competitive range and send a new summary report to the contracting officer. The summary report may or may not include a recommendation for award, depending on agency procedures.

Some agencies (the U.S. Army, for example) include in their evaluation and summary report forms an Item for Negotiation (IFN) form, which can be used to document matters that must be clarified, communicated, or discussed. The Army requires this form for "each weakness, significant weakness, deficiency, or uncertainty."

A number of agencies have automated systems in which evaluation data can be entered as appropriate and then arrayed in a user-friendly fashion. Users of these systems still have to address all the issues and follow all the rules discussed in this book.

MATCHING THE WORDS WITH THE MUSIC

It is the responsibility of the contracting officer and the source selection authority to review evaluation reports carefully for errors, omissions, or anomalies. Too frequently, these officials receive reports in which the words do not match the music. For example, a report may show that a proposal has been given an outstanding rating, but there is a relatively long list of deficiencies and weaknesses. Or, conversely, a proposal receives a lesser rating, but there are no listed deficiencies or weaknesses.

RETAINING EVALUATORS AND EVALUATION FORMS

Competent and unbiased evaluation of meaningful evaluation factors is critical to the source selection process. Whenever possible, the same evaluators should be used throughout the process.

It is normal practice for most agencies to retain individual evaluator forms even after summary reports are prepared. However, those that do not retain them are apparently on safe ground, provided that final documentation can reasonably demonstrate the bases upon which the judgments were made. In Government Acquisitions Inc., B-401048, May 4, 2009, the Comp Gen opined:

> Although an agency must document its evaluation judgments in sufficient detail to show that they are not arbitrary, the necessary amount and level of detail will vary from procurement to procurement. U.S. Defense Sys., Inc., B-245563, Jan. 17, 1992, 92-1 CPD ¶ 89 at 3; Champion-Alliance, Inc., B-249504, Dec. 1, 1992, 92-2 CPD ¶ 386 at 6-7. For example, there is no requirement that the evaluation record must include narrative explanations for every rating assigned. Apex Marine Ship Mgmt. Co., LLC; American V-Ships Marine, Ltd., B-278276.25, B-278276.28, Sept. 25, 2000, 2000 CPD ¶ 164 at 8-9. Similarly, there is no requirement that an agency retain individual evaluator's notes or worksheets, provided the agency's final evaluation documentation reasonably explains the basis for the agency's judgments.

EVALUATING SMALL BUSINESS SUBCONTRACTING PLANS

One part of non-cost evaluation that is usually done separately from the evaluation of technical factors is the evaluation of small business subcontracting plans. FAR 19.705-4 and the solicitation provision at FAR 52.219-9 give the contracting officer the responsibility for determining the adequacy of submitted plans. Normally, the contracting officer will ask the procuring agency's small business advisors for assistance or guidance in evaluating these plans.

WHERE THE RUBBER MEETS THE ROAD

While the statutorily independent SSA does not have to comply with the evaluator findings, he or she does have to consider them. Even though the SSA does not have to agree with evaluator conclusions, it is clear that in the vast majority of cases, he or she does rely a great deal on the evaluators. If the evaluators do not do their jobs properly, all the careful planning and hard work expended to this point might be for naught. Proposal evaluation is truly where the rubber meets the road in the source selection process.

CHAPTER 27

ADHERENCE TO THE RATING METHODOLOGY

Acquisition officials are generally not required to evaluate proposals using the methodology described in the source selection plan. Both the Comptroller General and the Court of Federal Claims have recognized that source selection plans "generally do not give outside parties any rights." Thus, if a particular source selection plan calls for an evaluation methodology using numbers, source selection officials can later decide to evaluate merit factors using adjectives instead of numbers.

One exception to this general rule would be when the rating methodology is described in the solicitation (see Appendix II for an example). In that case, a promise has been made and should be kept unless the solicitation is amended and contractors are given an opportunity to resubmit any proposals already received. In Frank E. Basil, Inc., B-238354, May 22, 1990, the Comp Gen opined that "agencies do not have the discretion to announce in a solicitation that one evaluation plan will be used and then follow another in the actual evaluation" unless offerors are informed and given the "opportunity to restructure their proposals with the new evaluation scheme in mind."

Another exception is explained in USfalcon, Inc., No. 09-602C, reissued May 21, 2010, when the Court of Federal Claims found that it would be improper for the source selection authority to believe that evaluators were following source selection plan mandates regarding evaluation methodology when in fact they were using some other methodology. The court was concerned that this could create a disconnect between the SSA decision and the underlying facts. The court stated, "[T]o ensure there is no disconnect between the SSA's decision and its underlying assumptions, the choice to depart must have been made known to him so that it may receive at least implied approval."

In summary, the planned rating methodology may be changed at the point evaluations are to be made, provided that:

- The method originally planned for use was not described in the solicitation.
- The SSA is aware of (and presumably agrees with) any change.

CHAPTER 28

EVALUATION OF PAST PERFORMANCE

In evaluating past performance, members of the evaluation team, who are often a separate performance risk assessment group (PRAG), have some specific FAR guidance to take into account. FAR 15.305 provides:

- The government shall consider information obtained from an offeror and the customers identified by the offeror, as well as information obtained from any other sources, when evaluating an offeror's past performance.
- The contracting officer or source selection authority shall determine the relevance of similar past performance information.
- The evaluation should take into account past performance information regarding predecessor companies, key personnel who have relevant experience, or subcontractors that will perform major or critical aspects of the requirement when such information is relevant to the instant acquisition.
- If an offeror does not have a record of relevant past performance, or information on past performance is not available, the offeror may not be evaluated favorably or unfavorably on past performance.

- The evaluation should include the past performance of offerors in complying with subcontracting plan goals for small disadvantaged business (SDB) concerns.

GATHERING THE INFORMATION

Most frequently, evaluators conduct telephone interviews with the customers identified by the contractor or otherwise known to the government. Less frequently they correspond with the identified customers by email or regular mail. In both cases they normally use standardized questionnaire forms developed by their agency. They also search the Past Procurement Information Retrieval System (PPIRS) and any other available government databases for relevant data. If additional information is needed, evaluators may gather it from external sources such as the Better Business Bureau.

DETERMINING RELEVANCE

One rather tricky part of the FAR guidance on evaluating past performance concerns the relevance of the competing contractor's past performance and the relevance of information on predecessor companies, key personnel, and subcontractors. Because it is the source selection authority who must determine the relevance of this past performance information, it may be necessary for the evaluation group to communicate with the source selection authority during the evaluation process and before preparing an official report. Alternatively, the evaluation group could include all available past performance information in its report and allow the source selection authority to make his or her determination of relevancy after evaluations are complete. The evaluation group may or may not make a recommendation regarding relevancy depending on the rules of the agency, the wishes of the source selection authority, or both.

WHEN THERE IS NO PAST PERFORMANCE INFORMATION

The most controversial part of the FAR guidance on past performance concerns competing contractors that have no discernible relevant past performance. They are to be treated neither favorably nor unfavorably. (Earlier FAR coverage indicated that competing contractors without past performance must be given a "neutral" evaluation.) There was, and to some extent still is, confusion about how this should be accomplished.

Those who publish the FAR apparently hoped to minimize the need for a neutral rating (a rating that is neither favorable nor unfavorable) by opening the door to consideration of predecessor companies, key personnel, and subcontractors when a competing contractor has no relevant past performance as a prime contractor.

The Office of Federal Procurement Policy (OFPP), in its *Best Practices for Collecting and Using Current and Past Performance Information* (May 2000), states that it expects that offerors will "very rarely" have to be rated as having no past performance.

Despite this broadening of FAR guidance and the opinion of OFPP, the issue keeps surfacing in online forums and in protests by disappointed offerors.

The two most common methods of evaluation when a competing contractor has no relevant past performance seem to be a technique called *splitting the difference* and a technique in which past performance is not considered at all. The techniques are used when determining the competitive range and/or when making the source selection decision.

To illustrate the first method, presume that a competing contractor could get up to 5 points for exceptional performance and

0 points for poor past performance. A competing contractor with no past performance would get 2.5 points. While it may seem that this technique is not compatible with a literal reading of the FAR guidance (because it is treating the contractor with no past performance unfavorably when competing with excellent performers and favorably when competing with poor performers), splitting the difference has been upheld by the Comptroller General, and it is used by a number of agencies. In one instance, the Comp Gen opined:

> We have held that, when FAR sect. 15.305(a)(2)(iv) applies, ratings of zero generally cannot be reasonably viewed as neutral ratings, and they thus violate the requirement that an offeror without past performance information may not be evaluated favorably, or unfavorably. Meridian Mgmt. Corp., B-285127, July 19, 2000, 2000 CPD ¶ 121 at 3 n.2. As explained above, however, the agency recalculated Chicataw's score using a rating of 2.5 for neutral. That score is the mid-point of the five-point range used to rate an offeror's prior performance, and appears to be consistent with the above-cited FAR requirement, and with our prior decisions (Chicataw Construction, Inc., B-289592; B-289592.2, March 20, 2002).

To demonstrate the other technique used, presume that a solicitation called for the evaluation of proposals based on technical merit, past performance, and cost. Also presume there were a number of competing contractors and that one has no past performance. In determining the competitive range, the contracting officer would identify the most highly rated offerors among those being evaluated on all three factors. Then past performance would be removed as an evaluation factor when comparing these contractors against the competing contractor with no past performance before determining the competitive range. The same method would then be used in establishing final ratings before a source selection decision. This procedure seems to comply more fully with the FAR requirement.

THE RELATIVE WORTH OF PAST PERFORMANCE

The Comptroller General has also consistently held that, notwithstanding a literal interpretation of the FAR, a source selection authority may consider a contractor with a good record of past performance to be more attractive than a contractor with no past performance. In Phillips Industries, Inc., B-280645, September 17, 1998, the Comptroller General opined:

> [T]he use of a neutral rating approach, to avoid penalizing a vendor without prior experience and thereby enhance competition, does not preclude, in a best value procurement, a determination to award to a higher-priced offeror with a good past performance record over a lower-cost vendor with a neutral past performance rating. Indeed such a determination is inherent in the concept of best value.

In American Floor Consultants, Inc., B-294530.7, June 15, 2006, the Comptroller General took a similar approach when he opined:

> Although agencies may not rate an offeror that lacks relevant past performance favorably or unfavorably with regard to past performance, an agency may in a price/technical tradeoff determine that a high past performance rating is worth more than a neutral past performance rating. See CMC & Maint., Inc., B-292081, May 19, 2003, 2003 CPD ¶ 107 at 4. We believe that the agency's source selection was reasonable and consistent with the RFP award criteria, which stated that past performance was less important than price. The protest provides no reasonable basis to challenge the agency's determination.

Past performance evaluation forms and summary reports, including any recommendations given by evaluators, can best serve the contracting officer and source selection authority if they indicate how the lack of past performance does or does not contribute to the risk of successful contract performance. This information can be invaluable in making, documenting, and defending the source selection decision.

SOLICITATION CONSTRAINTS

How the solicitation was worded can, of course, limit the flexibility of the source selection authority. For example, the solicitation provisions in Appendix II (Section M.4.2.5) indicate that the lack of past performance will have "no positive or negative evaluation significance." It could be argued that these words preclude the source selection authority in this case from determining that a high past performance rating is "worth more than a neutral past performance rating."

OTHER EVALUATOR RESPONSIBILITIES

Those evaluating past performance must also point out situations in which clarifications or communications are desired or required regarding past performance (see Chapters 30 and 32). And they must properly categorize each contractor—for example, as high risk or low risk—and furnish the source selection authority with supporting rationale. Just as with other evaluation factors, there may be differences of opinion among evaluators as to how contractors are to be rated/scored. These differences may require meetings of past performance evaluators to develop, where feasible, consensus opinions and consensus recommendations for submission to the contracting officer and source selection authority.

CHAPTER 29

EVALUATION OF COST OR PRICE

At the same time that the non-cost portions of the proposals are distributed to the technical evaluators, the contracting officer asks an individual or a group, such as a separate cost evaluation team that is a part of a source selection evaluation board, to evaluate the price or cost proposals.

A decade or more ago, price/cost evaluation was normally done by one or more price analysts or cost analysts who specialized in price/cost issues. But in recent years austere personnel restrictions were put in place, and cost/price analysts were deemed a luxury rather than a necessity. Now, cost/price evaluations are often performed by contract specialists or financial personnel borrowed from comptroller offices who often do not possess the specialized expertise of cost/price analysts. This loss of specialized corporate expertise has had a perceived negative impact on the depth and quality of cost and price analyses. A number of agency managers have recognized this shortcoming and are striving to remedy the situation by including cost/price analysts on procuring-office staffs, so that the contracting officer or other SSA can once again assign cost or price evaluations to these specialized professionals.

As we learned in Chapter 18, either price analysis or cost analysis is undertaken when proposals are evaluated. The FAR has a definite preference for price analysis. It indicates that cost analysis will be used in "limited situations." Guidance can be found in FAR 15.305(a)(1):

> *Cost or price evaluation.* Normally, competition establishes price reasonableness. Therefore, when contracting on a firm-fixed-price or fixed-price with economic price adjustment basis, comparison of the proposed prices will usually satisfy the requirement to perform a price analysis, and a cost analysis need not be performed. In limited situations, a cost analysis ... may be appropriate to establish reasonableness of the otherwise successful offeror's price. When contracting on a cost-reimbursement basis, evaluations shall include a cost realism analysis to determine what the Government should realistically expect to pay for the proposed effort, the offeror's understanding of the work, and the offeror's ability to perform the contract. (See 37.115 for uncompensated overtime evaluation.) The contracting officer shall document the cost or price evaluation.

WHEN COST ANALYSIS IS ESSENTIAL

Despite the apparent FAR preference for price analysis, many situations exist in which some sort of cost analysis is essential. These include situations in which technical factors are important to the selection decision and costs can vary depending on the quality and approach of the proposal. For example, a reasonable cost for one technical approach may be quite different than a reasonable cost for a competing technical approach. Thus, determining reasonableness through comparison of proposed prices would not pass the common sense test. Cost analysis should also be performed for source selections for cost-reimbursement contracts.

COST REALISM ANALYSIS

FAR 15.404-1(d) defines cost realism analysis as "the process of independently reviewing and evaluating specific elements of each offeror's proposed cost estimate to determine whether the estimated proposed cost elements are realistic for the work to be performed; reflect a clear understanding of the requirements; and are consistent with the unique methods of performance and materials described in the offeror's technical proposal."

The FAR requires that cost realism analysis *shall* be performed on cost-reimbursement contracts to determine the probable cost of performance for each offeror. And it requires that the probable cost *shall* "be used for purposes of evaluation to determine best value." As stated in Chapter 18, this makes good business sense for the government because the government will ultimately pay (with some limited exceptions) actual costs reasonably incurred, rather than paying proposed costs.

The FAR also permits, but does not require, cost realism analysis on various types of fixed-price contracts. Among other uses, cost realism analysis permits the government to determine if a competing contractor fully understands the requirement. Cost realism analysis can also be used for contract performance risk assessments and responsibility determinations.

Exhibit 29-1 contains excerpts from a Comptroller General opinion involving the use of realism analysis on a fixed-price contract and the reasonableness of the government's conclusions. In the opinion, the Comptroller General points out:

Price realism is not ordinarily considered in the evaluation of proposals for the award of a fixed-price contract, because these contracts place the risk of loss upon the contractor. However, in light of various negative impacts on both the agency and the contractor that may result from an offeror's overly optimistic proposal, an agency may, as here, expressly provide that a price realism analysis will be applied in order to measure the offerors' understanding of the requirements and/or to assess the risk inherent in an offeror's proposal.

PROBABLE COSTS

FAR 15.404-1(d)(2)(ii) tells us that "probable cost is determined by adjusting each offeror's proposed cost, and fee when appropriate, to reflect any additions or reductions in cost elements to realistic levels based on the results of the cost realism analysis." In essence, this means that the government establishes an independent government cost estimate (IGCE) for each proposal undergoing cost realism analysis.

Experience has shown that contractors' proposed costs and probable costs can vary considerably and can have a significant impact on the source selection decision. Consider the proposed costs and probable costs, shown in Table 29-1, of competing contractors in an Army source selection for base operations and support at a Middle East location.

TABLE 29-1   Proposed and Probable Costs for Five Contractors' Proposals

Contractor	Proposed Cost	Probable Cost
A	$226 million	$278 million
B	$173 million	$268 million
C	$135 million	$256 million
D	$270 million	$290 million
E	$189 million	$337 million

The cost evaluation group used an independent government cost estimate as a baseline and, taking into account each individual technical approach, adjusted each cost proposal in the areas of staffing levels and labor categories.

Since probable cost, not proposed cost, is often used to select a source, there have, of course, been a number of protests regarding the manner in which the government determines probable cost. In reviewing the outcome of these protests, it appears that if the government has a reasonable basis for the probable costs, has taken into consideration the differing technical approaches in proposals, and has not made any grievous mathematical errors, the protests are generally not successful.

However, when the government does not, in the opinion of the Comptroller General, have a reasonable basis for its probable costs, the consequences can be severe. In the protest opinion shown in Exhibit 29-2, the Comptroller General asserts that the government failed to obtain the information it needed for a "meaningful" cost realism analysis. The impact on the government was substantial. In this case, the Comp Gen recommendations included:

- A new cost realism analysis
- A new source selection
- Possible termination of an existing contract and the award of a new one
- Payment of costs for filing and pursuing the protest.

ADDRESSING ISSUES OF COST OR PRICE WITH COMPETING CONTRACTORS

Cost or price evaluators should point out any need for clarifications whenever award is to be made without discussions. If a competitive range is to be established, then the evaluators should identify any need for communications. And, of course, if discussions are to be held, the evaluators must point out any areas of questioned cost or price. In no event should evaluators contact competing contractors except through the contracting officer. As noted previously, the contracting officer is the focal point for any exchanges with competing contractors that occur after the solicitation has been issued.

TECHNICAL ANALYSIS OF COST PROPOSALS

While cost evaluators tend to be contracting or financial experts, technical experts also may be needed to participate in a cost analysis. This is so because cost analysis frequently requires judgments about the technical elements of an offeror's cost proposal. These technical elements could include matters such as the number of labor hours proposed, the categories of labor, the types and quantities of material, tooling, scrap rates, and other issues requiring some degree of technical expertise. In some cases, especially those involving "other than formal" selection procedures, experts who participated in the evaluation of technical/merit factors will be asked to do a technical analysis of the cost proposals after the initial evaluation of non-cost factors has been completed. In many more formal source selections, technical experts will be a part of the cost evaluation team.

DETAILED FAR COVERAGE

There is a great deal of guidance on price and cost matters in FAR Part 15. Topics addressed include obtaining field pricing support from resident auditors, subcontracting pricing considerations, certification of cost and pricing data, unbalanced pricing issues when multiple contract line items are involved, and polices for establishing profit or fee. The FAR also touches on a number of issues more appropriate for a pricing guide than an examination of the source selection process. For detailed guidance on these matters, FAR 15.404-1(a)(7) suggests that pricing and negotiation personnel consult a five-volume set of *Contract Pricing Reference Guides* that were jointly prepared by the Air Force Institute of Technology and the Federal Acquisition Institute. The guides are available at http://www.acq.osd.mil/dpap/cpf/contract_pricing_reference_guides.html.

THE COST/PRICE EVALUATION REPORT

Following their evaluation of cost proposals, including consideration of any need for clarifications or communications, evaluators submit a report to the contracting officer and source selection authority. The report may be submitted through an SSEB chairperson and any other assigned advisory individuals or groups. The report must identify any questions about an offeror's cost or price and, where appropriate, the results of cost realism analyses.

Often this report is combined with the summary report of non-cost factors before it is submitted to the contracting officer and source selection authority. When award is to be made without discussions, the individual reports (on non-cost factors and cost or price) or a combined technical/cost report should give the contracting officer and source selection authority all the information needed to make a selection decision. Reports may or may not, depending on agency procedures or the wishes of the source selection authority, include a recommendation for award.

When a competitive range is to be determined, a combined report may also give a recommendation for the competitive range, again depending on agency procedures and any direction from the contracting officer and source selection authority.

PARTICIPATION IN DISCUSSIONS

When discussions are to be held with those in the competitive range, price/cost evaluators may be asked to help write letters to contractors, to participate in formulating a negotiation plan, and possibly to participate in face-to-face discussions.

After discussions are complete and final proposal revisions have been submitted, cost evaluators may again have to evaluate any changed proposals. Often, non-cost and cost evaluators do this together, and they submit a single report (with or without a recommendation for award) through established channels to the contracting officer and source selection authority.

* * *

Price or cost must by law be considered in every source selection, and the contracting officer must determine that the price is fair and reasonable before a contract is awarded. Acquisitions officials rely a great deal on the competence and expertise of price/cost evaluators in meeting these mandated requirements.

EXHIBIT 29-1   Comptroller General Decision: Pemco Aeroplex, Inc., B-310372.3, June 13, 2008

Price realism is not ordinarily considered in the evaluation of proposals for the award of a fixed-price contract, because these contracts place the risk of loss upon the contractor. However, in light of various negative impacts on both the agency and the contractor that may result from an offeror's overly optimistic proposal, an agency may, as here, expressly provide that a price realism analysis will be applied in order to measure the offerors' understanding of the requirements and/or to assess the risk inherent in an offeror's proposal. See, e.g., Wackenhut Servs., Inc., B-286037, B 286037.2, Nov. 14, 2000, 2001 CPD ¶ 114 at 3; Molina Eng'g, Ltd./Tri-J Indus., Inc. Joint Venture, May 22, 2000, B-284895, 2000 CPD ¶ 86 at 4. Although the Federal Acquisition Regulation (FAR) identifies permissible price analysis techniques, FAR sect. 14.404-1, it does not mandate any particular approach; rather, the nature and extent of a price realism analysis, as well as an assessment of potential risk associated with a proposed price, are generally within the sound exercise of the agency's discretion. See Legacy Mgmt. Solutions, LLC, B 299981.2, Oct. 10, 2007, 2007 CPD ¶ 197 at 3; Comprehensive Health Servs., Inc., B 310553, Dec. 27, 2007, 2007 CPD ¶ 9 at 8. In reviewing protests challenging an agency's evaluation of these matters, our focus is whether the agency acted reasonably and in a way consistent with the solicitation's requirements. See, e.g., Grove Res. Solutions, Inc., B 296228, B-296228.2, July 1, 2005, 2005 CPD ¶ 133 at 4-5.

Although xxxxx raises the full range of possibilities—that is, that the agency should not have considered certain information, that the agency should have considered certain other information, that the agency should have performed alternative analyses, and/or that the price realism and risk assessments should have been dispositively resolved by comparison to various benchmarks including xxxxx's own proposal—its protest fails to demonstrate that any of the agency's actions, inactions, or analyses are inconsistent with, or contrary to, the terms of the solicitation or applicable statute or regulation. As discussed above, an agency has considerable discretion in determining the nature and extent of required price realism and proposal risk assessments in the context of fixed-price contracts. Based on our review of the record, we conclude that xxxxx's various arguments challenging the agency's analysis and judgments reflect xxxxx's mere disagreement or dissatisfaction with the agency's determinations.

Accordingly, based on our review of the entire record, including the agency's documentation responding to our prior decision, we see no basis to question the adequacy or reasonableness of the agency's actions, its analysis, or its conclusions. Pemco's protest challenging the agency's cost/price evaluation is without merit (Pemco Aeroplex, Inc., B-310372.3, June 13, 2008).

EXHIBIT 29-2 Comptroller General Decision: National City Bank of Indiana (NCB), B-287608.3, August 7, 2002

Here, the agency had before it two technical proposals that received virtually identical technical evaluations. [Deleted.] In view of these evaluations, where [Bank of America] BOA's claimed cost savings could be expected to be, and were, in fact, dispositive in the award determination, and BOA's proposed savings were justified, in part, by [deleted], it was particularly important that the agency perform and document a meaningful realism assessment regarding the proposed savings. The record before our Office does not establish that the agency had a reasonable basis to accept BOA's proposed staffing costs as realistic. The agency clearly recognized that BOA needed to provide more support for its proposed staff reductions than it initially did; as discussed above, the agency repeatedly asked BOA to provide additional, detailed explanation regarding the bases for its proposed reductions. The agency did not, however, satisfy the requirement for a meaningful cost realism analysis simply by asking, repeatedly, for such support. The fact is that, despite the agency's repeated requests, BOA failed to provide the information requested. While BOA did provide a [deleted] of its proposed staffing reductions, it failed to provide any link between the majority of these reductions and any particular aspect of its technical approach. Rather, as the protester accurately points out, BOA's proposal revisions, including its [final proposal revisions] FPR, contain, primarily, vague and cursory explanations for its proposal to dramatically eliminate staff.

After a documented cost realism analysis has been performed, the SSA should make a new source selection decision. If NCB is selected for award, [Defense Finance and Accounting Service] DFAS should terminate the award to BOA. We also recommend that NCB be reimbursed the reasonable costs of filing and pursuing a protest, including attorney's fees (National City Bank of Indiana, B-287608.3, August 7, 2002).

CHAPTER 30

CLARIFICATIONS AND AWARD WITHOUT DISCUSSIONS

If the government so notified offerors in the solicitation, the government may, after proposals have been evaluated and summary report(s) issued, make award without discussions. The source selection authority takes into consideration evaluator comments, any advisor comments, and any recommendations from these parties.

FAR COVERAGE ON CLARIFICATIONS

Even when discussions will not be held, there is an exchange that is permitted prior to final evaluation and contract award. That exchange is called clarifications. FAR Part 15 explains clarifications as follows:

15.306 EXCHANGES WITH OFFERORS AFTER RECEIPT OF PROPOSALS.

(a) Clarifications and award without discussions

1. Clarifications are limited exchanges, between the Government and offerors, that may occur when award without discussions is contemplated.

2. If award will be made without conducting discussions, offerors may be given the opportunity to clarify certain aspects of proposals (e.g., the relevance of an offeror's past performance information and adverse past performance information to which the offeror has not previously had an opportunity to respond) or to resolve minor or clerical errors.

This FAR coverage requires a little parsing in order to fully appreciate it. First, it says that clarifications are "limited exchanges." This phrasing was presumably intended to end some agencies' practices of giving competing contractors page after page of clarification questions that, based on sheer magnitude alone, looked a lot like discussions.

Second, it says that "offerors may be given an opportunity to clarify certain aspects of proposals." "May" means that the contracting officer can choose whether or not to allow offerors this opportunity. "Certain aspects" is not defined, which means the contracting officer must decide on a case-by-case basis what "certain aspects" are. The examples of "certain aspects" provided in the FAR are related only to past performance, such as the relevance of past performance information and adverse past performance information to which the offeror has not had an opportunity to respond.

Finally, the FAR provides that clarifications can also be used to correct "minor or clerical errors." Again the contracting officer will have to use judgment to determine if an error is minor or clerical or, alternatively, if it constitutes a deficiency requiring discussions in order to correct it.

Clearly, there is no need at all for clarifications when the proposal being considered has no opportunity for award. For example, it would make no sense to ask for clarification from a contractor that has proposed the highest price in an LPTA source selection in which there are other acceptable offerors.

While it would appear from the FAR coverage that giving competing contractors the chance to clarify certain aspects of their proposals is completely discretionary, the Comptroller General has indicated that in the event of a protest, the record will be examined to determine if this discretion has been properly applied. When one contractor complained that the contracting officer should have allowed it to clarify certain adverse past performance information, the Comptroller General opined that the contracting officer was not obliged to seek clarification unless there was some reason to doubt the past performance information. The bottom line is that while contracting officers have discretion regarding clarifications, it is not unfettered discretion. The contracting officer must make a judgment call and defend it if necessary.

After the source selection authority has considered all information available to him or her, including any clarifications, he or she determines which offeror(s) will receive a contract. Documentation of this decision is required. See Chapter 36 for a fuller explanation of the requirements.

LPTA CONTRACT AWARDS

In an LPTA source selection, award is made to the lowest-priced responsible and responsive offeror that has been found acceptable on all evaluation factors. If an otherwise lowest-priced offeror is not deemed acceptable solely because of a past performance factor, and if that offeror is a small business, the offeror may request a certificate of competency (COC) from the Small Business Administration (SBA), since the government is making a de facto decision that the lowest-priced offeror is not responsible because of past performance. When the government finds a small business to be not responsible, the small business has the right under law to make this appeal to the SBA.

If the SBA announces an intent to issue a COC, contracting officers will either acquiesce to the decision and make award to that offeror or appeal the tentative COC decision to the SBA through the procuring agency's Office of Small and Disadvantaged Business Utilization (OSDBU). Most frequently, when the SBA announces an intent to issue a COC, the agency makes award to the offeror involved without making a formal agency appeal.

On a tradeoff procurement, an offeror that is not awarded a contract solely because of a low past performance score/rating does not have this right to a COC request. In that case, the contractor is not found to be "not responsible"; it is merely scored lower than other competing contractors.

CHANGING THE AWARD APPROACH

Even if the solicitation provided for award without discussions, the contracting officer can determine on a case-by-case basis that discussions are required. In that case, a competitive range is established, discussions are held, final proposal revisions are obtained, and final evaluations are performed before an award is made. Conditions that might prompt a contracting officer to choose this course of action include instances in which no acceptable proposal was received or all offered costs or prices could not be found to be fair and reasonable.

PART V

ESTABLISHING THE COMPETITIVE RANGE AND HOLDING DISCUSSIONS

This part addresses the establishment of the competitive range and examines the alternatives available to the contracting officer and the source selection authority. It also covers the exchange known as communications and identifies the situations in which communications may be required prior to the establishment of the competitive range. It explains the concept of meaningful discussions and the vulnerability of government contracting officials regarding meaningful discussions. Lastly, it addresses exchanges that are prohibited by the FAR.

CHAPTER 31

ESTABLISHING THE COMPETITIVE RANGE

If discussions are to be held, the contracting officer and source selection authority establish a competitive range. This simply means that they do not have to hold discussions with all contractors that have submitted proposals. Instead, they may limit the pool of offerors with which they will hold discussions to the cream of the crop. Some contractors refer to the competitive range as the *short list.*

Previously, the FAR required that the competitive range include all offerors that had a reasonable chance of receiving the award following discussions. If there was any doubt about whether a particular offeror should be included, that doubt was resolved by placing the offeror in the competitive range. The contracting officer and source selection authority were given great discretion here. It was relatively rare that a competing contractor prevailed when it protested being left out of the competitive range.

THE EFFECTS OF THE STAY PROVISIONS/ STAY RULES

When the Competition in Contracting Act became law in 1984, it required that in the event of a protest, the award should be delayed (stayed) until the protest was resolved. If the contract had already been awarded, then a stop work order was usually required. Exceptions to these stay provisions were difficult to obtain.

The stay provisions had a profound impact on the source selection process, and contracting offices began to apply preventive law in earnest. One of the measures taken was including more contractors in the competitive range simply to minimize the likelihood of a protest. In practice, the "reasonable opportunity" cutoff point for inclusion in the competitive range became "any opportunity." This approach made a burdensome source selection process even more burdensome, and both contractors and government voiced displeasure with this turn of events. Contractors that had little or no chance of receiving the award were being asked to hold discussions and revise their proposals. Government program offices suffered from longer delays in getting contracts awarded and were subject to additional expense in the evaluation process.

CURRENT FAR COVERAGE

Ultimately, the FAR was changed to provide for a more efficient competitive-range process. The current coverage at FAR 15.306 is as follows:

(c) Competitive range.

1. Agencies shall evaluate all proposals in accordance with 15.305 (a), and, if discussions are to be conducted, establish the competitive range. Based on the ratings of each proposal against all evaluation criteria, the contracting officer shall establish a competitive range comprised of all of the most highly rated proposals, unless the range is further reduced for purposes of efficiency pursuant to paragraph (c)(2) of this section.

2. After evaluating all proposals in accordance with 15.305 (a) and paragraph (c)(1) of this section, the contracting officer may determine that the number of most highly rated proposals that might otherwise be included in the competitive range exceeds the number at which an efficient competition can be conducted. Provided the solicitation notifies offerors that the competitive range can be limited for purposes of efficiency (see 52.215 (f)(4)), the contracting officer may limit the number of proposals in the competitive range to the greatest number that will permit an efficient competition among the most highly rated proposals (10 U.S.C. 2305(b)(4) and 41 U.S.C. 253b(d)).

3. If the contracting officer, after complying with paragraph (d)(3) of this section, decides that an offeror's proposal should no longer be included in the competitive range, the proposal shall be eliminated from consideration for award. Written notice of this decision shall be provided to unsuccessful offerors in accordance with 15.503.

4. Offerors excluded or otherwise eliminated from the competitive range may request a debriefing (see 15.505 and 15.506).

(Note: The paragraph (d)(3) referred to in this FAR excerpt concerns the minimum requirements for holding discussions and is addressed in Chapter 33.)

As shown above, the FAR requires that the evaluation leading to the competitive range be based on the ratings of each proposal against "all evaluation criteria." That means both merit and cost have to be considered in determining the "most highly rated proposals." Along this line, it has long been held that it is generally an inappropriate practice to establish arbitrary cutoff points for determining the competitive range—for example, determining that an offeror must receive a technical rating of 70 out of 100 to get into the competitive range, or that proposing a cost of $1 million or more will eliminate a competing contractor from the competitive range. Establishing such arbitrary cutoff points would preclude the integrated assessment of merit and cost that the FAR requires when it says that the competitive range is determined based on all evaluation criteria. (This matter is further addressed in Exhibit 31-1.)

INCLUSION OF UNACCEPTABLE PROPOSALS

It had long been acknowledged by the Comptroller General and the federal courts that an unacceptable proposal (one with deficiencies) could be kept in the competitive range while an acceptable proposal could be excluded when the "reasonable opportunity" criterion was applied. For example, a proposal that was not immediately acceptable because it lacked a piece of necessary information but that had high potential and an attractive cost could be kept in the range, while an acceptable proposal with a high cost could be excluded when it offered nothing of comparative worth to justify the higher cost. Presumably this can still be done, but only if the unacceptable proposal is among the most highly rated. In that sense, the new FAR rules may have taken away some of the flexibility formerly enjoyed by the contracting officer and source selection authority.

REDUCTIONS FOR THE SAKE OF EFFICIENCY

As can be seen in FAR 15.306, the contracting officer may further reduce the competitive range for the sake of efficiency. While this provision was apparently intended to be applied on a case-by-case basis, it appears that some agencies have more or less adopted a standard efficient number of proposals—three or five, for example.

CHARACTERISTICS OF THE COMPETITIVE RANGE

The competitive range is dynamic as opposed to static in that it can expand or contract. A contractor excluded from the competitive range can protest or complain about the exclusion and, if the contracting officer feels the contractor's position has merit, the contractor can be added to the competitive range. On the other hand, a competing contractor can be dropped if discussions held prior to final proposal revisions reveal that it should no longer be included in the competitive range.

There is no legally established minimum or maximum number of offerors for competitive range determinations. After the implementation of the current competitive range provisions in FAR 15.306, a contractor complained to the Comptroller General that it was eliminated from the competitive range even though it was rated the second best. The agency had decided to have a competitive range of only one offeror, notwithstanding the FAR guidance that used the plural when it said, "[T]he contracting officer shall establish a competitive range comprised of the most highly rated proposals…"

After examining the intent of the current FAR coverage, the Comptroller General opined: "[W]e conclude that the Part 15 rewrite does not require that agencies retain in the competitive range a proposal that is determined to have no reasonable prospect of award simply to avoid a competitive range of one. We have long held there is nothing inherently improper in a competitive range of one…" (SDS Petroleum Products, Inc., B-280430, September 1, 1998). The reader is cautioned, however, that while the Comptroller General finds nothing inherently wrong with a competitive range of one, he has traditionally given such circumstances "increased scrutiny."

A SUBJECTIVE DECISION

Just as is the case in many other elements of the source selection process, decisions regarding the size of and inclusion in the competitive range are largely subjective. Given identical circumstances, different individuals or groups can come to different conclusions about the size and composition of the competitive range. Not only is this obvious in the real world, but it has also consistently been demonstrated in source selection classrooms, where groups of acquisition professionals engage in practical exercises involving the competitive range.

Exhibit 31-1 is a Comptroller General decision that involves several of the issues we have discussed above as well as some other issues worthy of note, such as questionable documentation, averaging of scores, and failure to consider price. Reading it should help reinforce the material in this chapter.

EXHIBIT 31-1   Comptroller General Decision: Arc-Tech Inc.,
B-400325.3, February 19, 2009

The protester argues that both the evaluation of its own proposal and the agency's competitive range determination were unreasonable. In the latter connection, Arc-Tech contends that the agency failed to consider price in determining the competitive range and instead based its determination as to which proposals were included on an arbitrary technical cut-off score.

The determination of whether a proposal is in the competitive range is principally a matter within the reasonable exercise of discretion of the procuring agency. Smart Innovative Solutions, B-400323.3, Nov. 19, 2008, 2008 CPD ¶ 220 at 3. In reviewing an agency's evaluation of proposals and subsequent competitive range determination, we will not evaluate the proposals anew in order to make our own determination as to their acceptability or relative merits; rather, we will examine the record to determine whether the evaluation was reasonable and consistent with the evaluation criteria. *Foster-Miller, Inc.*, B-296194.4, B-296194.5, Aug. 31, 2005, 2005 CPD ¶ 171 at 6.

Here, based upon our examination of the record, we conclude that the agency's competitive range determination was unreasonable in that there is no evidence that price was considered in deciding whether a proposal should be included or excluded. In this connection, we recognize that an agency may properly exclude a technically unacceptable proposal from the competitive range regardless of its price. *TMC Dev. Corp.*, B-296194.3, Aug. 10, 2005, 2005 CPD ¶ 158 at 4. We also recognize that an agency has the discretion to exclude a technically acceptable proposal that is not among the most highly rated proposals where it determines that the number of most highly rated proposals that might otherwise be included in the competitive range exceeds the number at which an efficient competition can be conducted (provided that the solicitation notifies offerors, as the RFP here did, that the competitive range might be limited for purposes of efficiency). *See* FAR sect. 15.306(c)(2); *Computer & Hi-Tech Mgmt., Inc.*, B 293235.4, Mar. 2, 2004, 2004 CPD ¶ 45 at 6. An agency may not exclude a technically acceptable proposal from the competitive range, however, without taking into account the relative cost of that proposal to the government. *Kathpal Techs., Inc.; Computer & Hi-Tech Mgmt., Inc.*, B-283137.3 et al., Dec. 30, 1999, 2000 CPD ¶ 6 at 9; *Meridian Mgmt. Corp.*, B 285127, July 19, 2000, 2000 CPD ¶ 121 at 4. That is, an agency may not exclude a technically acceptable proposal from the competitive range simply because the proposal received a lower technical rating than another proposal or proposals, without taking into consideration the proposal's price. *A&D Fire Protection Inc.*, B 288852, Dec. 12, 2001 CPD ¶ 201 at 3. Similarly, an agency may not limit a competitive range for the purposes of efficiency on the basis of technical scores alone. *See Kathpal Techs., Inc.; Computer & Hi-Tech Mgmt., Inc., supra*, at 9-10.

In this case, the record shows that Arc-Tech's proposal was excluded from the competitive range not because it had been determined technically unacceptable, but because it was not among the most highly rated proposals technically. While the competitive range determination and the technical evaluation panel (TEP) report both label the protester's proposal "unacceptable," neither of those documents provides any explanation for such a finding, and there is no support for it anywhere else in the record. On the contrary, the score sheets of the individual evaluators reflect ratings of [deleted]. In fact, it is apparent from the TEP report—in particular, the statement that "the results [of the individual technical evaluations] were averaged to provide a total score to determine whether the company was in the competitive range or not," TEP Report, Oct. 6, 2008, at 1—that the evaluators used the offerors' technical scores to determine whether their proposals should be included in the competitive range, and that proposals excluded from the competitive range based on their technical scores were, simply as a consequence of their exclusion, labeled unacceptable. Further, there is no indication in the record that the agency considered the protester's proposed price as part of the competitive range determination. In sum, because the record shows that the agency's decision to exclude the protester's proposal from the competitive range was based on its technical score alone—without consideration of its relative cost to the government and without a documented finding that the proposal was unacceptable—the decision was improper, and on that basis we sustain Arc-Tech's protest.

We recommend that the agency make a new competitive range determination, taking into consideration offerors' proposed prices, as well as their technical scores. We also recommend that the agency reimburse the protester for its cost of filing and pursuing the protest, including reasonable attorneys' fees. 4 C.F.R. sect. 21.8(d) (1) (2008). The protester's certified claim for costs, detailing the time spent and cost incurred, must be submitted to the agency within 60 days after receiving this decision.

The protest is sustained.

CHAPTER 32

THE EXCHANGE KNOWN AS COMMUNICATIONS

The contracting officer may hold, and in some cases *must* hold, an exchange with competing contractors prior to the establishment of a competitive range. These exchanges are intended to address issues that must be explored to determine whether an individual offeror is among the most highly rated competitors and should be placed in the competitive range.

FAR COVERAGE

FAR 15.306 (see Exhibit 32-1) indicates that communications:

- Shall not provide an opportunity for a contractor to revise its proposal
- May be conducted to enhance government understanding of proposals, allow reasonable interpretation of the proposal, or facilitate the evaluation process
- May be held only with those whose inclusion in the competitive range is uncertain, pending the outcome of communications
- Shall be held with offerors whose past performance is the determining factor preventing them from being placed in the competitive range, and must address adverse past

performance information to which an offeror has not had an opportunity to respond

- May not constitute discussions.

CONDUCTING AND USING COMMUNICATIONS

Communications give competing contractors an opportunity to clarify but not change certain aspects (such as ambiguities or other concerns) of their proposals to enhance the government's understanding of the proposals so that they can be more accurately evaluated.

If a contractor is clearly not going to be in the competitive range, regardless of the outcome of any communications, then communications are not held. Obviously, in such a case, communications would be a waste of time. If a contractor clearly *is* going to be in the competitive range, regardless of the outcome of any communications, then communications are not held. In that case, any additional information needed from the competing contractor can be obtained when discussions are held with those in the competitive range. Accordingly, communications are held only when they would have an impact on whether a contractor is to be included in the competitive range.

While most communications are largely discretionary, it can be assumed that, in the event of a protest, the Comptroller General may ascertain whether that discretion was properly applied (just as is done with regard to a contracting officer's decision to seek or not seek clarifications when awarding without discussions).

There is one instance, however, in which communications are not discretionary. Communications are required when an offeror is being kept out of the competitive range *solely* because of an adverse past performance report, presumably one to which the offeror has not already had an opportunity to respond. The emphasis should be placed on the word *solely*. If the offeror's proposal is not highly rated and would not make the competitive range even with an improved past performance rating, then any communications would just be a waste of time. On the other hand, if the offeror would be in the competitive range regardless of the outcome of communications, then adverse past performance can be addressed during the discussion phase, and any delay that would be occasioned through conducting communications can be avoided.

IDENTIFYING THE NEED FOR COMMUNICATIONS

Normally, the merit and past performance evaluators inform the contracting officer in their evaluation reports of any need for communications. The evaluators' ratings are subsequently adjusted, if appropriate, after communications are held. The competitiverangeisthenestablishedbythecontractingofficer,source selection authority, or both after they take into consideration the ratings and the comments of the evaluators.

EXHIBIT 32-1   FAR Guidance on Communications (FAR 15.306) (b)

Communications with offerors before establishment of the competitive range. Communications are exchanges, between the Government and offerors, after receipt of proposals, leading to establishment of the competitive range. If a competitive range is to be established, these communications—

(1) Shall be limited to the offerors described in paragraphs (b)(1)(i) and (b)(1)(ii) of this section and—

   (i) Shall be held with offerors whose past performance information is the determining factor preventing them from being placed within the competitive range. Such communications shall address adverse past performance information to which an offeror has not had a prior opportunity to respond; and

(ii) May only be held with those offerors (other than offerors under paragraph (b)(1)(i) of this section) whose exclusion from, or inclusion in, the competitive range is uncertain;

(2) May be conducted to enhance Government understanding of proposals; allow reasonable interpretation of the proposal; or facilitate the Government's evaluation process. Such communications shall not be used to cure proposal deficiencies or material omissions, materially alter the technical or cost elements of the proposal, and/or otherwise revise the proposal. Such communications may be considered in rating proposals for the purpose of establishing the competitive range;

(3) Are for the purpose of addressing issues that must be explored to determine whether a proposal should be placed in the competitive range. Such communications shall not provide an opportunity for the offeror to revise its proposal, but may address—

(i) Ambiguities in the proposal or other concerns (e.g., perceived deficiencies, weaknesses, errors, omissions, or mistakes (see 14.407); and

(ii) Information relating to relevant past performance; and

(4) Shall address adverse past performance information to which the offeror has not previously had an opportunity to comment.

CHAPTER 33

HOLDING DISCUSSIONS

The government often uses common words in a very narrow way. We have already seen that what the general public would call *communications* between the government and contractor are called *exchanges* in the FAR. When the government intends to make award without discussions, the exchange is called *clarifications.* However, if a competitive range is to be established, any request for clarification of a proposal prior to the establishment of the competitive range is then called a *communication,* not a clarification.

FAR COVERAGE

After a competitive range has been established, the government must hold discussions with all the competing contractors in the competitive range. What are discussions? FAR 15.306(d) tells us that:

- Negotiations are exchanges that are undertaken with the intent of allowing an offeror to revise its proposal.
- Negotiations may include bargaining over price and other requirements of the proposed contract.
- When negotiations are conducted in a competitive acquisition, they take place after the establishment of the competitive range and are called discussions.

- The primary objective of discussions is to maximize the government's ability to obtain best value, based on the requirement and the evaluation factors set forth in the solicitation.

Thus, it is clear that any discussions held in a noncompetitive environment are called *negotiations,* and any negotiations held in a competitive environment are called *discussions.*

In holding discussions, the contracting officer must address the following matters with each offeror still being considered for award:

- *Deficiencies.* A deficiency is defined in FAR 15.001 as a material failure of a proposal to meet a government requirement, or a combination of significant weaknesses in a proposal that increases the risk of unsuccessful contract performance to an unacceptable level.
- *Significant weaknesses.* FAR 15.001 defines a significant weakness as a flaw in a proposal that appreciably increases the risk of unsuccessful performance.
- *Adverse past performance information*—to which the offeror has not had an opportunity to respond.

The "still being considered for award" caveat is significant. FAR 15.306(d)(5) provides that offerors may be eliminated from the competitive range whether or not material aspects of the proposal have been discussed or whether or not the offeror has been given an opportunity to submit a proposal revision. This means that, if it becomes clear during discussions that a proposal is no longer considered to be among the most highly rated and thus has no real chance of receiving a contract award, the proposal may be eliminated from the competitive range even if the full range of meaningful discussions has not occurred.

In addition to deficiencies, significant weaknesses, and certain adverse past performance information, FAR 15.306(d)(3) encourages the contracting officer to discuss "other aspects" of the proposal that could, in the opinion of the contracting officer, be altered or explained to materially enhance the proposal's potential for award. These other aspects certainly include any areas of questioned cost and presumably include weaknesses, which FAR 15.001 defines as flaws that increase the risk of contract performance. (A *weakness* is different from a *significant* weakness, in that it does not "appreciably" increase the risk of contract performance.)

DISCUSSING COST OR PRICE

Although the FAR does not address pricing or cost issues in any depth in its coverage of minimum requirements for discussions, it seems clear that any price issue that would make a contractor's proposal unacceptable should be considered a deficiency even though it may not contribute to the risk of contract performance. Further, the Comptroller General has in the past found that meaningful discussions were not held when the government did not inform a contractor that its price was too high or too low. In one instance, the Comptroller General found that "[D]iscussions cannot be meaningful if the offeror is not apprised that its cost exceeds what the agency believes to be reasonable." Along that line, FAR 15.306 coverage on discussions does provide that the government "may suggest" to offerors, when appropriate, that proposals might be more competitive if excesses in proposals were removed and the offered price decreased.

Exhibit 33-1 is an example of how the Comp Gen views the issue of cost during discussions. In this decision, the Comp Gen addresses the discretion afforded to the government on discussing cost issues. For example, he indicates that it is not necessary to tell a competing contractor that its price is high relative to other offerors if the government does not find the price to be unreasonable. However, he also indicates that "excesses" may have to be addressed in order for discussions to be meaningful. And he discusses the specificity with which the government should convey its cost concerns.

THE NEED FOR MEANINGFUL DISCUSSIONS

It would not be an overstatement to suggest that the component of government source selection that is most vulnerable to successful protest is the government's failure to hold meaningful discussions. This seems to stem from government employees being so intent on following regulations and procedures on matters such as agency-required forms and communication chains that they lose sight of what they are trying to accomplish.

The object of holding discussions is to allow a contractor in the competitive range to revise its proposal and make it more attractive to the government, thus giving the competing contractor a reasonable opportunity for receiving an award. If the matters that would keep a competing contractor from being a legitimate contender for an award are not discussed, then discussions with that contractor are likely to be a meaningless charade and a waste of everyone's time.

It might be helpful to look at the definitions for deficiencies and weaknesses that were generally accepted before the current FAR definitions. Substantially, they were:

- *Deficiency:* Anything in a proposal that would make it unacceptable. This would include things such as a too-risky technical approach, failure to meet a minimum government requirement as specified in the solicitation, failure to furnish all significant information required in the solicitation, and other such issues.

- **Weakness:** Anything in a proposal that is not a deficiency but that would cause one contractor to be rated lower than another.

If an agency is going to hold discussions with a competing contractor with the goal of giving the contractor an opportunity to improve its proposal, then those discussions should cover all deficiencies and enough weaknesses that a suitably improved proposal could legitimately be a contender for the award. This includes giving the contractor an opportunity to respond to adverse past performance reports where applicable, identifying areas where technical improvements are desirable, and pointing out any excesses that may have unnecessarily increased the proposed cost or price.

Although enough weaknesses should be discussed, including significant weaknesses (a mandatory requirement), it is not necessary to discuss all of them. The Comptroller General has consistently held that the government is not required to spoonfeed a contractor during discussions. Determining how many weaknesses are "enough" is again a matter of business judgment.

In addition to the above elements, it should go without saying that the government must discuss any cost issues that would otherwise preclude a competing contractor from getting the award, such as a cost that the government considers unreasonable.

When a deficiency, weakness, or questionable cost is identified in discussions, the competing contractor has three choices. It can revise its proposal, it can convince the contracting officer that the government's observation is incorrect, or it can do nothing. Those choices are business decisions that the competing contractor must make. By pointing these matters out, the government has met its obligations under the law and has given the contractor an opportunity to improve its proposal.

THE MANNER AND SPECIFICITY OF DISCUSSIONS

The FAR does not prescribe how discussions are to be held. This is a matter left to the discretion of the contracting officer. Discussions may be face-to-face; through letters; by telephone, computer, or videoconference; or through any combination of these formats. When determining how discussions will be held, the contracting officer takes into consideration time and expense constraints, the complexity and magnitude of the issues to be discussed, and the need to maintain a clear and complete record of the discussions.

FAR 15.306(d) requires that discussions be tailored to each offeror's proposal. Consequently, it is possible that the contracting officer could determine that only one or two issues will be discussed with one offeror, while a larger number of issues will be discussed with another. It is also possible that only one round of discussions will be held with one offeror but multiple rounds with another, as long as this disparity is not created to favor one offeror over another.

The contracting officer also gets to determine the specificity of discussions. For example, he or she may indicate that the government is concerned about the risk of the proposed technical approach. Or the contracting officer may not only tell the contractor that the source selection team is concerned about the risk of the proposed technical approach, but also explain specifically *why* the government is concerned. While the contracting officer has discretion here, a word of caution is in order. In the event of a protest, the Comptroller General may base an opinion on whether the discretion was properly applied.

AVOIDING PROTESTS

Like so many other elements of the source selection process, discussions require both compliance with law and regulation and the exercise of good business judgment. If acquisition officials wish to avoid successful protests concerning their failure to hold meaningful discussions, they will make certain that all deficiencies, all pertinent cost/price issues, and enough weaknesses are discussed so that each contractor remaining in the competitive range has had an opportunity to improve its proposal to a point at which it could be a legitimate contender for contract award.

While it is possible to get away with "charade discussions"— discussions that do not address the elements a competing contractor must improve in order to be a real contender for award—this may be too big a risk to take. In candor, however, it should be noted that charade discussions sometimes do stand up under protest. This is because the protest forums, in their opinions, sometimes make a distinction between meeting government needs and having a competitive proposal.

For example, in Standard Associates Inc./Comfort Systems USA, 09-372C, reissued December 3, 2009, the Court of Federal Claims issued a finding that "[m]andatory discussions ... are designed to point out shortcomings in an offeror's proposal as judged from the standpoint of the government's stated needs, rather than the standpoint of the proposal's competitiveness." The ruling also quoted a previous opinion that "aside from areas of significant weakness or deficiency, the contracting officer need not discuss areas in which a proposal may merely be improved."

While it may be presumptuous to disagree with the learned ladies and gentlemen of the federal courts, it appears obvious that the failure of a contracting officer to discuss matters that could enhance the competitiveness of a proposal that is placed in the competitive range but that is inferior in merit or costs (or both) to other proposals in the competitive range is a waste of both the contractor's time and the government's time. Further, if the solicitation contains evaluation factors or subfactors that do not relate directly to government needs, those factors probably shouldn't be there. FAR 15.304(b) requires that evaluation factors and significant subfactors:

Represent the key areas of importance and emphasis to be considered in the source selection decision, and

Support *meaningful* comparison and discrimination between and among competing proposals.

It is imperative that evaluators and advisors know the rules and issues regarding meaningful discussions so that they can better serve the contracting officer and source selection authority by pointing out both those matters that must be discussed and those that should be discussed. It is in the interest of both the government and the private sector to close this gap of protest vulnerability in discussions and to further increase the potential that any resulting contract fully meets government needs.

EXHIBIT 33-1 Comptroller General Decision: Creative Information Technology, Inc., B-293073.10, March 16, 2005

When contracting agencies conduct discussions with offerors in the competitive range, such discussions must be meaningful. Kaneohe Gen. Servs., Inc., B-293097.2, Feb. 2, 2004, 2004 CPD ¶ 50 at 3. In order for discussions to be meaningful, agencies must advise an offeror of weaknesses, excesses, or deficiencies in its proposal, correction of which would be necessary for the offeror to have a reasonable chance of being selected for award. In this regard, the actual content and extent of discussions are matters of judgment primarily for determination by the agency involved, and we generally limit our review of the agency's judgments to a determination of whether they are reasonable. J.G. Van Dyke & Assocs., B-248981, B-248981.2, Oct. 14, 1992.... Specifically, with regard to the adequacy of discussions of price, an agency generally does not have an obligation to tell an offeror that its price is high, relative to other offers, unless the government believes the price is unreasonable. State Mgmt. Servs., Inc.; Madison Servs., Inc., B-255528.6 et al., Jan. 18, 1995, 95-1 CPD ¶ 25 at 5-6; Marwais Steel Co., B-254242.2, B-254242.3, May 3, 1994, 94-1 CPD ¶ 291 at 6.

The issue here is whether the Army's discussions with [Creative Information Technology Inc.] CITI were meaningful where the Army advised CITI merely that its total price appeared "overstated," given the unique circumstances of this case—specifically, the extraordinary disparity between CITI's proposed level of effort and price as compared to the government estimate as well as the level of effort and prices of the other offerors in the competitive range. We conclude that they were not. In addressing this issue, we recognize that it is within the agency's discretion to decide whether to inform an offeror that its price is considered too high and to reveal the results of the analysis supporting that conclusion or to indicate to all offerors the cost or price that the government's price analysis, market research, and other reviews have identified as reasonable. See FAR 15.306(e). The question is whether the agency's judgment in this instance was reasonable.

While an agency is not required to "spoon-feed" an offeror during discussions as to each and every item that could be revised to improve its proposal, see ITT Fed. Sys. Int'l Corp., B-285176.4, B-285176.5, Jan. 9, 2001, 2001 CPD ¶ 45 at 6, agencies must impart sufficient information to afford offerors a fair and reasonable opportunity to identify and correct deficiencies, excesses or mistakes in their proposals. Matrix Int'l Logistics, Inc., B-272388.2, Dec. 9, 1996, 97-2 CPD ¶ 89 at 9. In this case, we conclude that CITI could not be reasonably expected to have understood the true nature and magnitude of the agency's concern with its proposal based upon the information provided by the Army during its discussions with CITI, thus rendering those discussions essentially meaningless (Creative Information Technology Inc., B-293073.10, March 16, 2005).

CHAPTER 34

PROHIBITED EXCHANGES

In the past, case law and the FAR identified three practices that were prohibited when holding discussions: technical leveling, technical transfusion, and auctioning. Generally, these practices were defined as follows:

Technical leveling. Successive rounds of discussions on the same issues with the intent to bring an inferior proposal up to the level of others. There was nothing improper about discussing deficiencies and weaknesses at least once; it was the successive rounds that could constitute technical leveling. Some also interpreted technical leveling as discussing every minute weakness in a proposal—the so-called "spoon-feeding" of a competing contractor. Unfortunately, in many cases, fear of technical leveling seemed to keep government officials from discussing weaknesses that probably should have been addressed in discussions. These officials seemed to overlook the successive rounds part of the generally accepted definition of technical leveling.

Technical transfusion. Introducing one competing contractor's ideas into another contractor's proposal. The government often did this by formulating leading questions during the discussion phase to coach a contractor to come up with the desired responses. Allegedly, it sometimes also occurred more overtly. For example, if an agency wanted to give a contract to a favored offeror, but another competing contractor had an idea the government wanted to exploit, the ideal solution seemed to be to infuse the good idea into the proposal of the favored contractor.

Another alleged aim of technical transfusion was to technically level competing contractors so that what the government really wanted from a technical proposal could be obtained from the competing contractor offering the lowest price.

Auctioning. The most common form of auctioning was setting one contractor against another to get a lower price without discussing any substantive price/cost issues. For example, Contractor A and B were competing for a contract. A would be told that its price was higher than other offerors'. A would drop its price below that of Contractor B, and Contractor B would then be told that its price was higher than competing prices, and so on. The now-obsolete FAR coverage described prohibited auctioning as:

- Indicating to an offeror a cost or price it must meet to obtain further consideration.

- Advising an offeror of its price standing relative to another offeror's. (However, it was (and still is) permissible to inform an offeror that the government considers its cost or price to be too high or unrealistic.)

- Otherwise furnishing information about other offerors' prices.

These three practices are no longer referenced in the FAR. In lieu thereof, the current version of the FAR, at FAR 15.306(e), lists several limits on exchanges:

Limits on exchanges. Government personnel involved in the acquisition shall not engage in conduct that—

(1) Favors one offeror over another;

(2) Reveals an offeror's technical solution, including unique technology, innovative and unique uses of commercial items, or any information that would compromise an offeror's intellectual property to another offeror;

(3) Reveals an offeror's price without that offeror's permission. However, the contracting officer may inform an offeror that its price is considered by the Government to be too high, or too low, and reveal the results of the analysis supporting that conclusion. It is also permissible, at the Government's discretion, to indicate to all offerors the cost or price that the Government's price analysis, market research, and other reviews have identified as reasonable;

(4) Reveals the names of individuals providing reference information about an offeror's past performance; or

(5) Knowingly furnishes source selection information in violation of [FAR] 3.104 and 41 U.S.C. 423(h) (1)(2)41.

Favoring one offeror over another has no well-defined limits. Most likely, technical leveling is one example. Giving a contractor an "unfair competitive advantage" might be another. Like pornography, favoring cannot always be readily defined, but one should be able to recognize it when one sees it.

The second limit on exchanges in FAR 15.306(e) replaces the prohibition on technical transfusion, but with greater clarity and an expanded scope.

The third limit on exchanges requires some in-depth analysis and parsing. This addition to the FAR helps clarify that the type of hard bargaining on price that takes place in the private sector can also take place in government acquisition. Foremost, it provides that the government cannot reveal an offeror's price without that offeror's permission. One situation in which the government requests offerors' permission to reveal price is in reverse auctioning, a price-oriented procurement method that does not ordinarily constitute a source selection as defined by the FAR.

Secondly, it also provides that the contracting officer may inform an offeror that its price is too high or too low and that the contracting officer may reveal the results of the analysis supporting that conclusion. The FAR does not limit the type of analysis used. Thus, it appears that the government can tell a contractor that in comparison to other prices offered, or in comparison to the government estimate, the proposed price is too high.

Finally, the third limit on exchanges provides that it is permissible, at the government's discretion, to indicate to all offerors the cost or price that the government's price analysis, market research, and other reviews have identified as reasonable. This seems to give the government the right to disclose the independent cost estimate to contractors and to use it as a bargaining tool.

The fourth limit on exchanges prohibits the government from releasing the names of individuals providing reference information about an offeror's past performance. This limitation can also be found elsewhere in the FAR—for example, in the FAR coverage on debriefings.

The last limitation concerns the protection of source selection information. FAR Part 2 defines source selection information as the following information, whenever it has not already been disclosed publicly:

- Bid prices
- Proposed costs or prices submitted in response to an agency solicitation
- Source selection plans
- Technical evaluation plans

- Results of technical evaluation of proposals
- Results of cost or price evaluation of proposals
- Competitive range determinations
- Rankings of bids, proposals, or competitors
- Reports and evaluations of source selection panels, boards, or advisory councils
- Other information marked as source selection information or as determined by the head of the agency or the contracting officer.

Failure to comply with the limitations on exchanges can result in sustained protests and/or other significant legal action against the government.

PART VI

OBTAINING FINAL REVISIONS AND SELECTING THE SOURCE

This part of the book addresses proposal revisions. It also explains the flexibility afforded to the sourse selection authority in making the source selection decision and the need for the source selection document to be rational, persuasive, and consistent with selection criteria in the solicitation.

CHAPTER 35

PROPOSAL REVISIONS

FAR 15.307 provides for the following with respect to proposal revisions:

- If an offeror is eliminated or otherwise removed from the competitive range, the contractor is notified that no further revisions to its proposal will be accepted or considered.
- The contracting officer may or may not request or allow interim proposal revisions to clarify and document understandings reached during negotiations (discussions).
- At the conclusion of discussions, each offeror still in the competitive range shall be given an opportunity to submit a final proposal revision.
- While the contracting officer is not required to establish a common cutoff date for any revisions permitted prior to a final proposal revision, the contracting officer is required to establish a common cutoff date for receipt of final proposal revisions.
- Requests for final proposal revisions shall advise offerors that the final proposal revisions shall be in writing and that the government intends to make award without obtaining further revisions.

Usually the government allows or requests interim proposal revisions when the issues being addressed during discussions are numerous or complex and the contracting officer wants to make sure the parties have a common understanding of what has been addressed and perhaps agreed upon.

As previously addressed in discussing the dynamic nature of the competitive range, a contractor can protest or otherwise appeal being dropped from the competitive range and not given the opportunity for proposal revision. If the contractor prevails, it can be placed back in the competitive range and interim and/or final proposal revisions can then be allowed or requested by the contracting officer.

REOPENING DISCUSSIONS

If, after receiving final proposal revisions, it becomes clear to the contracting officer that some issues still remain that must be resolved, discussions can be reopened, and each offeror still in the competitive range is given an opportunity for another final proposal revision. This procedure, however, should be used with great prudence—as discussed later in this chapter.

THE BAFO AND THE BARFO

In the distant past, competing contractors would get upset when they received a notice in the mail announcing that another competing contractor had received the contract award. These contractors complained, "Why didn't you tell us negotiations were over? We have been up all night working up a better price deal for the government." These kinds of complaints led to the government's giving notice to all competing contractors still in the competitive range that discussions were to be concluded for all contractors by a common date and time and that they should submit their "best and final offer" by that date and time. This best and final offer procedure was popularly called the BAFO.

Over time, the government began to misuse the BAFO procedure. In too many cases, after the government had received final offers, some advisory person or group (or perhaps even a source selection authority) would suggest that the contracting officer ought to be able to get a better price. So competing contractors were notified that they were being given an opportunity to submit *another* BAFO. Often these "opportunity letters" did not address any discussion issues, but contractors sensed they were being asked to sharpen their pencils and come up with a better price. In some cases, these new BAFO "opportunities" were given to competing contractors multiple times on the same source selections. Contractors bitterly began to distinguish between the BAFO, best and final offer, and the BARFO, best and *really* final offer.

Contractors subsequently complained to government officials about the way BAFO worked, and some government officials vowed to abolish it. However, when they set about to abolish the BAFO, it was obvious that a common cutoff date was still necessary. So the request for a BAFO by a common cutoff date became a request for a "final proposal revision" by a common cutoff date. Except for the language used, the procedures seem remarkably the same—and so does the potential for abuse. Asking for multiple "final" revisions without a compelling reason to do so would seem to be as questionable a practice as asking for multiple BAFOs.

Although the term *best and final* offer no longer appears in the FAR, many contractor personnel and government officials still refer to the final proposal revision as the BAFO in general conversation.

EVALUATION AFTER FINAL PROPOSAL REVISIONS

Once final proposal revisions are received, the government conducts evaluations to take into account any changes and additional information furnished by the competing contractors, and the evaluators submit a new summary report to the contracting officer and source selection authority. Depending on the regulations or practices of the agency and/or the wishes of the source selection authority, the final summary report may or may not contain a recommendation for award. Some source selection authorities prefer to have a recommendation to consider. Others prefer that there not be a recommendation so that if the source selection authority does not agree with the recommendation, there is no paper trail showing disagreement. Regardless, the source selection authority has autonomy in selecting the source, and there is nothing improper in making an independent decision that may be different from the decision that evaluators and advisors would have made.

The Comptroller General decision in Exhibit 35-1 reinforces the need for proper documentation of the evaluation of final proposal revisions. This opinion is included in its entirety in view of the many interesting aspects of the source selection discussed. These include:

- Sustainment of the protest
- Redaction of the public release to protect contractor-sensitive information
- The use of a peer committee to evaluate proposals
- Evaluator bias
- Reaffirmation that point scores are useful as guides to decision-making but are not controlling
- An inadequate source selection memorandum.

EXHIBIT 35-1 Comptroller General Decision: Biospherics
Incorporated, B-278508.4; B-278508.5; B-278508.6,
October 6, 1998

Document for Public Release

The decision issued on the date below was subject to a GAO Protective Order. This redacted version has been approved for public release.

Matter of: Biospherics Incorporated

File: B-278508.4; B-278508.5; B-278508.6

Date: October 6, 1998

Digest

Protests are sustained where there is no documentation of the agency's evaluation of final revised proposals, that is, there is no information in the record regarding proposal strengths and weaknesses after discussions, and as a result, the reasonableness of the agency's evaluation upon which the award decision was made cannot be determined....

Decision

Biospherics Incorporated protests the award of a contract to Logistics Applications Inc. [LAI] under request for proposals (RFP) No. AHCPR-98-0001, issued by the Agency for Health Care Policy and Research (AHCPR), Department of Health & Human Services, for the operation of a publications clearinghouse. Biospherics challenges the agency's evaluation of proposals and the agency's selection decision.

We sustain the protests.

The RFP, issued on June 5, 1997 as a small business set-aside, contemplated the award of a cost-plus-fixed-fee contract for the base period and four 1-year option periods. RFP sec. L.2., at 62. The RFP described warehousing and distribution (fulfillment) tasks and automated call center and database management function tasks. The RFP required the contractor to store and distribute AHCPR publications; to maintain and manage AHCPR's automated mailing/inventory control systems; and to manage the storage and shipping of AHCPR exhibits.

The RFP stated that the "Government reserves the right to make an award to the best advantage of the Government, cost and other factors considered." RFP sec. M.1.A., at 80. The RFP contained the following technical evaluation factors and respective weights: (1) understanding the problem—25 points; (2) technical approach—25 points; (3) management plan—20 points; (4) key personnel—20 points; and (5) facilities—10 points. RFP sec. M.2.A.—E., at 81-82. The RFP stated that a peer review technical committee would consider offerors' proposals in light of these technical evaluation factors and make a recommendation concerning the technical acceptability/unacceptability of each proposal. RFP sec. M.2., at 81. Offerors whose proposals were determined technically acceptable would then be evaluated for past performance, weighted at 25 points, based on the firm's performance under existing and prior contracts for similar services. RFP sec. M.2.F., at 82. The RFP stated that technical proposals would receive paramount consideration in the selection of the awardee. RFP sec. M.1.A., at 80. Cost would only become a significant factor if two or more proposals were determined approximately technically equal. Id.

Three firms, including Biospherics and LAI, submitted proposals by the amended closing date of July 11, 1997. Under the prior contract, LAI was the prime contractor performing the warehousing and distribution tasks, and Biospherics was LAI's subcontractor performing the call center and database management tasks. For the current procurement, LAI submitted a proposal to basically perform all required tasks, and Biospherics submitted a proposal as the prime contractor teamed with another firm which would serve as a subcontractor for the warehousing and distribution tasks. The three proposals were evaluated by a peer review panel made up of six individuals. This panel determined that two proposals, including that of Biospherics, were technically acceptable, and that LAI's proposal was technically unacceptable. Following discussions with Biospherics and the other offeror and the submission of revised proposals, the agency awarded a contract to Biospherics.

LAI subsequently protested to our Office, contending among other things that the peer review panel was biased because two of the six reviewers were former employees of Biospherics and had failed to disclose in their conflict of interest certificates their prior employment relationships with Biospherics. The agency took corrective action by convening a new peer review panel to reevaluate proposals. Our Office dismissed LAI's protest as academic in light of the agency's corrective action.

The agency's new peer review panel, made up of three individuals,[1] convened on March 23, 1998. This panel reviewed the three technical proposals as initially submitted, that is, none of the offerors was permitted to revise its proposal at this time. All three proposals were determined technically acceptable. The panel then considered the project officer's evaluation of each offeror's past performance which was based on questionnaires completed by references listed in each offeror's proposal. As relevant to these protests, Biospherics and LAI received the following scores:

	Biospherics	LAI
Technical	[deleted]	[deleted]
Past Performance	[deleted]	[deleted]
TOTAL	[deleted]	[deleted]

Technical scores were supported by narratives of the strengths and weaknesses in each offeror's technical proposal. At this time, the proposed cost of Biospherics was [deleted] than LAI's proposed cost [deleted].

The proposals of Biospherics and LAI (as well as that of the third offeror) were included in the competitive range. Following discussions with each competitive range offeror, which focused on technical and cost issues, the offerors submitted final revised proposals. The agency made no adjustments to the technical scores of any of the offerors, and therefore, as relevant to these protests, the final scores for the revised proposals of Biospherics and LAI remained as reflected in the above chart. The agency produced no documentation reflecting an analysis of the offerors' revised proposals. With respect to cost, the Biospherics proposed cost now was [deleted] than LAI's proposed cost. The agency selected LAI as the most advantageous offeror since it submitted the highest technically rated, [deleted] proposed cost proposal.

Biospherics challenges the agency's evaluation of its proposal, contending that its proposal should have been rated technically superior to LAI's proposal. Biospherics further challenges the agency's decision to award a contract to LAI as a technically superior offeror.

In reviewing protests against allegedly improper evaluations, it is not our role to reevaluate proposals. Rather, our Office examines the record to determine whether the agency's judgment was reasonable and in accord with the RFP's stated evaluation criteria. Engineering and Computation, Inc., B-261658, Oct. 16, 1995, 95-2 CPD ¶ 176 at 2-3. In order for us to review an agency's selection determination, an agency must have adequate documentation to support that decision. Arco Management of Washington, D.C., Inc., B-248653, Sept. 11, 1992, 92-2 CPD ¶ 173 at 3. While adjectival ratings and point scores are useful as guides to decision-making, they generally are not controlling, but rather, must be supported by documentation of the relative differences between proposals, their weaknesses and risks, and the basis and reasons for the selection decision. FAR sec. 15.608(a)(3), 15.612(d) (2) (June 1997); Century Envtl. Hygiene, Inc., B-279378, June 5, 1998, 98-1 CPD ¶ 164 at 4; Engineering and Computation, Inc., supra, at 3.

Here, the record is devoid of any documentation of the agency's evaluation of final revised proposals. There is no indication of an analysis of the revised proposals, no information in the record regarding proposal strengths and weaknesses after discussions, and no discussion as to why the strengths and weaknesses from the initial evaluation remained the same.[2] In the absence of such documentation, we are unable to determine the reasonableness of the agency's evaluation upon which the selection of LAI for award was made.

In responding to these protests, the agency states:

The [Biospherics] proposal, as amended [by its final revised proposal], was considered improved (though no rescoring was performed), but not enough to be considered technically equal with LAI. The judgment of the source selection official that LAI's proposal was superior was not based on a numerical rescoring, but rather on a comprehensive look at the final results of the technical, cost and past performance evaluations. Agency Report, letter dated August 17, 1998, at 1-2.

In view of the inadequacy of this conclusory statement that LAI's proposal was technically superior to Biospherics' proposal, we asked the agency to point out where the record documented a "comprehensive look at the final results of the technical, cost and past performance evaluations." The agency responded, again with conclusory statements, in a letter dated August 27, 1998:

The Source Selection Memorandum (Tab Q) represents the "comprehensive" assessment of the three major factors of cost, technical and past performance. Before preparing this document, the contract specialist had a comprehensive discussion with the project officer, during which the relative technical strengths and weaknesses of the offerors were reviewed. Also covered in that discussion was the weight to be afforded to estimated cost and past performance. This oral discussion was not reduced to writing directly except, as mentioned above, as it is reflected in the Source Selection Memorandum. As the contracting officer has stated in her most recent submission, Biospherics would not have been selected for award even if its technical merit had been considered equal to LAI's (which was not the case), since LAI was more highly ranked in both estimated cost and past performance.

The record shows that the agency's source selection memorandum consisted of a chronology of the procurement; a listing of the technical evaluation factors; the technical, past performance, and total scores for each offeror; the offerors' proposed costs before and after discussions; a statement that all three proposals were included in the competitive range because the three offerors submitted technically acceptable proposals and were determined capable to perform the RFP requirements; a statement repeating that the RFP required paramount consideration to be given to technical quality rather than cost, unless the proposals were determined essentially technically equal; and the contracting officer's statement that the proposal of LAI scored highest for the technical evaluation factors and past performance and represented the best value (highest technical score and [deleted] proposed cost).

The source selection memorandum, however, contained no discussion of the results of the evaluation of the Biospherics and LAI revised proposals after discussions. In the absence of such narratives, we cannot discern the basis for the agency's conclusion that LAI's proposal was technically superior to that of Biospherics or, in other words, that the Biospherics proposal was, essentially, technically inferior to LAI's proposal.

In sum, the evaluation and source selection record furnished to our Office—numerical scores and a blanket determination of acceptability, no post-discussion narratives, and the source selection memorandum which contains no explanation of how the revised proposals affected the initial evaluation—is insufficient for our Office to determine the reasonableness of the agency's evaluation of proposals and the reasonableness of the agency's selection decision. See, e.g., Labat-Anderson Inc., B-246071, B-246071.2, Feb. 18, 1992, 92-1 CPD ¶ 193 at 5-8.

We recommend that the agency, in accordance with the applicable FAR provisions, reevaluate the proposals, document its evaluation, and make a new selection decision. If after reevaluation the agency believes further discussions with offerors are warranted, it may reopen discussions and request another round of revised proposals. If the agency decides that LAI is no longer in line for award, the agency should terminate the award to LAI and make another award. We also recommend that Biospherics be reimbursed its costs of filing and pursuing the protests, including reasonable attorneys' fees. Bid Protest Regulations, 4 C.F.R. sec. 21.8(d)(1) (1998). Biospherics should submit its certified claim, detailing the time expended and costs incurred, directly to the contracting agency within 60 days of receipt of this decision. 4 C.F.R. sec. 21.8(f)(1).

The protests are sustained.

Comptroller General of the United States

Notes

1. This panel consisted of a registered nurse with a Ph.D. degree who teaches nursing theory and research and is a freelance technical writer; an individual who is a freelance editor/writer, owns his own publications company, and teaches college-level mass communications and communications studies; and an individual who owns his own company dealing with corporate communications. The protester contends that the selection of these individuals for the panel demonstrates the agency's bad faith. While these individuals may not have had direct publications clearinghouse experience, Biospherics has presented no evidence that these individuals lacked the competence and skills necessary to reasonably evaluate proposals. In fact, we agree with the agency that the collective expertise of these individuals in the areas of communications, publications, health services research, and information technology provided relevant and appropriate background for them to be able to reasonably evaluate proposals.

2. The materials provided to Biospherics as part of its debriefing included a statement of the strengths and weaknesses resulting from the initial evaluation.

CHAPTER 36

MAKING AND DOCUMENTING THE SOURCE SELECTION DECISION

The FAR makes crystal clear that the source selection authority has autonomy in making the source selection decision:

15.308 Source selection decision.

The source selection authority's (SSA) decision shall be based on a comparative assessment of proposals against all source selection criteria in the solicitation. While the SSA may use reports and analyses prepared by others, the source selection decision shall represent the SSA's independent judgment. The source selection decision shall be documented, and the documentation shall include the rationale for any business judgments and tradeoffs made or relied on by the SSA, including benefits associated with additional costs. Although the rationale for the selection decision must be documented, that documentation need not quantify the tradeoffs that led to the decision.

As shown above, the source selection decision must represent the SSA's independent judgment. On occasion SSAs have asked for reevaluations, performed reevaluations themselves, or have otherwise gone against the advice of evaluators. And these are perfectly acceptable things to do when the source selection authority has a reasonable basis for doing them. Case law makes clear that when making the source selection decision, the source selection authority is normally held to only two standards:

1. The decision must be reasonable (sometimes the Comptroller General says "rational").

2. The decision must be consistent with the promises the government made or implied in the solicitation.

A PERSUASIVE SALES DOCUMENT

FAR 15.308 tells us that the source selection decision must be documented and that the documentation shall include the reasoning behind business judgments made, including any benefits associated with additional costs. In an LPTA source selection, this is relatively easy to do. But for tradeoff selections, the documentation requires greater thought and greater clarity. The source selection document in that case should be looked upon as a sales document designed to convince others that a rational decision was made. It should be accurate, complete, and persuasive. It may turn out to be the only significant defense the government has in the event of a protest against the source selection decision.

QUANTIFICATION OF THE DECISION

FAR 15.308 also tells us that although the rationale for selection must be documented, it is not necessary to quantify the tradeoffs that led to the decision. Nonetheless, some agencies do have a longstanding practice of quantifying tradeoffs. Those agencies that historically have quantified tradeoff decisions usually did so in one of two ways:

- By "scoring" costs (as shown in Chapter 16). The contractor with the highest combined total of non-cost points and cost points normally received the contract award.
- Explaining specific estimated cost impacts in a narrative fashion. For example, a source selection document might say:

> Contractor A has far more favorable past performance ratings and more experience in the maintenance and repair of test equipment and has been rated higher than other competing contractors by the technical evaluation team. By selecting Contractor A, it can be expected that the agency would experience at least 20 percent less equipment downtime and avoid the consequent expensive testing delays, especially in the early months of the contract. Since schedule delay can cost the agency as much as $50,000 per day, the adverse cost impact of choosing any of the other competitors could possibly exceed $750,000. The proposed cost of Contractor A's proposal is only $250,000 more than any other competitor's. Thus, it is clear that award to Contractor A is the best value.

Some skeptical observers have characterized this type of approach as an attempt to draw a mathematically precise line from unwarranted assumptions to foregone conclusions. Nonetheless, it is an acceptable method of quantification if the assumptions made are reasonable and defensible.

All that would really be necessary to justify the selection of Contractor A in our abbreviated and simplified example would be a statement of the strengths of its proposal, without any precise quantification. For example:

> The proposal of Contractor A was the best-rated proposal and received a rating of "outstanding" on all evaluation factors. It was particularly strong in the areas of past performance and relevant experience. Taking advantage of these strengths will

most assuredly result in significant reduction in equipment downtime and reduction of delays in critical and expensive testing. These advantages more than offset any differences in proposed cost when compared to other proposals considered.

Of course, the source selection authority could have opted for a lower-priced proposal even if non-cost factors were significantly more important than costs. And, as might be noted, the source selection authority in our example did not address all the evaluation factors, only those that were significant in making the selection. A Comptroller General opinion addresses both the source selection authority's freedom to choose a lower-priced proposal and to discuss some evaluation factors but not others when documenting the reasons for making a source selection decision:

> Notwithstanding a solicitation's emphasis on technical merit, an agency may properly select a lower-priced, lower technically rated proposal if it decides that the cost premium involved in selecting a higher-rated, higher-priced proposal is not justified, given the acceptable level of technical competence available at the lower price....
>
> An agency need not address each and every feature of a proposal in documenting a source selection decision, but must show only that its evaluation conclusions are reasonably based (ViroMed Laboratories, Inc., B-310747.4, January 22, 2009).

THE INDEPENDENCE OF THE SSA

FAR 15.305 requires that source selection records include an assessment of each offeror's ability to accomplish the technical requirements based on a summary, matrix, or quantitative ranking, along with an appropriate supporting narrative assessment of each technical proposal, using the evaluation factors. When properly prepared, the summary reports of evaluators and or advisors may be sufficient to fulfill this requirement. However, the SSA is not bound by such reports, and this FAR requirement can be met through documents independently prepared by the SSA.

The independence of the source selection authority is well established in case law, which clearly indicates that the SSA may deviate from the advice of evaluators. For example, in National Steel and Shipbuilding Company, B-281142.2, January 4, 1999, the Comptroller General found:

> Under a best value evaluation scheme, evaluation ratings and scores are only guides to assist source selection officials in evaluating proposals. PRC, Inc., B-274698.2, B-274698.3, Jan. 23, 1997, 97-1 CPD 115 at 12. Source selection officials, which includes officials at an intermediate level, are not bound by the recommendations or evaluation judgments of lower-level evaluators, even though the evaluators normally may be expected to have the technical experience required for such evaluations.

The significant flexibility and discretion afforded the source selection authority in making cost/merit tradeoffs was again demonstrated in DynCorp et al., B-257037.2 et al., December 15, 1994. The Comptroller General addressed the protest of an award made under a solicitation for base operations and support in the Middle East. In that case, the source selection authority selected a contractor that had received an evaluation score of 82.48 points, as opposed to a contractor that received an evaluation score of 80.37 points, even though the probable cost of the selected contractor was $22 million more than that of the contractor that received 80.37 points. Source selection documentation indicated that the primary advantage the winning contractor offered was a more realistic staffing level.

All the four unsuccessful contractors that had been in the competitive range joined together to protest the award. Among other issues, the protestors maintained that it was unreasonable for the Army to conclude that the small numerical technical superiority (about 2 points out of 100) was worth up to $22 million in additional costs, especially since the evaluation scheme in the RFP granted only slightly more importance to technical quality. In his opinion, the Comptroller General stated:

> Agencies may make cost/technical tradeoffs in deciding between competing proposals; the propriety of such a tradeoff turns not on the difference in technical scores or ratings *per se*, but on whether the selection official's judgment concerning the significance of that difference was reasonable and adequately justified in light of the RFP evaluation scheme.... [W]e cannot conclude that the Army acted unreasonably in determining that ITT's ... proposal ... represented the best value to the government.

In the decision, the Comp Gen also noted that the compression in point scores may have been caused in part by "the multitude of evaluated areas."

ADVICE FROM SUPERIORS

In some agencies, source selection authorities announce a decision only after they first brief and presumably get advice from a superior. The Comptroller General has cautioned that SSAs should tread lightly when asking for this advice, to avoid any actual or perceived impediment to their independence. If it can be shown that an SSA's decision was coerced, the decision will be overturned.

If the source selection authority is not the contracting officer, the contracting officer is still the one who must sign the contract and bind the government to the terms and conditions of the contract. Government contracting officials often have hypothetical discussions about what would happen if the contracting officer and the source selection authority did not agree on a source selection. There does not appear to be any public evidence of this having occurred, probably because the parties must work together so closely during the selection process and because source selection officials typically rely a great deal on the advice of experienced contracting officers. If such a situation did occur, the obvious choice would be to bring the matter to the attention of higher officials within the agency and to involve agency legal counsel. If there is merely a difference of opinion about which proposal offers the best value, then the agency could appoint another contracting officer, assuming that the SSA's decision was rational and in accordance with the solicitation provisions.

THE SUBJECTIVE NATURE OF DECISIONS

The source selection decision for tradeoff procurements is much like many other elements of the process. It tends to be very subjective, and in many cases, different people could come to different conclusions. As we have seen, other such subjective elements of the process include:

- Determining whether to use LPTA or tradeoff
- Selecting the evaluation factors
- Establishing the relative weight of evaluation factors
- Selecting a rating method
- Determining scores or ratings of proposals
- Seeking clarifications
- Holding communications

- Determining the competitive range
- Deciding on the extent and specificity of discussions.

Despite the huge number of regulations and all the guidance that acquisition officials must follow in the source selection process, sound business judgment remains a prerequisite to a successful and competent source selection. It must be demonstrated throughout the process, including in the selection of the source and the documentation of the decision.

When judgment calls are questioned in the source selection process, there are no instant replay cameras available. The courts and the Comptroller General occasionally use witnesses but are more apt to rely on the written record.

PART VII

NOTIFICATIONS, DEBRIEFINGS, AND PROTESTS

This part addresses notifications that must be made during the pre-award phase and those that must be made after contract award. It also addresses contractors' rights to a debriefing and the sensitive nature of debriefings and gives suggestions on how to conduct a debriefing. Finally, it discusses protests and their significant, potentially adverse effects.

CHAPTER 37

NOTIFICATIONS TO OFFERS

FAR 15.503 provides for two types of notifications to unsuccessful offerors when using the source selection processes described in FAR Part 15: preaward notices and postaward notices.

PREAWARD NOTICES

There are two types of preaward notices:

1. The FAR requires that "[t]he contracting officer shall promptly notify offerors in writing when their proposals are excluded from the competitive range or otherwise eliminated from competition. The notification shall state the basis for the determination and that a proposal revision will not be considered."

2. The FAR requires a preaward notice at completion of negotiations (discussions) and completion of determinations of responsibility, but *before award,* whenever there was one or more of the following:

   - A small business set-aside
   - A benefit given to a small disadvantaged business concern
   - Use of HUBZone procedures
   - Use of service-disabled veteran-owned small business procedures.

This latter preaward notice shall state:

- The name and address of the apparently successful offeror
- That the government will not consider any further proposal revisions
- That no response is required unless a basis exists to challenge the small, disadvantaged, HUBZone, or service-disabled status of the apparently successful offeror.

The only exceptions to the requirement to issue this latter type of preaward notice are in instances in which the procurement was set aside under the 8(a) program for small disadvantaged businesses or when the contracting officer has determined in writing that urgency necessitates award without delay.

In addition to giving unsuccessful offerors an opportunity to challenge the claimed socioeconomic status of the apparently successful contractor before the contract award is made, this latter preaward notice may also give the unsuccessful offerors an opportunity to seek out subcontracting opportunities before the contract award is made and announced to the public.

POSTAWARD NOTIFICATION

Pursuant to FAR 15.503(b), the contracting officer must, within three days after award, provide written postaward notices to each offeror whose proposal was in the competitive range but was not selected for award. This notice shall include:

- The number of offerors solicited
- The number of proposals received
- The name and address of each offeror receiving an award
- Items, quantity, and price information for the award

- In general terms, the reasons the offeror's proposal was not accepted, unless the price information reveals the reason, as is the case in an LPTA selection.

FAR 15.504 provides also that the successful contractor is notified "by furnishing the executed contract or other notice of award."

CHAPTER 38

DEBRIEFINGS

Many of the rules of source selection are there to protect the interests of the seller and go far beyond protections that would normally be found in private-sector buyer-seller relationships. One of these special perks is the furnishing of a detailed debriefing by the buyer when a seller requests it in a timely manner. Debriefings may be given to a competing contractor before a source selection is made or after a source selection is made, but a competing contractor is not entitled to both.

As is immediately obvious when reading the coverage of debriefings in FAR Subpart 15.5, much more information is given to a competing contractor in a postaward debriefing than is given in a preaward debriefing, and the range of that information is now far greater than was the case in the past. The information content of postaward debriefings was expanded in the hope that if competing contractors had greater access to factual information, they would be less likely to protest to the Comptroller General. No one knows for sure if this change has had the desired impact, because agencies are also using alternative dispute resolution (ADR) techniques, such as mediation, to consider and resolve protests and preempt their being submitted to the Comptroller General or the Court of Federal Claims.

One interesting facet of this expanded coverage on debriefings is the requirement that the ranking of all offerors be disclosed if any ranking was developed by the agency. The original proposed language was "the ranking of all offerors," without any further qualification. But many agencies pointed out that they just pick a winner; they do not determine win, place, and show. Consequently, "when any ranking was developed" was added to the FAR coverage.

PREAWARD DEBRIEFINGS

FAR 15.505 includes these provisions for preaward debriefings:

- They may be requested by offerors within three days after receipt of notification that they have been excluded from the competitive range or otherwise eliminated from the competition.

- The contracting officer must furnish the debriefing as soon as practicable but can delay the debriefing until after award if such delay is determined to be in the best interest of the government.

- Preaward debriefings are limited to discussion of the offeror's proposal (e.g., deficiencies and weaknesses) and issues involving the source selection process.

- The excluded offeror may instead request a postaward debriefing, at which it could obtain more information than it would be given in a preaward debriefing. However, this delay may impair the ability of the offeror to submit a "timely protest" should it wish to protest after the debriefing.

In a preaward debriefing, there is no discussion at all about the content or rating of other proposals nor any discussion of relative standing. The FAR prohibits the disclosure of:

- The number of offerors
- The identity of other offerors

- The content of other offerors' proposals
- The ranking of other offerors
- The evaluation of other offerors
- The release of any of the information that would be prohibited in a postaward debriefing.

POSTAWARD DEBRIEFINGS

FAR 15.506 sets forth the following provisions for postaward debriefings:

- The competing contractors that were not eligible for a pre-award debriefing must request a postaward debriefing within three days after receiving a notice that an award has been made. Requests submitted after this time do not have to be honored, but the contracting officer has the discretion to honor them and furnish a debriefing if he or she wishes to do so.
- The contracting officer should arrange for the debriefing within five days after receipt of a request. If this is not practicable, the debriefing should be given as soon as circumstances permit. (Note: If a contractor learns of a protestable issue at a debriefing, the clock on its ability to submit a timely protest starts ticking at that moment. Protest rules generally provide that a contractor has to submit a protest within 10 days of the time it knew or should have known of the protestable issue. For this reason, it is usually to the advantage of the government to schedule debriefings as quickly as possible to minimize the potential cost impact of any subsequent protest.)

Offerors are given much more information in a postaward debriefing than they would have been in a preaward debriefing. In a postaward debriefing, the government must discuss:

- Significant weaknesses and deficiencies in the offeror's proposal.
- The overall evaluated price and technical rating of both the successful contractor and the contractor being debriefed. (Point-by-point comparisons are not permitted.)
- Past performance information on the debriefed offeror. This may not include the names of individuals providing information about the offeror's past performance.
- The ranking of offers, if a rank order was developed.
- A summary of the rationale for award.
- For commercial items, the make and model of the item to be delivered by the successful offeror.

REASONABLE RESPONSES

In both preaward and postaward debriefings, the debriefed offerors are also entitled to "[r]easonable responses to relevant questions about whether source selection procedures contained in the solicitation, applicable regulations, and other applicable authorities were followed." Here, offerors can further explore government actions taken during the source selection process to determine if, in their opinion, the contracting officer and the source selection authority followed the rules and case law in such matters as consistency with solicitation promises, the conduct of meaningful discussions, and reasonable decisions.

INFORMATION THAT MAY NOT BE FURNISHED

Information that may not be made available in either preaward or postaward debriefings includes:

- Point-by-point comparisons of the debriefed offeror's proposal with those of other offerors.

- Competing contractors' proposals.

- Information not available under the Freedom of Information Act.

- Trade secrets.

- Privileged or confidential manufacturing processes and techniques.

- Commercial and financial information that is privileged or confidential. This includes cost breakdowns, profit, indirect cost rates, and other similar information.

- The names of individuals providing reference information about an offeror's past performance.

Both preaward and postaward debriefings must be summarized in official documents that are made a part of the contract file.

THE SENSITIVITY OF DEBRIEFINGS

Ostensibly, debriefings are given to help competing contractors do better in future acquisitions, and they can be very valuable in this regard. However, there is no question that contractors often come to debriefings in a less-than-conciliatory frame of mind. They have invested blood, sweat, tears, and money in a proposal. Sometimes, losing a contract can have a profoundly adverse impact on a company and those who work for that company. If an offeror is not convinced at the debriefing that it was treated fairly and in accordance with the rules, a protest may follow.

The manner in which a debriefing is conducted can help defuse this potentially volatile situation. Contracting officers get to determine how the debriefing will be given (for example, by mail, by telephone, or face-to-face). In selections involving a substantial amount of money or that are otherwise of significant sensitivity or import, most contracting officers seem to opt for face-to-face debriefings, during which they can relate more personally with contractor personnel.

When preparing and conducting a face-to-face debriefing, government contracting officers should:

- Ask for the offeror's questions in advance so that the government can be better prepared to answer them.
- Ask key government personnel to assist in preparing for and presenting the debriefing. This may include evaluators, program officials, contract specialists, and legal counsel.
- Prepare for any additional questions that might arise during the debriefing.
- Prepare an agenda beforehand to keep the meeting on track and to address matters in a logical sequence.
- Impress on team members the potential sensitivity involved and the need to treat contractors with courtesy and respect.

It is important that the contracting officer control the government's share of dialogue during a debriefing to avoid any slips of the tongue that might precipitate a protest. For example, characterizing a weakness as a deficiency, or technical personnel pointing out flaws that evaluators perceived in a proposal when those perceived flaws had no bearing on evaluation ratings or the source selection decision.

Such slips of the tongue may not be fatal in that they are unlikely to result in a sustained protest. For example, in Keystone Sealift Services, Inc., B-401526.3, April 13, 2010, the Comptroller General opined:

[Keystone Sealift Services] KSS asserts that the agency unreasonably evaluated its proposal under the contract administration and property management subfactors. As with its other protest grounds, KSS's assertions are based on statements allegedly made by the agency during the debriefing. Specifically, KSS understood that the agency did not consider its proposal to be as "compelling" as [General Dynamics American Overseas Marine] AMSEA's due to unspecified "past problems" with contract administration and its failure to provide specific examples of how it used its property management system. Protest at 12-13.

The evaluation record, not the agency's alleged statements during a debriefing, is the basis for our review. We are concerned with the manner in which the evaluation was conducted, notwithstanding the protester's understanding of the agency's subsequent explanation of how it conducted the evaluation. In this regard, a debriefing is only an explanation of the agency's evaluation and source selection decision, not the evaluation or decision itself. Del-Jen Int'l Corp., B 297960, May 5, 2006, 2006 CPD ¶ 81 at 4.

Still, while such slips may not result in a sustained protest, they can precipitate the protest itself and cause the delay, cost, and ill will that will be occasioned by a protest.

In summary, competing contractors are entitled to a debriefing. It is their right under the law. Debriefings can be valuable as lessons learned for those competing contractors that did not receive the contract award. Properly conducted, they can also offer reassurance to those contractors that they were treated fairly and in accordance with law and regulation.

Unless a protest is received, postaward debriefings mark the completion of the source selection process. To help the reader review the process, the exhibits shown in Chapter 2 that outlined the key steps in the process are repeated as exhibits 38-1, 38-2, and 38-3.

EXHIBIT 38-1   The Normal Sequence of Events in Source Selection

When award is to be made without holding discussions

1. Identify the requirement.
2. Planning begins; assign responsibilities.
3. Market research begins.*
4. Prepare the acquisition plan (AP) and the source selection plan (SSP).
5. Issue the draft request for proposal (RFP), if any, and conduct other presolicitation exchanges.**
6. Issue a synopsis of the requirement at www.fedbizopps.gov, the government-wide point of entry (GPE). This notifies the public that a solicitation is to be issued and often occurs at the same time as activity 7, preparation of the solicitation..
7. Prepare the solicitation. A request for proposal is used for most source selections other than simplified acquisitions. Simplified acquisitions often are accomplished using a request for quotation (RFQ).
8. Issue the solicitation.
9. Conduct the preproposal conference or site visit, if any.
10. Receive proposals.
11. Evaluate proposals.
12. Obtain clarifications, where appropriate.
13. Select the source, document the rationale, and make the award.***
14. Notify competitors, and offer debriefings.
15. Hold debriefings.

When discussions are to be held

1. Identify the requirement.
2. Planning begins; assign responsibilities.
3. Market research begins.*
4. Prepare the acquisition plan and the source selection plan.
5. Issue the draft RFP, if any, and conduct other presolicitation exchanges.**

6. Issue a synopsis of the requirement at www.fedbizopps.gov, the government-wide point of entry (GPE). This notifies the public that a solicitation is to be issued and often occurs at the same time as activity 7, preparation of the solicitation.

7. Prepare the solicitation. A request for proposal is used for most source selections other than simplified acquisitions. Simplified acquisitions often are accomplished using a request for quotation.

8. Issue the solicitation.

9. Conduct the preproposal conference or site visit, if any.

10. Receive proposals.

11. Evaluate proposals.

12. Conduct communications, where appropriate.

13. Establish the competitive range.

14. Notify those not placed in range; offer debriefings.

15. Hold debriefings at a time determined by the contracting officer. They may be delayed until after award at the request of a competing contractor or if the contracting officer chooses to do so.

16. Hold discussions with those in the competitive range.

17. Receive interim proposal revisions, if permitted or required.

18. Request and receive final proposal revisions.

19. Reevaluate proposals.

20. Select the source, document the rationale, and make the award.***

21. Notify competing contractors of the award, and offer debriefings.

22. Hold debriefings.

* Steps 3 through 5 may be concurrent.

** Presolicitation activities may be synopsized at the GPE.

*** Advance notifications before award may be given to competing offerors when certain socioeconomic programs are involved, such as set-asides for small businesses.

EXHIBIT 38-2   Flow Chart for Award without Discussions

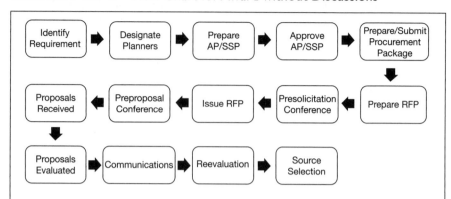

- Requests for information or draft requests for proposal may be issued at any time before the final RFP is prepared.

- Presolicitation conferences may be held before or following preparation of the RFP.

- Clarifications are obtained at the discretion of the contracting officer.

- Synopsis at the governmentwide point of entry (GPE) is normally required before the RFP is issued and after the contract is awarded.

EXHIBIT 38-3 Flow Chart for Award after Discussions

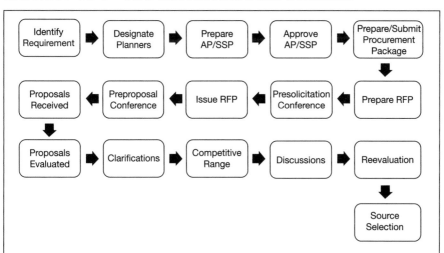

- Requests for information (RFIs) or draft RFPs may be issued at any time before the final RFP is prepared.
- Presolicitation conferences may be held prior to or following preparation of the RFP
- Communications are conducted as required.
- Synopsis at the governmentwide point of entry (GPE) is normally required before the RFP is issued and after the contract is awarded.

CHAPTER 39

PROTESTS

FAR 33.101 defines a protest as a written objection by an interested party to any of the following:

1. A solicitation or other request by an agency for offers for a contract for the procurement of property or services

2. Cancellation of the solicitation or other request

3. Award or proposed award of a contract

4. Termination or cancellation of an award of a contract when it is alleged that the termination or cancellation is based in whole or part on improprieties concerning the award of the contract.

The impact of a protest on the government became more significant with the passage of the Competition in Contracting Act. This act generally requires that when a protest is filed before a contract is awarded, award be delayed until the protest is resolved. If award has already been made and a protest is lodged, then some sort of stop work order must usually be issued. These provisions of CICA are known as the stay provisions or stay rules (see Chapter 31).

If a protest has been submitted to the Government Accountability Office (GAO), the government may proceed to award or continue contract performance regardless of the stay provisions only in cases of documented urgency and approval by the head of the contracting activity. In most cases, the government does not seek documentation of urgency and approval, and the stay provisions prevail. If the government does decide to use the override procedure based on urgency, the protester has the right to challenge the override in the Court of Federal Claims.

INTERESTED PARTIES

An interested party is an actual or prospective offeror whose direct economic interest would be affected by award of a contract or failure to award a contract. When a competing contractor protests, the protestor must show that were it not for the agency's actions, it would have had a substantial chance to receive the award. If that is not the case, no harm was done to the protester as a result of government action, and the Comp Gen or the courts usually will not address the issue being protested. This has been called the "no harm, no foul rule" by some in the business.

An interested party may file a protest with:

- The agency conducting the acquisition
- The GAO (Comptroller General)
- The Court of Federal Claims.

The Court of Federal Claims does not have an automatic stay provision, and there is no established time limit for it to issue an opinion. For these and other reasons, the overwhelming majority of protests are filed with the agency or with the GAO.

PREAWARD AND POSTAWARD PROTESTS

There are two basic types of protests: a preaward protest that is made before a contract is awarded, and a postaward protest that is made after a contract has been awarded. Matters that may be addressed in preaward protests include challenging solicitation provisions (including evaluation factors or their relative importance), challenging limitations on competition, and any other instances in which an offeror believes that the government is acting in violation of law, regulation, or basic issues of fairness.

Postaward protests often address matters such as erroneous or biased evaluations, the government's failure to act in accordance with the provisions of the solicitation, failure to hold meaningful discussions, unequal treatment of offerors, and the like.

TIMELINESS

If a preaward protest involving the solicitation provisions is to be considered, the interested party generally must file the protest before the closing date established for receipt of proposals. If a postaward protest is to be made, it should be filed within ten days of the time the protestable issue was known or should have been known. For example, if the protestable issue is not discovered until a debriefing, the contractor has ten days from the debriefing to file a protest. There is a rule, however, that in order to invoke the CICA stay provision, the contractor must file a protest based on information discovered at a debriefing within *five* days after the debriefing was held or offered to be held.

WHEN INTERESTED PARTY OR TIMELINESS STANDARDS ARE NOT MET

If a protester does not meet the criteria for an interested party, timely submission, or both, it is likely that the protest will not be considered. However, there have been relatively rare occasions in which the Comp Gen did consider and publish an opinion on protests that did not meet these standards. In those instances, the Comp Gen felt that the issue involved was "significant to the procurement system," or "of widespread interest to the procurement community." In other words, the Comp Gen felt that establishing case law for the issue or issues involved would benefit the system.

COMPTROLLER GENERAL DECISION PERIOD

The Comptroller General normally has 100 days from the date a protest is filed to issue a decision. If the protestor chooses an "express option," the Comp Gen will expedite consideration of the matter and will normally issue a decision within 65 days.

AGENCY RESPONSIBILITIES

The FAR suggests that agencies avoid protests by making their best efforts through open and frank discussions at the contracting officer level to resolve concerns raised by an interested party. Protests are expensive and time-consuming, and they can have significant adverse effects on the orderly progression of government programs. Obviously, every reasonable effort should be made to avoid them.

If a protest is made to the agency, FAR 33.103 advises that the agency "should provide for inexpensive, informal, procedurally simple, and expeditious resolution of protests." It also suggests that alternative dispute resolution (ADR) techniques, third-party neutrals, and enlisting another agency's personnel to help might be appropriate. Many agencies have adopted and successfully used ADR procedures for protests.

Pursuing an agency protest does not extend the time for obtaining a stay if the agency denies a protest and the protester subsequently files at the GAO, although agencies are permitted to include a voluntary suspension period as a part of their process. This voluntary period could encourage more contractors to choose an agency-level protest as their first forum of redress.

The protest coverage in FAR Part 33 is extensive and includes instructions to contractors for submitting protests and coverage for the government on the handling of protests.

IMPACT OF PROTESTS

To demonstrate the impact protests can have on government operations, consider the following actual sequence of events (a synopsis of the events previously described in Exhibit 35-1).

A government agency issued a solicitation for operation of a publications clearinghouse.

- The selection was to be based on technical acceptability, past performance, and cost.
- Two of the contenders for this competitive small-business set-aside were firms named Logistics Applications Inc. (LAI) and Biospherics Incorporated.
- A review panel reviewed each proposal for acceptability. LAI's was found technically unacceptable, and Biospherics was awarded the contract.
- LAI protested that the review panel was likely biased because two of the six members of the panel were former employees of Biospherics.
- The agency convened a new panel and, because corrective action had been taken, the Comp Gen dismissed the LAI protest as academic.

- A new panel considered both of the firms to be acceptable, and both were included in the competitive range.
- Discussions were held, and final revised proposals were received.
- LAI was given the award.
- Biospherics then submitted a protest to the GAO contending that its proposal should have been found technically superior (Biospherics Incorporated, B-278508.4; B-278508.5; B-278508.6, October 6, 1998).

In reviewing the agency documentation, the Comp Gen found, "[T]he record is devoid of any documentation of the agency's evaluation of final revised proposals.... In the absence of such documentation, we are unable to determine the reasonableness of the agency's evaluation upon which the selection of LAI for award was made." The Comp Gen made the following recommendations:

- Reevaluation of proposals and a new selection decision.
- If after reevaluation, the agency believes further discussions are warranted, it may reopen discussions and request another round of revised proposals.
- If the agency determines that LAI is no longer in line for award, the agency should terminate the award to LAI and make another award.
- Biospherics should be reimbursed for its cost of filing and pursuing the protests, including reasonable attorneys' fees.

This situation, unfortunately, is far from a worst-case scenario. Many sustained protests have caused far more severe delays and had far worse monetary consequences. It was selected as an example because, in retrospect, it appears that the issues involved were clear cut and might have been avoided with the application of better business judgment. The solicitation was issued on June 5, 1997, and the Comp Gen opinion was issued on October 6, 1998. That means that about 480 days had already elapsed since issuance of the solicitation, and the source selection process was still far from over. The government incurred significant expenses, including the costs associated with defending against the protest, costs it reimbursed to the protester, and the costs associated with any termination of contracts.

REIMBURSEMENT OF ATTORNEY FEES AND BID AND PROPOSAL COSTS

Government payment of protestors' attorney fees and the payment of bid and proposal costs can often be in order. In some cases, these costs are substantial. For example, in Alabama Aircraft Industries, Inc.–Birmingham, No. 08-470C, reissued February 3, 2009, the Court of Federal Claims found the protestor was entitled to $1,003,288.23 in bid and proposal costs. In another case, CourtSmart Digital Systems Inc., B-292995.7, March 18, 2005, the Comptroller General found that attorney fees of $475.00 per hour (for 324.15 hours) were reasonable.

MINIMIZING PROTESTS

Obviously, a government agency should strive to avoid receiving a protest whenever it can, and it should strive to avoid a *successful* protest if despite its efforts to avoid it, a protest is filed. Government source selection personnel can help minimize the incidence of protests or avoid successful protests by learning and adhering to the rules and principles discussed in this book, by creating and maintaining accurate and complete documentation, and by making reasonable, defensible business decisions.

PART VIII

STREAMLINING

This part of the book addresses a number of streamlining techniques and provides information on the award and use of task order contracts.

CHAPTER 40

STREAMLINING THE SOURCE SELECTION PROCESS

Procurement administrative lead time (PALT) is usually defined as the time that elapses from receipt of a proper and complete procurement request at the contracting office until a contract is signed. Total acquisition lead time is much longer because it includes all the planning processes discussed in Part II of this book.

It often appears to government contracting officers that program managers and others on the acquisition team focus too much on PALT as the culprit when they miss projected program target dates. Not that PALT isn't extensive. Most contracting offices estimate that it will take 180 days or more before a negotiated contract is awarded using conventional source selection. For example, in March 2010, a government directorate of contracting (DOC) established and published estimated PALT times to be used by its customers for planning purposes. It informed the customers that "[t]hese timelines assume the customer provides a procurable requirement, responds to DOC or other inquiries in a prompt manner and that no litigation such as a GAO protest occurs." The DOC estimated a PALT of 180 days for noncommercial items and services over $500,000. For complex negotiated requirements exceeding $5.5 million, the DOC estimated 360 days. In the latter case, that means that PALT may consume a year of the total acquisition cycle. The DOC was apparently seeking to be very candid with customers and to prevail upon them the need for early planning.

An acquisition team can take a number of steps to potentially reduce the time it takes to execute a source selection and to avoid the severe delay that can be occasioned by a successful protest. Many are just common sense.

- Acquisition team members should work together and be mutually supportive. Any wagon goes faster and farther if everyone pulls at the same time and in the same direction.

- Spend an adequate amount of time on planning, and plan carefully. Market research as described herein can be particularly valuable. Contractor participation in planning is critical. Remember that planning begins with the identification of the requirement.

- Use planning tools such as RFIs and draft RFPs. Even though this may add time to the front end, it will reduce time at the back end. As any competent carpenter will tell you, "If you measure twice, you'll only have to cut once."

- Program officials and contracting personnel should work closely together during the planning phase and during preparation of a procurement package so that the package represents a realistic procurable requirement. It was once too often true that the first time a contracting officer saw a contracting requirement was when the project officer "threw it over the wall" and asked that a solicitation be prepared. We hope that this type of lone-wolf behavior is now an anachronism.

- Take advantage of the tools available to shorten PALT whenever it makes sense to do so. These include task order contracts, the combined synopsis/solicitation, oral presentations in lieu of written material, and the flexibility given to acquisition personnel in the FAR. (They can be creative so long as they stay within the bounds of law and regulation.) Do not let one bad experience deter your agency from using available tools. Instead, learn from the experience and make better use of the tools in the future.

- Limit the evaluation factors to true, requirement-based discriminators between competing contractors. Each unnecessary evaluation factor adds cost, time, and complexity to the process.

- For the same reasons, limit the amount of information that is to be required from competing contractors to that needed to make a proper selection and to execute a proper contract.

- Consider using past performance as a primary discriminator between competing contractors. Many acquisition professionals believe that this will reduce or eliminate the need for many other evaluation factors such as key personnel, management plans, and the like.

- Limit the number of evaluators to a reasonable number commensurate with the range of expertise needed to competently evaluate proposals.

- Avoid any unnecessary layering of evaluators, overseers, and advisors when organizing for source selection. Having too many layers can add static and distortion to communications between evaluators and the source selection authority, and it most assuredly takes up more time.

- Ensure that evaluators are properly briefed on their role in the process and are familiar with the need to protect procurement information. Improper release of procurement information can abort or otherwise seriously delay a source selection effort.

- Ensure that evaluators understand the meaning of words such as *clarifications, communications, discussions, deficiencies, significant weaknesses,* and *weaknesses* so that required evaluations will not have to be redone.
- Plan for award without discussions whenever feasible.
- Establish reasonable deadlines (target dates), and gain team commitment to meeting them.
- Avoid successful protests through careful evaluations, meaningful discussions, and reasonable (rational) source selection decisions consistent with the promises the government made in the solicitation.
- Prepare well-thought-out and persuasive source selection documentation to further decrease the probability of a successful protest.
- Carefully prepare for and conduct debriefings so that contractors will know that they were treated fairly and in accordance with law and regulation.

CHAPTER 41

AWARDING TASK ORDER CONTRACTS

Before 1994, the government had for many years used indefinite delivery contracts almost solely for supplies. Under this mechanism, the government could execute a contract with a supplier and issue delivery orders against the contract as supplies were needed. Three types of indefinite delivery contracts were permitted:

- *Indefinite delivery/definite quantity (ID/DQ) contracts.* A contract was written for a specific quantity (such as 20 tons of gravel) to be delivered in smaller increments whenever the government issued a delivery order.
- *Requirements contracts.* The government did not commit itself to a specific quantity but promised that it would get all the supplies (gravel, for example) that the contracting activity needed during the term of the contract from the single-requirement contract holder.
- *Indefinite delivery/indefinite quantity (ID/IQ) contracts.* The government did not commit itself to a specified quantity (beyond a minimum quantity specified in the contract) but provided that the government could issue delivery orders up to a stated maximum.

THE FEDERAL ACQUISITION STREAMLINING ACT

When the Federal Acquisition Streamlining Act (FASA) was passed in 1994, it provided for indefinite delivery contracts for services as well as supplies. This transformed the way much of government contracting was conducted.

Up until that time, an agency that needed an environmental study, for example, would go through the entire acquisition process with a PALT of up to 180 days or more. Then it would have to do the same thing again when it needed to remove contaminated soil or restore a damaged ecosystem or study the flow of contaminants in an aquifer. With the changes in law and regulation, an indefinite delivery contract could now be awarded for environmental remediation services, with task orders (the service-contract equivalent of a delivery order) being issued as environmental remediation needs arose. Thus, PALT for each individual requirement could be reduced to a small fraction of what it was before.

The utility of task order contracts was exploited immediately, and there has been explosive growth in their use, especially indefinite delivery/indefinite quantity (ID/IQ) task order contracts. Some of these contracts are designed and used specifically for the agency that executed the contract. Others, such as many executed by the General Services Administration (GSA), are for government wide use. While task order contracts were at first primarily used for tasks of modest dollar value and duration, it was not long before agencies began awarding individual tasks requiring years of effort and costing millions of dollars.

THE SOURCE SELECTION PROCESS FOR TASK ORDER CONTRACTS

The source selection process for selecting contractors for ID/IQ contracts is essentially the same as the general process we have discussed throughout this book, with two significant exceptions:

1. The preference for multiple awards

2. The use of sample task orders.

FAR Part 16 established a preference for multiple awards of ID/IQ contracts under a single solicitation for the same services (except for certain advisory and assistance services and some other limited exceptions) so that there will be competition for later task orders when the occasion permits. The FAR does not address how many contracts should be awarded but leaves this matter up to acquisition planners. Among the factors to be considered are:

- The scope and complexity of the requirement
- Expected duration and frequency of task orders
- The mix of resources a contractor must have to perform task requirements
- The ability to maintain competition among awardees.

SAMPLE TASKS

Because there may not be a specific task that encompasses the general range of services that will be needed under an ID/IQ contract, or there may not be any immediate tasks at all, it is common practice for agencies to ask contractors to base their proposals in part on government-prepared "sample tasks" that encompass a reasonable range of the expected services. Competing contractors are then evaluated in part on how they would propose to perform the sample tasks.

The use of sample tasks has been the topic of some academic discussion. Some contracting officers felt that asking competing contractors to submit proposals for make-believe work could result in overly optimistic proposals because competing contractors would not have to live up to the promises made. Because of this some agencies attempt to have actual tasks ready to be awarded at the time the basic contracts are awarded. This helps to ensure that task proposals are more realistic, especially in the area of costs, since competing contractors must commit themselves to doing the work for a specific sum.

Because of the perceived drawbacks of using sample tasks, especially the potential for over-optimistic pricing, one agency attempted to have competing contractors commit to markup rates alone rather than pricing out sample tasks. Markup rates were to be on a not-to-exceed basis and included overhead, general and administrative costs, bonds, insurance, other indirect costs, profits, and other fees that the firm would commit to for use on later actual tasks. Working from the premise that labor hours would depend on the specific requirements of later tasks and that material costs would depend on market conditions at the time a task was ordered, the contracting officer believed that offerors' committing to markup rates provided the one common basis for comparison of cost proposals.

But an offeror, S. J. Thomas Co., Inc., protested the use of markup rates as the sole cost factor in a General Services Administration RFP. The Comp Gen sustained the protest (B-283192, October 20, 1999), opining:

> We recognize the legitimacy of some of the contracting officer's concerns about using sample tasks to estimate the relative costs to the government of the competing proposals. We have previously acknowledged the artificial nature of prices offered in the context of sample tasks. See, e.g.,

SCIENTECH, Inc., supra, at 7-8. Moreover, we agree with the contracting officer that where, as here, there is the expectation of binding price competition when the contractors compete for actual tasks under individual task orders, the non-binding character of sample-task prices makes their use appear of limited value. The limitations of sample tasks, however, do not provide reasonable justification for an agency, as GSA has done here, to use mark-up rates as the sole cost factor that may eliminate a proposal from consideration for an umbrella contract, thus preventing that offeror from competing in the price competitions for actual task orders. We recognize that GSA does not at this time know exactly what repair and alteration services it will order under these contracts during the next 5 years. However, that is the case with all indefinite-quantity contracts and does not relieve GSA of its obligation to evaluate cost to the government here. If used intelligently, sample tasks can provide insight into competing offerors' technical and staffing approach and thus provide a reasonable basis to assess the relative cost of the competing proposals.

PREPARING FOR THE AWARD OF TASK ORDERS

Whatever evaluation factors are used to select contractors, the contracts awarded must describe the procedures the government will use in issuing orders, including the criteria to be used to provide contract holders a "fair opportunity to be considered," as provided for in FAR 16.504. The contract must also provide for a minimum and a maximum amount for any task orders that might be issued. The sample solicitation provisions shown in Appendix II are for a proposed task order contract. Procedures for selecting the source for individual task orders are discussed in Chapter 42.

CHAPTER 42

AWARDING INDIVIDUAL TASKS

FAR Part 16 contains the guidance used for selecting a task order contract holder (an awardee that received a task order contract for specified services) for a particular task. This guidance can be summarized as follows:

- The contracting officer must provide each contract holder a "fair opportunity to be considered" for each order exceeding $3,000.
- The contracting officer has broad discretion in developing order-placement procedures and should keep contractor submission requirements to a minimum. If architect-engineer (AE) services are involved, the contracting officer must use procedures prescribed in FAR Part 36.
- Streamlining procedures, including oral presentations, can be used.
- If the contracting officer has information available to ensure each of the multiple awardees was provided a fair opportunity, then it is not necessary to contact each awardee unless the order is expected to exceed $5 million. If the order is expected to exceed $5 million, each awardee must be notified of the requirement and the significant factors and subfactors (and their relative importance) to be used

in selecting a contract holder for the task. Further, each unsuccessful awardee is entitled to receive a notification of the task order award and may receive a debriefing.

- Order-placement procedures must be consistent with the placement guidance given to contractors in the contract. Accordingly, these contract procedures should be carefully tailored to provide for realistic ordering of anticipated task orders under anticipated conditions.

- Generally, formal evaluation plans or scoring of quotes and offers are not required. However, a number of agencies routinely follow the source selection procedures laid out in FAR Part 15 when awarding large tasks.

- Documentation of the basis for award is required.

The manner in which a contractor is given a "fair opportunity to be considered" may vary widely from contract to contract and from agency to agency. In one case, the contracting officer may, for example, examine all basic contract awardees and determine that only one or two have the wherewithal to perform a given task. Excluded contractors were given a "fair opportunity" in that their qualifications, past performance, experience, and perhaps current workload were considered by the contracting officer. In another situation, the contracting officer may determine that all basic contract awardees should be given an opportunity to compete for the task.

Some streamlining techniques lend themselves well to awarding of tasks on a competitive basis. Returning to the example of an environmental services contract (Chapter 41), assume that four contracts have been awarded. Thus, the government has already gathered information on each contractor's past performance, corporate experience, and personnel, among other factors. To award a task for an environmental study, the government might ask the four contractors for only a signed price offer and an oral presentation on how each plans to accomplish the task. On the strength of this information, the government could select a contractor to receive the task order award. A process that once took months can be completed in a few weeks. This scenario presumes, of course, that the basic task order contracts permit this streamlined technique.

With two exceptions, protests from basic task order contract holders are not permitted. These two exceptions are:

1. A protest on the grounds that an order increases the scope, period, or maximum value of a contract.

2. The task order was in excess of $10 million, in which case a protest may be filed with only the Government Accountability Office. (This is a temporary provision of law, and the reader should check FAR Part 16 to see if it still applies in the event this becomes an issue in the awarding of a task).

The head of each agency must appoint an ombudsman to review complaints from contractors and ensure that they are given a fair opportunity to be considered. The ombudsman must be a senior agency official who is independent of the contracting officer.

While they may not have the right to protest, some contractors have alleged that failure to be given a fair opportunity is a breach of contract and is subject to the Contract Disputes Act (CDA). Both the Armed Services Board of Contract Appeals (ASBCA) and the Court of Federal Claims have found that this approach may have merit and that a CDA claim properly submitted might be considered by either of these bodies.

PART IX

VARIATIONS IN SOURCE SELECTION

This part of the book addresses:

- The advisory multistep selection process
- Selection of architect-engineer (AE) contractors
- Obtaining best value in simplified acquisitions
- Source selection in commercial item procurement
- The streamlined synopsis/solicitation
- Selections under broad agency announcements.

CHAPTER 43

THE ADVISORY MULTISTEP SELECTION PROCESS

Over the years, agencies have used a number of source selection processes that allow or encourage the winnowing down of potential competing contractors before the government requests and receives full-blown proposals. One of these processes is the Brooks Act selection process for architect-engineer services, which will be discussed in Chapter 44. Another was a four-step selection process once used by the Department of Defense for major systems acquisitions. Contractors would be eliminated from the process during earlier steps before spending the large sum of money needed to prepare a complete cost proposal. Still another is a system in use by the Federal Aviation Agency (which has its own acquisition management system regulations that differ from the FAR) in which one or more screening information requests (SIRs) may be used to narrow the field of competitors.

When the FAR was being amended in 1997, the government planned to provide for two multistep source selection processes. Both would solicit a limited amount of information from contractors. One process was an advisory process in which the agency would perform an evaluation of solicited information, then inform potential offerors whether the government considered them to be viable competitors. Even if the government did not consider them to be viable competitors, they were still permitted to participate in the planned acquisition if they saw fit to do so. In the other process, called a mandatory process, an offeror that was informed that it was not considered to be a viable competitor could not continue to participate in the planned acquisition as a prime contractor.

Industry, in general, was not opposed to the idea of realistically reducing the list of potential contractors and saving money on proposal preparation. However, some felt that the mandatory process was not needed. If the government informed potential offerors that they were not considered to be viable competitors and told them the reasons the government believed this to be true, then the offerors could make a business decision about whether to continue in the process. Obviously, it would not be a good business decision for a contractor to continue if the government gave compelling reasons why the contractor was not considered a viable competitor for a particular acquisition.

Ultimately, only the advisory multistep process was included in the FAR, at FAR 15.202. The advisory process allows an agency to publish a presolicitation notice describing the planned acquisition and invite potential offerors to submit the information that the government feels it needs in order to properly advise offerors about their potential to be viable competitors. The notice should identify the information that potential offerors must submit and the criteria that will be used in making the government determination of viability.

If offerors are subsequently advised that they are not considered to be viable competitors, the government must inform the offerors of the general basis for that opinion. Offerors must also be notified that, notwithstanding the advice furnished by the government, they may participate in the resultant acquisition.

The FAR requires that access to the presolicitation notice be provided through the GPE but does not specify any particular format for the presolicitation notice. Exhibit 43-1 is an example in which the GPE requirement and the advisory multistep notice itself are combined, a procedure that has the potential for saving time and money.

While the example in the exhibit is lengthy, it should be noted that only a relatively small part of the notice pertains to the information the potential contractors must submit (i.e., specialized corporate capability and experience). The remainder explains the process to be used, describes the requirement to be procured, and defines relatively stringent minimum qualification requirements. This particular example is also interesting because it informs potential offerors that it will employ the services of private-sector firms to help the government determine the viability of interested contractors.

Clearly, a properly executed advisory presolicitation notice can save contractors time and money when they are required to submit only the limited information needed for the government to determine whether it will consider them to be viable competitors for an upcoming acquisition. Such a notice also allows the government to save time and money when contractors elect not to participate in the upcoming acquisition, since the government will not have to evaluate proposals that have no realistic potential of receiving a contract award.

EXHIBIT 43-1 Combined Synopsis and Presolicitation Notice

Solicitation Number:

BIOMETRICS

Notice Type:

Presolicitation

Synopsis:

COMBINED PRESOLICITATION ANNOUNCEMENT AND ADVISORY MULTI-STEP NOTIFICATION FOR IDENTITY INTELLIGENCE (I2) BIOMETRICS SERVICES

1.0 Description:

This publication serves as a combined pre-solicitation announcement and Advisory Multi-Step (AMS) notification by the United States Army Intelligence and Security Command (INSCOM). INSCOM intends to issue a solicitation on behalf of the INSCOM G3 Biometrics Division. This requirement will be solicited as a multiple award Indefinite Delivery Indefinite Quantity (IDIQ) contract. The award will be based on the best value to the Government. The exact closing date and time of the Request for Proposal (RFP) will be identified in the solicitation release. It is the sole responsibility of the offeror to review the Army Single Face to Industry (ASFI) webpage frequently for any updates/amendments to the solicitation. All prospective offerors must have a Commercial and Government Entity (CAGE) code and be registered with the Central Contractor Registration (CCR) at http://www.ccr.gov. Interested vendors of this combined pre-solicitation AMS announcement should submit their Capabilities Statement with the intention of submitting a proposal. The respondent should possess NAICS Code 541690.

This combined pre-solicitation notice and AMS announcement requests corporate qualifications from offerors responding to the INSCOM I2 Biometrics Services Acquisition. This announcement requests information from prospective offerors allowing the INSCOM G3 Biometrics Division to review and assess the likelihood of each respondent's ability to provide the services and supplies needed to fulfill the I2 Biometrics requirements. Based on an assessment of each prospective offerors response to this notice, the firm will be notified as to whether it is considered a viable competitor for the I2 Biometrics contract. Notification of a prospective offerors non-viability is advisory, and respondents so notified may submit proposals should they so choose.

The authority and basis for utilizing the AMS process is contained in Federal Acquisition Regulation (FAR) Part 15.202.

2.0 Advisory Multi-Step (AMS)

This combined pre-solicitation notice and AMS announcement is being conducted to allow potential offerors to submit qualifying documentation demonstrating their corporate qualifications which will allow the Government to advise them about their potential to be viable competitors for the I2 (Biometrics) acquisition. The AMS process is accomplished at minimal cost to the potential offerors and the Government by asking interested organizations to submit limited information that focuses on their corporate capability and experience. The Government will assess all responses in accordance with the published criteria, and advise each offeror, in writing, whether they will be viable candidates. Those offerors considered unlikely to be viable candidates will be notified and provided a general basis for that assessment. Notwithstanding the advice provided by the Government, respondents identified as unlikely to be viable competitors may still participate in the resultant acquisition, as long as they recognize the inherent risks and costs of doing so.

3.0 Introduction to the I2 Biometrics Acquisition

INSCOMs intention is to continue acquisitions of I2 and Biometrics support services and technologies at the current contracted levels and at higher levels if required by future conditions, and also to provide the capability to acquire new I2 and Biometrics technologies and services as they become available in the marketplace through the contract resulting from this acquisition.

3.1 Identity Intelligence

INSCOMs Biometrics mission is to conduct I2 Operations to include staff oversight, biometrics and forensics analysis, tools, training, watchlist management and operational support to Department of Defense (DoD), interagency and multinational partners in denying adversaries anonymity.

I2 is defined as the information produced by the discovery, management, and protection of identity attributes (the biographic, biometrics, behavioral, relational, and/or systemic characteristics, by which an individual, person, persona, system, or discrete group thereof, can be distinctly recognized or known) in support of U.S. national and homeland security interests. I2 provides critical intelligence information that helps map and understand the human terrain. Analysis consists of the integration of Identity Intelligence efforts within DoD and the United States Government. Current capabilities and future technologies will be utilized to identify critical intelligence gaps and develop and apply fixes, develop theater/regional watchlists, and develop all-source products that enhance I2 related efforts.

4.0 Services to be Provided

4.1 I2 Biometric Services

Interested offerors for the I2 Biometrics program will provide a complete range of technical and professional support to provide INSCOM a worldwide contract to help manage I2 (Biometrics). Offerors should be able to provide biometric intelligence subject matter expertise ensuring direct linkage between tactical units CONUS and OCONUS, produce various reports from biometric data collection, and manage the ongoing awareness of innovative and developing new ideas for future requirements. Additionally, the offeror(s) will assist in support of, but not limited to the following activities:

- Program Management, Identity Intelligence Resource Management, and Strategic Planning
- Intelligence Analysis, Production and Dissemination
- Forensic-related Biometric Operations Support and Production
- Identity Intelligence Education and Training
- Deployed Biometric and Forensics Subject Matter Expertise (SME)
- Architecture and Enterprise Services Support
- Data Sharing Development, Management and Support
- Information Assurance and Intelligence Oversight Support
- Counter Biometric Capability Support
- Biometric Modality Development.

4.1.1 Contingency Environment Operations

Interested offerors of the I2 Biometrics requirement will be tasked to perform the services to support the activities listed in section 3.1 in a high-pressure, contingency-area deployment type environments. The contractor will be required to logistically support the personnel performing these services.

4.1.2 Security

The interested offerors should include personnel involved in I2 Biometrics with Top Secret (TS) clearances and must have a current Single Scope Background Investigation (SSBI) with eligibility for Sensitive Compartmented Intelligence (SCI) access.

4.1.3 Rapid Response

The contractor shall have the capability to rapidly deploy worldwide to perform the services to support the activities listed in section 4.1.

5.0 Submission Instructions

5.1 Format for Submissions

Interested offerors are requested to provide the information as outlined below.

- Information beyond that requested is neither desired, nor will it be considered in the assessment.

- All page limitations are based on single sided pages, 8 × 11 inch paper, single spaced, Arial or Times New Roman typeface no smaller than 12 point (smaller fonts are acceptable for graphics, figures, tables, footnotes and legends), 1 margins.

- Costly, complex presentations are neither required nor desired.

- Offerors will not be reimbursed for the cost of preparation of their responses to this AMS notice.

5.1.1 Submission Date, Time and Location

Electronic submissions shall be received no later than 11:00 a.m. EST on 05-14-10 at the following email address _biometrics@mi.army.mil__. Any questions concerning this combined pre-solicitation notice and AMS announcement should be directed to the email address above and be limited to the process of responding to this announcement only.

5.2 Content Requirements

All submissions must include the information described sufficient to permit an assessment of all criteria identified within this combined pre-solicitation notice and AMS announcement.

5.2.1 Corporate Capability

Describe your organizations current established corporate capability discussing why your company is well qualified to perform on the I2 Biometrics acquisition in accordance with I2 Biometric Services. The corporate capability statement must address the following topics:

- Organizational Structure to include company size, and facility security level;

- Financial Capability to support a program of this size;

- Personnel Management Strategy to include methodology for employee recruitment, training, and retention;

- Project Team, Management and Composition to include a description of the number of qualified and cleared personnel available for OCONUS assignment with a 60-day advance notice; and

- Organization's Geographical Coverage to include whether the organization has facilities capable of supporting a broad geographical scope including CONUS, and OCONUS locations.

Page limitation: 10 pages

5.3.2 Experience

Describe your organizations experience and past performance in the last three years in providing identity intelligence and biometrics products and services to the intelligence community. The respondent shall identify contracts on which it and/ or its team have experience during the past three years. All categories and circumstances in section 4 must be addressed in the discussion of past experience. Not all functional categories or circumstances need to be addressed by a single contract. Each contract identified shall have at least a $1,000,000 annual dollar value (including equipment and services). The contracts identified shall demonstrate the respondents performance or responsibility for performance of the functional categories and circumstances as stated in section 4.0. The government reserves the right to contact any other government offices to validate information provided as part of this submission.

For each identified contract, provide the following (this information may be provided in table format): PLEASE ENSURE THAT ALL INFORMATION IS PROVIDED: ITEMS WITH MISSING INFORMATION WILL NOT BE ASSESSED.

- Contract number
- Contract name
- Contract type
- Contract period of performance
- Performance based (Y or N)
- Contracting vehicle (i.e. ITES, GSA)
- Customer agency (i.e. Army, other DoD, other Federal Agency (i.e. DHS, FAA)
- Total dollar value of contract that respondent, to include subcontractors and team members, were responsible for; includes equipment and services
- Total dollar value of equipment and services for each contract year
- Respondents role/status on contract (prime or subcontractor)
- Place(s) of Performance
- Security Level(s)
- Summary of the contract (include depth and breadth of the work performed to include type of services performed under each functional categories as listed in section 4.)
- Customer points of contact (i.e. the program/project manager, contracting officer and a major end-user), name, phone number, and e-mail address.
- Identify key personnel and their level of experience throughout the Identity Intelligence community.
- Page limit: 2 pages per each contract identified.

5.3.3 Special Notice Use of Consultant Contractor

The Government will use Acquisition Solutions, Inc. (ASI) or their follow-on replacement and Davis Paige Management Systems (DPMS) Limited Liability Corporation (LLC) for administrative, technical, subject matter expertise during the capabilities assessment. The exclusive responsibility for capabilities assessment will reside with the government. Proprietary information submitted in response to this combined pre-solicitation notice and AMS announcement will be protected from unauthorized disclosure as required by subsection 27 of the Office of Federal Procurement Policy Act as amended (41 United States Code (U.S.C.) 423) (hereinafter referred to as the act) as implemented in the Federal Acquisition Regulation (FAR). ASI or their follow-on replacement and DPMS LLC are contractually bound by organizational conflict of interest (OCI) and disclosure clauses with respect to proprietary information. Contractor personnel assisting in the assessment of capabilities statements are procurement officials within the meaning of the act and will take all necessary action to preclude unauthorized use or disclosure of a competing contractor's proprietary data. Nondisclosure and OCI certificates for all contractor support personnel participating in this source selection are on file at the respective contracting activities.

6. Assessment of the AMS Corporate Capability and Experience

The Government will assess the respondents viability based on Corporate Capability (Section 5.0), the depth of demonstrated Corporate Experience and the ability to support the I2 services requirements (Section 4.1).

7. Viability Notification

It is the Governments intent to provide advice to each respondent by letter whether or not considered to be a viable competitor. Viability notifications will be sent to respondents in advance of release of RFP.

Those respondents who are notified that they have been determined to be unlikely candidates will not be debriefed. Such debriefings are not required nor contemplated by the applicable regulations. Moreover, a debriefing at this time which notes the strengths and weaknesses which formed the basis for the determination that the respondent would likely not be a viable candidate allows the offeror the opportunity to adjust their approach to correct their deficiencies and weaknesses and gain an unfair competitive advantage over other offerors.

8. Place of Performance:

INSCOMs global command with major subordinate commands and a variety of smaller units with personnel dispersed over 180 locations worldwide.

CHAPTER 44

ARCHITECT-ENGINEER SERVICES

The procedures for selecting a source for architect-engineer, or AE, services are described in FAR Part 36, not in FAR Part 15. While AE acquisitions are considered to be competitive for the purposes of the Competition in Contracting Act, competing contractors for AE services do not normally compete on cost, only on non-cost factors. These procedures are based on a law commonly referred to as the Brooks Act, which seeks to make sure that quality AE services are acquired at a fair and reasonable cost, instead of merely acceptable services being acquired at a lower cost.

FAR 36.602-1 requires the following selection criteria for AE selections:

- Professional qualifications
- Specialized experience and technical competence in the type of work required
- Capacity to perform on time
- Location in the general geographical area of and knowledge of the locality of the project (unless this would result in an inappropriate number of competitors)
- Conceptual design, when appropriate and when approved by the agency head or designee
- Other appropriate evaluation criteria.

The AE selection process can be summarized in eight steps:

1. An agency issues a public notice for a requirement, and an evaluation board reviews responses to this public notice and reviews current data files on eligible firms.
2. At least three firms are selected as the most highly qualified. These contractors constitute what is commonly called the short list.
3. The evaluation board prepares a detailed report for the source selection authority and recommends, in order of preference, at least three of the evaluated competitors.
4. The source selection authority may go along with the order of preference recommended or may establish one of his or her own.
5. The contracting officer conducts negotiations with the most preferred contractor, or, when multiple awards are to be made, with the most preferred contractors.
6. If agreement is reached, the agency awards a contract or contracts.
7. If agreement cannot be reached, then negotiations begin with the next firm or firms on the preferred list.
8. If the preferred list is exhausted without agreement being reached, the selection authority may direct the evaluation board to recommend additional firms.

FAR 36.602-2 requires that members of the evaluation board "shall be appointed from among highly qualified professional employees of the agency or other agencies" and may include "private practitioners."

A simpler, shortened procedure is used for AE source selections for contracts that will not exceed the simplified acquisition threshold. The evaluation board acts essentially as the selection authority, and the chairperson may even perform all the functions of the evaluation board.

Exhibit 44-1 is a detailed example of agency procedures for a regular AE selection. (Note that this civilian agency uses *CO* as an acronym for contracting officer, while the military agencies use *KO* for contracting officer and *CO* for commanding officer).

Exhibit 44-2 is an example of an agency notice issued to gather input for later use in an AE short selection process.[1]

In contemporary practice, it is common for one or more task order (indefinite delivery) contracts to be awarded using the full AE process and subsequent individual task orders to be awarded in an expedited fashion, consistent with whatever ordering procedures are described in the task order contract(s).

EXHIBIT 44-1   Standard Operating Procedures

Department of Agriculture Facilities Division Facilities Contracts Branch
DATE: October 10, 2003; Revised June 15, 2009
SUBJECT: Source Selection Procedures for Architect-Engineering (A-E) Services— Project Specific or Indefinite Quantity Contracts
NUMBER: CSOP-04-001
EFFECTIVE DATE: Immediately Until Replaced or Superseded

1. References

The Brooks Act, Public Law 92-582

FAR Part 15, Contracting by Negotiation

FAR Part 19, Small Business Programs

FAR Part 36.6, Architect-Engineering Services

(Note: Others omitted for the sake of brevity)

2. Purpose

This document provides Facilities Contracts Branch (FCB) procedures for source selection in acquiring Architect-Engineer (AE) services.

3. Policy

Contracting Officers shall initiate a source selection for AE services for projects whose estimated cost of construction is greater than $10 million per phase, or there is a need to have an Indefinite Quantity Contract (IQC) contract in place to accomplish various smaller projects.

4. Procedures

A. AE firms are selected for IQC's (Nation-wide or Area-wide) or for project specific requirements in accordance with FAR Part 36.6.

B. The Engineering Project Manager (EPM) will develop an Action Plan/ Fact Sheet for project specific AE selections. IQC awards do not require an Action Plan/Fact Sheet. The Action Plan/Fact Sheet provides detailed information regarding the project background and budget.

C. In accordance with FAR Part 19.10, the U.S. Department of Agriculture is a participant in the Small Business Competitiveness Demonstration Program (Comp Demo) Program. The Architect and Engineer Services category is identified in the Program as one of the applicable Designated Industry Groups (DIGs). Each year the Department's Office of Small and Disadvantaged Business Utilization (OSDBU) reviews each Agency's data from the Federal Procurement Data System-Next Generation (FPDS-NG) to assess the ability of small businesses to compete successfully with large businesses for Agency contracts in certain DIGs without competition being restricted to only small firms. But where procurement preference goals have not been met, the OSDBU will impose set-asides for that specific NAICS code.

The Contracting Officer (CO) shall determine the applicable NAICS code for each requirement and conduct market research. If it is determined that a requirement cannot be completed as a set-aside in accordance with the USDA policy, the CO shall forward the pertinent information to FD's OSDBU Coordinator for review and submission to the [Agricultural Research Services] ARS OSDBU Coordinator in the Acquisition & Property Division (APD) for their review. The APD OSDBU will review and forward their concurrence to the Department's OSDBU Office for their review and subsequent clearance by the Small Business Administration Procurement Center Representative (SBA-PCR). OSDBU clearances must be submitted to and approved by the Department prior to synopsizing the requirement in FedBizOpps (FBO).

D. The CO shall prepare a procurement plan which shows the milestone dates for each stage of the procurement. The procurement plan is a living document and should be kept up-to-date. If a milestone date cannot be met, a revised plan shall be prepared with new dates and copies given to all interested parties. The procurement plan in the Facilities Division Management Information System (FDMIS) is to be updated as well.

E. The CO shall submit a request via e-mail to the Chief, Facilities Engineering Branch (FEB), to identify a Chairperson and the members of the Evaluation Board. The Chairperson should be the EPM in charge of the project and the remaining Board members should be from the appropriate Area for an Area-wide project, or FEB for a nation-wide project. The Chief, FEB, will e-mail the names of the appointees to the CO.

F. The CO and Evaluation Board should work together to develop the evaluation factors and methodology, as well as the synopsis for the FBO announcement. The announcement shall identify the requirements, the evaluation factors and any subfactors, the scoring method for each factor and subfactor, whether there will be multiple awards, any geographic considerations, and the number of copies of Standard Form (SF)-330s, Architect-Engineer Qualifications, to be submitted. Once the announcement has been developed, the CO shall post the announcement to FBO.

G. Release of information during the process is restricted in accordance with FAR Parts 5.4, 15 and 36.607. See paragraph Q for additional guidance.

H. Prospective firms will submit their SF-330s to the CO. The CO shall collect and store the documents in a locked cabinet until the date established for receipt. After that date, the CO shall provide the SF-330s to the Evaluation Board members for initial screening.

I. The initial screening by the Evaluation Board shall be conducted using the established evaluation criteria and scoring method. The scoring method shall be consistent throughout the process.

J. The Evaluation Board Chairperson will provide a written report to the CO detailing the Board's findings and recommendation for the short-list. The CO shall review this report and recommend the short-list to the Selection Authority, normally the Chief, Facilities Contracts Branch (FCB).

K. After the Selection Authority has approved the short-list, those firms not making the short-list shall be notified in writing that their submission will not be evaluated further.

L. After the Selection Authority has approved the short-list, the CO shall schedule interviews with the short-listed firms and confirm the interview by letter. The letter should discuss the interview structure, any questions that need to be responded to prior to the interview, and advise that all presentation materials must be in writing.

M. The Evaluation Board shall conduct interviews based on the evaluation criteria. After the interview is complete, the panel members will discuss each firm's qualifications in order to come to a consensus. Each firm is evaluated against the stated selection criteria and not against each other.

N. The Chairperson shall prepare a comprehensive final report and provide it to the CO. The report shall include each firm's strengths and weaknesses, their scores, and clearly identify the most highly qualified firm, or firms if there will be multiple awards in the case of an IQC.

O. The CO shall review the report, ensuring that the established evaluation criteria were used properly, and recommend the AE firm(s) to the Selection Authority who will either concur with the CO's recommendation or recommend another firm(s). If the Selection Authority recommends another firm(s), he/she must provide a written justification to the CO.

P. The CO shall notify the successful firm(s) of their selection and follow-up with a letter. The CO shall also notify, by letter, the unsuccessful firms and thank them for their continued interest in ARS projects.

Q. In accordance with FAR Part 15.505, unsuccessful firms may request a debriefing either before award or after, but not both. The CO shall conduct all debriefings with the assistance of the Chairperson.

Pre-award debriefings shall include, at a minimum, the agency's evaluation of significant elements in the offeror's proposal, a summary of the rationale for eliminating the offeror from the competition, and reasonable responses to relevant questions about whether source selection procedures contained in the solicitation, applicable regulations, and other applicable authorities were followed in the process of eliminating the offeror from the competition.

Pre-award debriefings *shall not* disclose the number of offerors, the identity of other offerors, the content of other offeror's proposals, the ranking of other offerors, the evaluation of other offerors, or any information that is considered proprietary.

Post award debriefings shall include, at a minimum, the Government's evaluation of the significant strengths and weaknesses or deficiencies in the offeror's proposal, reasonable responses to relevant questions about whether source selection procedures contained in the solicitation, applicable regulations, and other applicable authorities were followed in the process of eliminating the offeror from the competition.

Post award debriefings *shall not* include point-by-point comparisons of the debriefed offeror's proposal with those of other offerors or any information that is considered proprietary.

R. The CO shall issue a Request for Proposal (RFP) to the successful firm (utilizing the Integrated Acquisition System (IAS) to prepare the document) requesting their current labor, overhead, and profit rates for the list of disciplines necessary for the contract, and any other costs as applicable (e.g., travel, other direct costs, etc.). The letter transmitting the RFP shall include a request for a copy of a recent audit of the firm's overhead rate, financial statements, and any other information deemed necessary to determine responsibility. For project specific contracts, the RFP will include a copy of Section J, Statement of Work, which details of the specific requirements for the project. The project specific Statement of Work will be submitted to the CO by the EPM.

S. Upon receipt of the proposal, the CO and the Evaluation Board shall review the proposal and develop the negotiation position. The pre-negotiation memorandum shall include the firm's fee proposal, the government's estimate, pre-negotiation objective, and the rationale for negotiation.

T. The Evaluation Board shall provide a technical analysis of the firm's proposal. The analysis shall state, at a minimum, which disciplines are technically acceptable, the rationale for others not being technically acceptable, what a technically acceptable fee would be for that discipline, whether the labor mix is correct, whether the amount of travel and ODCs are correct, etc. For IQCs, it should address whether the escalation factor, other direct, and indirect costs are appropriate.

U. The CO shall review the overhead rate and subsequent documentation for accuracy and completeness. If a recent audit is included and substantiates the overhead rate, the CO can accept the proposed rate. If no documentation substantiating the rate is received and the CO determines the rate unreasonable, he/she shall negotiate a reasonable rate.

V. For project specific AE contracts and IQCs, a subcontracting plan is required if the total value of the contract exceeds $500,000. Subcontracting plans must be negotiated prior to award. After the CO has negotiated the plan, it is to be submitted to FD's OSDBU Coordinator for review and then to the APD OSDBU who will review and submit it to the Department OSDBU. All subcontracting plans must be approved by the Department's OSDBU Office prior to award

W. Negotiations can be held face-to-face or via telephone. Upon completion of negotiations, a memorandum documenting the session(s) shall be prepared for the file. The memorandum shall show the AE fees, the pre-negotiation objective, and the final negotiated fee.

X. The CO shall prepare the award document for the signature of the AE firm. The award document shall consist of the Standard Form (SF)-252 with Sections B, C, D, E, F, G, H, I and J. Section K is to be incorporated by reference. Section L shall be retained in the file.

Y. After receipt of the signed documents, the CO shall sign the SF-252, release it in IAS, and post the Notice of Award on FBO. For project specific awards exceeding $1 million, the CO shall also follow the Procurement and Property Policy Memorandum No. 5-01, Information for Public Announcement of Contracts Valued at Over $1 Million, and FD's CSOP-02-004, Contract and Task Order Award Announcements (as applicable).

Z. After award, the CO and the EPM will conduct a pre-performance orientation/pre-design meeting. This meeting will provide the AE with direction on how ARS does business, such as ARS design standards, partnering, management reviews, task order procedures, anticipated type of task order workload, funding, submittals, payment methods, and payment submittal schedules. For project specific AE selections, this meeting will be the pre-design meeting and will begin the Program of Requirements (POR) effort. The CO shall document this meeting and place a copy in the file.

EXHIBIT 44-2   Sources Sought Notice

C—AE Firms Qualifications Data Sought for Short Selection Process—Request for Information

Notice Date
2/25/2010

Notice Type
Sources Sought

NAICS
541330—Engineering Services

Contracting Office
Department of Agriculture, Forest Service, R-9 Lake States Acquisition Team (LSAT), Federal Building, 68 S. Stevens St., Rhinelander, Wisconsin, 54501

ZIP Code
54501

Solicitation Number
AG-569R-S-10-0005

Small Business Set-Aside

Total Small Business

Description

SF330—Firms should submit Part 2 AE Request for Information—Firms should return Page 1 of this form, their CCR details, and Part 2 of the SF330. Pursuant to FAR Part 36, we are updating our qualifications data for Architect-Engineer (AE) contractors interested in doing work in northern Wisconsin and Michigan. This data is used to establish a list of interested and qualified AE firms primarily for projects that will be awarded utilizing AE short selection procedures (for projects [less than] $100,000). Please Note: For fiscal year 2010, pursuant to the USDA Annual Set-Aside Policy, AE firms must be an emerging small business to receive consideration for USDA Forest Service contract awards for AE projects less than $50,000.00. For AE projects between $50,000 and $100,000 only small business AE firms are eligible. Dependent upon the socioeconomic status of respondents to this Sources Sought, individual AE projects may be set aside for 8(a), Hubzone, or Service Disabled Veteran Owned small business firms. Accordingly, large business concerns will not be included on our short selection lists. Furthermore, there are many Wisconsin and Michigan AE small businesses interested in doing business with the Forest Service. Because "[l]ocation in the general geographical area of the project and knowledge of the locality of the project" is an evaluation factor used in the short selection process, selection of out-of-area firms under these procedures is unlikely.

Web Link

https://www.fbo.gov/spg/USDA/FS/569R/AG-569R-S-10-0005/listing.html

Place of Performance

Address: Northern Wisconsin and Michigan, Rhinelander, Wisconsin, 54501, United States

Zip Code: 54501

Note

1. FBO Daily Issue of February 27, 2010 [FBO #3017]. Department of Agriculture, Forest Service, "AE Firms Qualifications Data Sought for Short Selection Process – Request for Information." Online at http://www.fbodaily.com/archive/2010/02-February/27-Feb-2010/FBO-02077068.htm (accessed October 21, 2010).

CHAPTER 45

OBTAINING BEST VALUE FOR SIMPLIFIED ACQUISITIONS

FAR Part 13 contains special procedures and guidance for procuring items and services that fall within the simplified acquisition threshold. Threshold refers to a dollar amount. FAR 2.101 defines the following as simplified acquisition thresholds:

- $150,000, except for those acquisitions described below
- $300,000 for any contract awarded and performed or purchase made inside the United States to support a contingency operation or to facilitate defense against or recovery from nuclear, biological, chemical, or radiological attack
- $1 million for any contract awarded and performed or purchase made outside the United States to support a contingency operation or to facilitate defense against or recovery from nuclear, biological, chemical, or radiological attack.

FAR Part 13 provides that, under a test program, the following simplified acquisition thresholds will also apply:

- Procurements of $6.5 million when market research creates the expectation that offers received will include only commercial items

- Procurements of $12 million in support of a contingency operation or to facilitate the defense against or recovery from nuclear, biological, chemical or radiological attack when commercial items are being procured or the procurement is being treated as if it were a commercial item procurement.

EXECUTING A SIMPLIFIED ACQUISITION

In simplified acquisition, competition is sought to the "maximum extent practicable." FAR 13.104 provides that this can include full and open competition, but quite often competition is limited to a lesser number. For example, oral quotations for a relatively routine simplified acquisition may be solicited from only a small number of sources.

Simplified acquisitions are executed in a wide variety of ways. When written solicitations are used in lieu of an oral solicitation, the solicitation is often a request for quotation (RFQ) and not the RFP that is used for most source selections for new contracts above the simplified acquisition threshold.

Simplified acquisitions may involve any number of procurement instruments such as purchase orders, blanket purchase agreements, indefinite delivery contracts, purchase cards, third-party drafts, or imprest funds.

When appropriate, best value source selection techniques can be used for simplified acquisitions. In fact, FAR 13.106-1 tells contracting officers that they are "encouraged to use best value." When this is done, FAR Part 13 gives buyers certain latitude not available under the source selection process guidance in FAR Part 15. FAR Part 13 provides that while the contracting officer is required to notify quoters or offerors of the basis on which award is to be made (price alone or price and other factors such as past performance and quality), "solicitations are not required to state the relative importance assigned to each evaluation factor and subfactor, nor are they required to include subfactors."

EVALUATING PROPOSALS

FAR 13.106-2 also provides that the contracting officer has broad discretion in fashioning suitable evaluation procedures for simplified acquisitions. It provides that one or more, but not necessarily all, of the evaluation procedures in FAR Part 15 may be used. Because the FAR anticipates that simplified acquisition procedures will promote less procedurally expensive and faster acquisitions, FAR 13.106-2 provides, "If using price and other factors, ensure that quotations or offers can be evaluated in an efficient and minimally burdensome fashion. Formal evaluation plans and establishing a competitive range, conducting discussions, and scoring quotations or offers are not required."

The FAR also provides that, "[c]ontracting offices may conduct comparative evaluations of offers. Evaluation of other factors, such as past performance... [d]oes not require the creation or existence of a formal [database]" and may be based on one or more of several factors:

- The contracting officer's knowledge of and previous experience with the supply or service being acquired
- Customer surveys and past performance questionnaire replies
- The Governmentwide Past Performance Information Retrieval System (PPIRS; www.ppirs.gov)
- Any other reasonable basis.

Thus, it appears that the contracting officer has great latitude. If, for example, quoters were notified that award would be made on the basis of past performance and cost, the contracting officer look at three quotes and, based on personal experience with the vendors, pick a higher-priced quote because the contracting officer knows that quoter (company) is more dependable.

However, contracting personnel should be aware that the Comp Gen has on several occasions held that rules of fairness must still be applied. This appears to be especially relevant for higher-dollar simplified acquisitions, when multiple evaluation factors are used and contractors must expend significant time and effort in preparing a proposal or quote. In Finlen Complex, Inc., B-288280, October 10, 2001, the Comp Gen opined:

> [W]e are sensitive to the fact that the thrust of FAR parts 12 and 13 is to avoid the use of procedures that constrict and complicate the acquisition process, and that FAR §§ 12.602(a) and 13.106-1(a)(2) do not, on their face, limit a contracting officer's discretion to disclose, or not disclose, the relative weight of evaluation criteria in a commercial item procurement conducted using simplified procedures. Nonetheless, basic principles of fair play are a touchstone of the federal procurement system, and those principles bound even broad grants of agency discretion. See Intellectual Properties, Inc., supra. In addition, even when using simplified procedures—and before them, when using small purchase procedures—federal procurements must be conducted with the concern for a fair and equitable contest that is inherent in any competition. Discount Mach. and Equip., Inc., B-220949, Feb. 25, 1986, 86-1 CPD ¶ 193 at 3.
>
> Here, where the agency required the commercial offerors to prepare detailed proposals addressing unique government requirements, withholding the relative weight of evaluation factors denied the offerors one of the basic tools used to develop the written, detailed proposals called for in the solicitation.

DOCUMENTING THE AWARD DECISION

Even for simplified acquisitions, documentation of the award decision is required. While the FAR indicates that award documentation of simplified acquisitions is kept to a minimum, it also requires that this documentation include information supporting the award decisions if factors other than price-related ones were considered in selecting a supplier. When non-cost factors are used, care should be taken to create a document that readily discloses the evaluation factors that the contracting officer took into consideration in the selection and that clearly demonstrates that a reasonable (rational) decision was made. Failure to do so could result in a sustained protest.

In a case in which persuasive documentation was lacking, the Comp Gen opined:

"Although we recognize that the procurement was conducted under ... simplified acquisition procedures, it is a fundamental principle of government accountability that an agency be able to produce a sufficient record to allow for meaningful review where its procurement actions are challenged" (e-LYNXX Corporation, B-292761, December 3, 2003).

Thus, caution is recommended when agencies use what are substantially FAR Part 15 source selection procedures to execute simplified acquisitions. Acquisition officials may not be able to avoid some of the fairness requirements and documentation issues that are inherent in FAR Part 15 selections simply because the item or service happens to be under a simplified acquisition threshold. The Comp Gen may decide that if it looks like a duck and it quacks like a duck, then the rules pertaining to ducks apply.

CHAPTER 46

COMMERCIAL ITEM PROCUREMENT

The FAR's definition for a commercial item is extensive and appears in Exhibit 46-1. It includes not only products sold to the general public, but many services as well. It even includes products that are evolving from items sold to the general public but have not yet been offered for sale. And, as you can see in the exhibit, it includes certain categories of nondevelopmental items (NDI).

The FAR requires that acquisitions of commercial items be made pursuant to FAR Part 12. While the simplified source selection procedures found in FAR Part 13 or the more complex source selection procedures in FAR Part 15 may be used for commercial items, as deemed appropriate by the contracting officer, in the event of any conflict in the FAR guidance, FAR Part 12 will apply.

Substantively, the source selection processes that we have discussed at length in this book apply to source selections for commercial item acquisitions. Two of the major differences are in forms and formats and in solicitation provisions. Rather than using the uniform contract format (UCF) common in RFPs for source selections, written solicitations for commercial items (other than combined solicitation/synopses; see Chapter 47) use Standard Form (SF) 1449. This standard form may be used as a request for quotations, a request for proposals, or an invitation for bid. (IFBs do not use non-cost evaluation factors other than bid samples that are sometimes used to show the offeror's responsiveness to the requirement and thus do not involve the source selection procedures described in this book.)

FAR PROVISIONS

Instead of the Sections L and M found in the uniform contract format, there are standard commercial item provisions in the FAR. When appropriate, the contracting officer may tailor these provisions. Tailored provisions are attached to the SF 1449 and form a part of the solicitation.

One of the provisions the contracting officer may or may not tailor for a specific acquisition is entitled Instructions to Offerors—Commercial Items. Another provision, Evaluation—Commercial Items, must be tailored for the specific acquisition.

INSTRUCTIONS TO OFFERORS— COMMERCIAL ITEMS

The provision Instructions to Offerors—Commercial Items, found at FAR 52.212-1, includes in its non-tailored form:

- Information pertaining to the small business size standard
- How offers may be submitted (format and content)
- The period established for the acceptance of offers
- Information regarding product samples if any are required
- Encouragement for the submission of multiple offers
- Information pertaining to late submissions, modifications, revisions, and withdrawal of offers
- Notification that the government intends to award without discussion but may hold discussions if felt necessary

- Information pertaining to debriefings
- Other information.

In the non-tailored provision, content information pertinent to the source selection process calls for a technical description of the items being offered (with product literature where appropriate) and past performance information on recent and relevant contracts when past performance is an evaluation factor.

FAR 12.205(a) offers the following guidance on the use of technical information in commercial item source selection:

Where technical information is necessary for evaluation of offers, agencies should, as part of market research, review existing product literature generally available in the industry to determine its adequacy for purposes of evaluation. If adequate, contracting officers shall request existing product literature from offerors of commercial items in lieu of unique technical proposals.

Clearly, the FAR considers that technical non-cost factors often will not require "unique technical proposals." If a unique technical proposal is to be required as a part of the source selection process, then the provision at FAR 52.212-1 will have to be modified (tailored) accordingly.

This provision also requires that offerors in commercial item acquisitions provide past performance information on recent and relevant contracts when past performance is an evaluation factor. Regarding the use of past performance when procuring commercial items, FAR 12.206 says: "Past performance should be an important element of every evaluation and contract award for commercial items. Contracting officers should consider past performance data from a wide variety of sources both inside and outside the Federal Government."

While FAR 52.212-1 does ask for past performance information, it does not (unless it is tailored by an agency), put offerors on
notice that other sources of information may be used.

EVALUATION—COMMERCIAL ITEMS

The other provision pertaining especially to source selection,
Evaluation—Commercial Items, is found at FAR 52.212-2 and
reads, in part, as follows:

(a) The Government will award a contract resulting from this
solicitation to the responsible offeror whose offer conforming to the solicitation will be most advantageous to the Government, price and other factors considered. The following
factors shall be used to evaluate offers:

_____

_____

_____

*[Contracting Officer shall insert the significant evaluation fac-
tors, such as (i) technical capability of the item offered to meet
the Government requirement; (ii) price; (iii) past performance
(see FAR 15.304); (iv) small disadvantaged business participation; and include them in the relative order of importance of the
evaluation factors, such as in descending order of importance.]*

Technical and past performance, when combined, are
_____ *[Contracting Officer state, in accordance with
FAR 15.304, the relative importance of all other evaluation fac-
tors, when combined, when compared to price.]*

Perhaps this provision and the instructions therein could have
been more artfully worded. It should be noted that the provision
uses "descending order of importance" as an example. However,

as is suggested in Chapter 15, it may not be wise to use "descending order of importance" without further explanation unless there are more or less equal gradients between the factors or there is a reasonable downward progression. It should also be noted that price is cited in the example in the provision both as an integrated factor with past performance and technical factors and then again as a factor against which all other factors are measured. It may not be advisable to use price both ways, as we saw in the beef stew example in Chapter 19.

It should also be noted that the example given in the FAR includes consideration of a small business subcontracting plan as a non-cost factor but only measures price against technical and past performance, with no mention at all of small business subcontracting. The FAR coverage on this point is rather confusing. It says the contracting officer "shall" include significant factors such as technical capability, price, small disadvantage business participation, and past performance. Then it goes on to provide as part of the standard clause that only technical ability and past performance are compared to price; leaving out the small business aspects mentioned earlier.

ACCOUNTABILITY

The issues of fairness and accountability apply to the acquisition of commercial items just as they apply to the acquisition of non-commercial items and services. The Comptroller General made this clear in Tiger Enterprises, Inc., B-293951, July 26, 2004, when he opined:

> Under FAR subpart 12.6, Streamlined Procedures for Evaluation and Solicitation for Commercial Items, the contracting officer is required to [s]elect the offer that is most advantageous to the Government based on the factors contained in the

solicitation, and to [f]ully document the rationale for selection of the successful offeror including discussion of any trade-offs considered. FAR 12.602(c). Although the FAR does not specify what is required for compliance with the mandate that the contracting officer [f]ully document the rationale for the source selection, the fundamental principle of government accountability dictates that an agency maintain a record adequate to allow for meaningful review. Checchi and Co. Consulting, Inc., B-285777, Oct. 10, 2000, 2001 CPD ¶ 132 at 6; Matrix Int'l Logistics, Inc., B-272388, B-272388.2, Dec. 9, 1996, 97-2 CPD ¶ 89 at 5. An agency which fails to adequately document the rationale for its source selection, including any trade-offs considered, bears the risk that its determinations will be considered unsupported, and that absent such support, our Office may lack a basis to find that the agency had a reasonable basis for its determinations. Matrix Int'l Logistics, Inc., supra; see Universal Bldg. Maint., Inc., B-282456, July 15, 1999, 99-2 CPD ¶ 32 at 5.

Here, the contemporaneous record of the evaluation of the five quotations and the agency's source selection consists of a 1-1/2 page "evaluation determination" memorandum, and a matrix setting forth the past performance ratings of the vendors as reported by their respective references. We find that these documents fail to adequately explain the basis for the agency's source selection or any trade-offs the agency considered in selecting B&Es lower-priced quotation for award.

Clearly, even for a commercial item procurement, the source selection document should be complete and persuasive.

EXHIBIT 46-1 Definition of a Commercial Item (FAR 2.101)

"Commercial item" means—

1. Any item, other than real property, that is of a type customarily used by the general public or by non-governmental entities for purposes other than governmental purposes, and—

    (i) Has been sold, leased, or licensed to the general public; or

    (ii) Has been offered for sale, lease, or license to the general public;

2. Any item that evolved from an item described in paragraph (1) of this definition through advances in technology or performance and that is not yet available in the commercial marketplace, but will be available in the commercial marketplace in time to satisfy the delivery requirements under a Government solicitation;

3. Any item that would satisfy a criterion expressed in paragraphs (1) or (2) of this definition, but for—

    (i) Modifications of a type customarily available in the commercial marketplace; or

    (ii) Minor modifications of a type not customarily available in the commercial marketplace made to meet Federal Government requirements. Minor modifications means modifications that do not significantly alter the nongovernmental function or essential physical characteristics of an item or component, or change the purpose of a process. Factors to be considered in determining whether a modification is minor include the value and size of the modification and the comparative value and size of the final product. Dollar values and percentages may be used as guideposts, but are not conclusive evidence that a modification is minor;

4. Any combination of items meeting the requirements of paragraphs (1), (2), (3), or (5) of this definition that are of a type customarily combined and sold in combination to the general public;

5. Installation services, maintenance services, repair services, training services, and other services if—

    (i) Such services are procured for support of an item referred to in paragraph (1), (2), (3), or (4) of this definition, regardless of whether such services are provided by the same source or at the same time as the item; and

    (ii) The source of such services provides similar services contemporaneously to the general public under terms and conditions similar to those offered to the Federal Government;

6. Services of a type offered and sold competitively in substantial quantities in the commercial marketplace based on established catalog or market

prices for specific tasks performed or specific outcomes to be achieved and under standard commercial terms and conditions. For purposes of these services—

(i) "Catalog price" means a price included in a catalog, price list, schedule, or other form that is regularly maintained by the manufacturer or vendor, is either published or otherwise available for inspection by customers, and states prices at which sales are currently, or were last, made to a significant number of buyers constituting the general public; and

(ii) "Market prices" means current prices that are established in the course of ordinary trade between buyers and sellers free to bargain and that can be substantiated through competition or from sources independent of the offerors.

7. Any item, combination of items, or service referred to in paragraphs (1) through (6) of this definition, notwithstanding the fact that the item, combination of items, or service is transferred between or among separate divisions, subsidiaries, or affiliates of a contractor; or

8. A nondevelopmental item, if the procuring agency determines the item was developed exclusively at private expense and sold in substantial quantities, on a competitive basis, to multiple State and local governments.

CHAPTER 47

STREAMLINED SOLICITATION FOR COMMERCIAL ITEMS

When an agency plans to issue a written solicitation for a commercial item, it can use a streamlined method of solicitation that combines the synopsis requirement at the governmentwide point of entry (GPE) and the solicitation itself. When properly executed, this procedure can significantly reduce procurement administrative lead time (PALT).

FAR Part 12 has the following guidance:

12.603 Streamlined solicitation for commercial items.

(a) When a written solicitation will be issued, the contracting officer may use the following procedure to reduce the time required to solicit and award contracts for the acquisition of commercial items. This procedure combines the synopsis required by 5.203 and the issuance of the solicitation into a single document.

(b) When using the combined synopsis/solicitation procedure, the SF 1499 is not used for issuing the solicitation.

(c) To use these procedures, the contracting officer shall—

(1) Prepare the synopsis as described at 5.207.

(2) In the Description, include the following additional information:

(i) The following statement:

This is a combined synopsis/solicitation for commercial items prepared in accordance with the format in Subpart 12.6, as supplemented with additional information included in this notice. This announcement constitutes the only solicitation; proposals are being requested and a written solicitation will not be issued.

(ii) The solicitation number and a statement that the solicitation is issued as an invitation to bid (IFB), request for quotation (RFQ) or request for proposal (RFP).

(iii) A statement that the solicitation document and incorporated provisions and clauses are those in effect through Federal Acquisition Circular _____.

(iv) A notice regarding any set-aside and the associated NAICS code and small business size standard. Also include a statement regarding the Small Business Competitiveness Demonstration Program, if applicable.

(v) A list of contract line item number(s) and items, quantities and units of measure, (including option(s), if applicable).

(vi) Description of requirements for the items to be acquired.

(vii) Date(s) and place(s) of delivery and acceptance and FOB point.

(viii) A statement that the provision at 52.212-1, Instructions to Offerors—Commercial, applies to this acquisition and a statement regarding any addenda to the provision.

(ix) A statement regarding the applicability of the provision at 52.212-2, Evaluation—Commercial Items, if used, and the specific evaluation criteria to be included in paragraph (a) of that provision. If this provision is not used, describe the evaluation procedures to be used.

(x) A statement advising offerors to include a completed copy of the provision at 52.212-3, Offeror Representations and Certifications— Commercial Items, with its offer.

(xi) A statement that the clause at 52.212-4, Contract Terms and Conditions—Commercial Items, applies to this acquisition and a statement regarding any addenda to the clause.

(xii) A statement that the clause at 52.212-5, Contract Terms and Conditions Required To Implement Statutes or Executive Orders— Commercial Items, applies to this acquisition and a statement regarding which, if any, of the additional FAR clauses cited in the clause are applicable to the acquisition.

(xiii) A statement regarding any additional contract requirement(s) or terms and conditions (such as contract financing arrangements or warranty requirements) determined by the contracting officer to be necessary for this acquisition and consistent with customary commercial practices.

(xiv) A statement regarding the Defense Priorities and Allocations System (DPAS) and assigned rating, if applicable.

(xv) The date, time and place offers are due.

(xvi) The name and telephone number of the individual to contact for information regarding the solicitation.

(3) Allow response time for receipt of offers as follows:

(i) Because the synopsis and solicitation are contained in a single document, it is not necessary to publicize a separate synopsis 15 days before the issuance of the solicitation.

(ii) When using the combined synopsis and solicitation, contracting officers must establish a response time in accordance with 5.203 (b) (but see 5.203 (h)).

(4) Publicize amendments to solicitations in the same manner as the initial synopsis and solicitation.

The rules of source selection that have been described in preceding chapters for simplified acquisitions (FAR Part 13) and negotiated procurements (FAR Part 15) will still apply, as appropriate, in commercial item procurement using this streamlined procedure.

Exhibit 47-1 is an example of a combined synopsis/solicitation for acquiring shotguns by brand name.[1] The sample was chosen because we may be able to learn a few things from it. The technical evaluation factor is presumably for the required modifications to the shotguns, since the government is mandating that the shotguns be a particular brand name and model for compatibility reasons, and, except for any permitted modifications, all the items will be technically the same.

However, it is not clear exactly what "detailed technical" information competing contractors must submit. The synopsis/solicitation does not state the relative importance of price and technical aspects, so in accordance with Comptroller General precedent, offerors have a right to assume that these factors are equal in importance. This may or may not be what the procuring agency intended.

It is also apparent that the FAR provided internal government instruction for use of an evaluation provision—"As prescribed in FAR 12.301(c), the contracting officer may insert a provision substantially as follows"—was included in the notice in error.

EXHIBIT 47-1 Combined Synopsis/Solicitation: Department of Education Solicitation for Shotguns

---

Solicitation Number:
EDOOIG-10-000004

Notice Type:
Combined Synopsis/Solicitation

Synopsis:
The U.S. Department of Education (ED) intends to purchase twenty-seven (27) REMINGTON BRAND MODEL 870 POLICE 12/14P MOD GRWC XS4 KXCS SF. RAMAC #24587 GAUGE: 12 BARREL: 14" - PARKERIZED CHOKE: MODIFIED

SIGHTS: GHOST RING REAR WILSON COMBAT; FRONT - XS CONTOUR BEAD SIGHT STOCK: KNOXX REDUCE RECOIL ADJUSTABLE STOCK FORE-SPEEDFEED SPORT-SOLID - 14" LOP are designated as the only shotguns authorized for ED based on compatibility with ED existing shotgun inventory, certified armor and combat training and protocol, maintenance, and parts.

The required date of delivery is March 22, 2010.

Interested sources must submit detailed technical capabilities and any other information that demonstrates their ability to meet the requirements above, no later than March 12, 2010 at 12 PM, E.S.T. Any quotes must be submitted electronically to the attention of (deleted)

The following clauses are applicable to this requirement:

52.212-1 Instruction to Offerors—Commercial Items

52.212-2 Evaluation—Commercial Items

52.212-3 Offeror Representations and Certifications—Commercial Items

52.212-4 Contract Terms and Conditions—Commercial Items

52.212-5 Contract Terms and Conditions Required [to Implement] Statutes or Executive Orders—Commercial Items.

In accordance with 52.212-2, the fill-in applicable to this requirement is below:

52.212-2 Evaluation—Commercial Items. As prescribed in 12.301(c), the Contracting Officer may insert a provision substantially as follows:

Evaluation—Commercial Items (Jan 1999)

(a) The Government will award a contract resulting from this solicitation to the responsible offeror whose offer conforming to the solicitation will be most advantageous to the Government, price and other factors considered. The following factors shall be used to evaluate offers:

(i) Technical Capability

(ii) Price

In accordance with 52.212-5, the following clauses are applicable to this requirement:

52.225-1 Buy American Act—Supplies (February 2009)

52.232-33, Payment by Electronic Funds Transfer-Central

New equipment only; no remanufactured products. No partial shipments[.]

Offer must be good for 30 calendar days after submission.

Offerors must have current Central Contractor Registration (CCR) at the time offer is submitted. Information can be found at www.ccr.gov.

This is a combined synopsis/solicitation for commercial items in accordance with Federal Acquisition Regulation Part 12, Acquisition of Commercial Items. The Government will award a commercial item purchase order to the offeror with the most advantageous offer to the government. All offerors must submit their best price and delivery capabilities.

Note

1. Department of Education, "Remington Shotguns." Solicitation Number EDOOIG-10-000004. Online at https://www.fbo.gov/spg/ED/OCFO/CPO/EDOOIG-10-000004/listing.html (accessed October 22, 2010).

CHAPTER 48

BROAD AGENCY ANNOUNCEMENTS

FAR 35.016 tells us that the broad agency announcement (BAA) is a competitive solicitation procedure used to obtain proposals for basic and applied research. It is also used "for that part of development [that is] not related to the development of a specific system or hardware procurement." The type of research solicited under a BAA is aimed at increasing knowledge in science and/or advancing the state of the art rather than the immediate practical application of knowledge.

BAAs offer a great deal more flexibility to the scientific and technical community than is available under conventional source selection procedures. It allows the government buyer to go window shopping in the marketplace of ideas. Even though the BAA source selection process is different from conventional source selection, contracts awarded as a result of a BAA competition are considered to have met the full and open competition requirements of the Competition in Contracting Act.

Adapting from a publication of the Defense Advanced Research Project Agency (DARPA), some of the differences between a FAR Part 15 source selection for research and development and a BAA include:[1]

Type of Research and Development

RFP: Normally focuses on a specific system or hardware solution.

BAA: Scientific study and experimentation directed toward advancing the state of the art or increasing knowledge or understanding.

Statement of Work

RFP: The government drafts a common requirements document setting forth a purchase description or performance objectives against which all offerors must propose.

BAA: The government drafts a statement of a problem to be addressed or of general research interest. Each offeror then proposes its own statement of work (SOW) and technical approach.

Proposal Comparison

RFP: Successful contractor is selected by comparing proposals.

BAA: Proposals contain standalone, unique solutions. They are not compared with one another.

Nature of the Competition

RFP: Proposals address a common requirements document and compete, one against another. Award is made to the lowest-priced technically acceptable offer or to the offer determined through tradeoff to be the best value.

BAA: Each proposal presents a separate approach to solving the problem. This is technical competition in the marketplace of ideas. Cost or price is rarely the deciding factor in selecting the winning proposal, but decisions are limited by the availability of funds.

Evaluation Process

RFP: Evaluators follow a predetermined source selection plan very closely.

BAA: Proposals undergo a scientific review process. A proposal that is otherwise weak could be selected if it shows great technical promise, such as a risky but perhaps revolutionary approach.

Notwithstanding these differences, there are three major similarities between FAR Part 15 source selection and BAA source selection. Both generally require that:

- The solicitation be publicized on FedBizOpps
- Criteria for selection be included in the solicitation
- Cost realism and reasonableness be considered.

THE MARKETPLACE OF IDEAS

An example that has been used in acquisition training classes to explain the concept of the marketplace of ideas is the following scenario:

The Army issues a BAA looking for alternative solutions to using traditional charcoal media in chemical agent filtration devices. A university has an idea that will involve the use of various fibrous plants and proposes a laboratory study of modest scope for $250,000. A consortium of filtration device manufacturers proposes to continue studies already begun to explore the use of various petroleum-based materials as chemical agent filtration media. The cost proposed is $1,000,000.

Following scientific review, and assuming fund availability, the Army could decide to award a contract to either, neither, or both of the offerors.

VARIATIONS IN BROAD AGENCY ANNOUNCEMENTS

A BAA source is selected in a number of ways. In a contractor guide, the U.S. Air Force lists the following as common BAA processes:

- *One-Step:* The one-step process is used to request full technical and cost proposals from each offeror. The proposals are evaluated in accordance with the solicitation criteria, and all of a selected proposal, part of a selected proposal, or none of the proposals are selected for individual negotiation.

- *Two-Step:* The two-step process is commonly used when the government is anticipating a large number of proposals. Potential offerors are invited to submit brief descriptive white papers or abstracts in lieu of full proposals. The government evaluates these, then requests full proposals from selected offerors. The full proposals are then evaluated and, where appropriate, proposals are selected for negotiation.

- *Open BAA:* This approach allows for white paper/proposal submission at any time within a specified period (usually 12 months). Open BAAs must be publicized no less frequently than annually. White papers/proposals are evaluated when received during the period that the BAA is open.

- *Closed BAA:* This approach allows for white paper/proposal submission at a specified date and time as set forth in the BAA. Late bid and proposal provisions are usually included in the BAA.

Other variations are also permissible as long as they are consistent with law and regulation. Exhibit 48-1 is an example of a BAA notice using a combined synopsis/solicitation.[2]

EXHIBIT 48-1   Sample Broad Agency Announcement

Title:	BAA for Chemical and Biological Technologies Directorate New Initiatives FY2010–FY2011 Program Build (Continuation of HDTRA1-08-CBDIF CBT-BAA)
Solicitation #:	HDTRA1-09-CHEM-BIO-BAA
Post Date:	10/17/2008
Response Date:	
Document Type:	Combined Synopsis/Solicitation
NAICS Code:	541—Professional, Scientific, and Technical Services/541711—Research and Development in Biotechnology

The purpose of this Broad Agency Announcement (BAA) is to solicit proposals for the Chemical and Biological Technologies Directorate New Initiatives Fiscal Year (FY) 2010–FY2011 Program Build[.]

Scope: This solicitation is an extramural endeavor focused on applied research and advanced technology development objectives encompassing a broad spectrum of topics in the chemical and biological science to include Physical Science and Technology, Medical Science and Technology, including the Transformational Medical Technologies Initiative, Threat Agent Science, and Information Systems Capabilities Development topics. [11]

Purpose: The purpose of this Broad Agency Announcement (BAA) is to solicit research proposals for Chemical and Biological Defense Program, Defense Threat Reduction Agency [DTRA] requirements for the Chemical and Biological Technologies Directorate New Initiatives BAA for the FY2010–2011. The Chemical and Biological Technologies Directorate, in its continuing mission, seeks new and innovative ideas for experimental and theoretical development of technologies to fill DOD requirements for chemical and biological defense. The goal is to identify and select science and technology projects that can be transitioned to joint acquisition programs.

Solicitation Overview and Purpose: This BAA is a continuation of the multi-year HDTRA1-08-CBDIF-CBT-BAA dated 29 Jan 08, remaining effective for three years from the initial date of issuance, unless amended otherwise. Multiple calls for proposals may occur in conjunction with this BAA. Ongoing, new or emerging requirements may necessitate amendment of the BAA to include new or different topics. At any time that the topics are amended, new proposal submission milestones will be specified and as applicable any limitations specific to the topics will be noted. These amendments are expected to occur, in general, annually, and may occur more frequently, in both cases on an as-needed basis. Over the span of its term, this BAA will solicit applied research and advanced technology development proposals for the topics presented in Attachment 8 and in effect at the time. Depending on the nature of requirements and/or available funding, each of these research categories may or may not be included in the most current List of Topics. Proposals may each address Applied Research and/or Advanced Technology Development as specified in each topic. Proposals will not be accepted or considered that combine Basic Research with Applied Research and/or Advanced Technology Development. The Government encourages proposals that span a wide spectrum of possible technical and business solutions in response to the specific technology topics stated in Attachment 8 of this BAA. The Government reserves the right to award any combination of approaches which offer the best overall value to the Government, and to oversee any and all processes and approaches once ongoing. The full range of flexible assistance and acquisition related statutory authority arrangements available to DTRA are possible results from this announcement including but not limited to contracts and Other Transaction Agreements; there is a strong preference for the award of FAR-based contracts. The Government does not intend to award grants under this solicitation. However, the Government reserves the right to negotiate and award the types of procurement instruments determined most appropriate under the circumstances. The technical point of contact for this BAA is [deleted]. All questions (administrative or technical) related to this BAA must be e-mailed to CB-FY10-11BAA@dtra.mil.

Notes

1. This list has been adapted from DARPA's material. See DARPA, Contracts Management Office, "Broad Agency Announcements." Online at http://www.darpa.mil/cmo/baa.html (accessed October 22, 2010).
2. Defense Threat Reduction Agency, "BAA for Chemical and Biological Technologies Directorate New Initiatives FY2010-FY2011 Program Build." Solicitation Number: HDTRA1-09-CHEM-BIO-BAA. Online at https://www.fbo.gov/spg/ODA/DTRA/DTRA01/HDTRA1-09-CHEM-BIO-BAA/listing.html (accessed October 22, 2010).

PART X

ETHICS

This part of the book examines some ethical considerations involved in acquisition, in general, and in source selection, in particular. It examines laws pertaining to on-the-job conduct and laws that apply to post-government employment. In addition to examining the rules, it addresses the human aspects in ethical behavior.

CHAPTER 49

ETHICAL CONSIDERATIONS IN SOURCE SELECTION

It often seems that barely a week or two goes by without news of some alleged or actual illegal activity involving federal government contracting. And I suppose we shouldn't be surprised. Willie Sutton, a career criminal, once said he robbed banks because "that's where the money is." And there is a great deal of money involved in government contracting.

ETHICAL PRINCIPLES

The Office of Government Ethics developed a list of principles that apply to the ethical conduct of all government employees, not just those involved in contracting. These principles were made applicable to all government employees by an executive order of the president. Because a number of these principles have a direct bearing on people involved in source selection, the list is shown in Exhibit 49-1.[1] One of the more pertinent principles states, "Employees will report waste, fraud, abuse, or any illegal activity to the appropriate authority." Depending on the circumstances of a specific source selection, that appropriate government author- ity might be the immediate supervisor, the contracting officer, the agency ethics advisor or official, the inspector general of the agency, or the Department of Justice. Most agencies have hotlines to which even anonymous reports can be made (hopefully by people who are not too careless with any accusations or suspicions.)

Other listed ethical principles that are especially pertinent to the source selection process include:

- Public service is a public trust, requiring employees to place loyalty to the Constitution, the laws, and ethical principles above private gain. (While unethical source selection activities are relatively rare by comparison, the hundreds, perhaps thousands, of abuses of government credit cards create a rather disturbing vision of human nature.)
- Employees shall not hold financial interests that conflict with the conscientious performance of duty. (If a member of the source selection team has a financial interest in one or more of the competing contractors, he or she should bring the matter to the attention of the appropriate supervisor and the contracting officer. The employee may then be recused from participating in the source selection, or other appropriate action may be taken, such as limiting the role of the member in source selection activities.)
- Employees shall not engage in financial transactions using nonpublic government information or allow the improper use of such information to further any private interest. (Relative to source selection, this means that a member of a source selection team may not invest in a contractor that is about to get an award, nor can the member tell relatives or friends that the contractor is going to get the award until the award has been publicly disclosed.)

- An employee shall not, except pursuant to such reasonable exceptions as are provided by regulation, solicit or accept any gift or other item of monetary value from any person or entity seeking official action from, doing business with, or conducting activities regulated by the employee's agency, or whose interests may be substantially affected by the performance or nonperformance of the employee's duties. (FAR 3.101-2 indicates that "certain limited exceptions may be permitted by agency regulation.")

THE PROCUREMENT INTEGRITY ACT

There is one law designed to specifically address the source selection process. In response to highly publicized situations in which competing contractors were given inside information by government employees and to situations in which it was perceived by those critical of government contracting practices that contractors were being treated favorably so that government officials could later gain employment with the contractors, Congress passed the Procurement Integrity Act. A Department of Justice outline of the provisions of the act is shown in Exhibit 49-2,[2] and further coverage can be found in FAR Part 3.

The Procurement Integrity Act, as outlined in this exhibit, deals with three major ethical concerns regarding source selection.

1. The responsibility of a source selection team member who receives a job offer from a competing contractor
2. The protection of contractor bid and proposal information and source selection information, both of which are defined in the exhibit

3. Time restrictions on accepting compensation from a competing contractor (for example, earning money as an employee or consultant).

Of course, source selection officials and contractors can violate a variety of other laws during a source selection, such as those dealing with the making of false statements and those dealing with bribery.

PERSONAL INTEGRITY

Notwithstanding any efforts to legislate ethics, proper conduct in source selection always comes down to personal integrity. Some people just seem to be more disposed toward unethical behavior than others. Not infrequently, major fraud on government contracts is committed by people who are especially hard-working and capable. These people apparently delude themselves into thinking that the value of the contribution that they make to government business far exceeds the salaries that they get, and thus it is only fair that they take advantage of opportunities to improve their financial position. Other times, employees who feel they have been dealt with unfairly on some issue or another may be seeking a way to "get even." Still others may have gotten themselves hopelessly in debt and are looking for a way out. The impact on their lives and the lives of their families when they are tried and convicted is devastating—as is the sense of betrayal felt by their coworkers.

It should go without saying that everyone involved in the source selection process must be very conscientious in following the established rules and should scrupulously avoid any impropriety or even the appearance of impropriety. FAR 3.101-1 tells us, "While many Federal laws and regulations place restrictions on the actions of Government personnel, their official conduct must, in addition, be such that they would have no reluctance to make a full public disclosure of their actions." FAR 3.1002 addresses the conduct of government contractors, stating, "Government contractors must conduct themselves with the highest degree of integrity and honesty.... Contractors should have a written code of business ethics and conduct."

With regard to the FAR reference that there "be no reluctance to make a full public disclosure," many who conduct ethics training advocate using the *Washington Post* rule of thumb (sometimes called the *New York Times* rule of thumb) in day-to-day performance of duties. This rule of thumb provides that officials make only those decisions or take those actions that they would not be reluctant to have reported the next day on the front page of the *Washington Post*.

EXHIBIT 49-1   Excerpt from Executive Order 12731, issued October 17, 1990

PRINCIPLES OF ETHICAL CONDUCT

FOR GOVERNMENT OFFICERS AND EMPLOYEES

a. Public service is a public trust, requiring employees to place loyalty to the Constitution, the laws, and ethical principles above private gain.[13]

b. Employees shall not hold financial interests that conflict with the conscientious performance of duty.

c. Employees shall not engage in financial transactions using nonpublic Government information or allow the improper use of such information to further any private interest.

d. An employee shall not, except pursuant to such reasonable exceptions as are provided by regulation, solicit or accept any gift or other item of monetary value from any person or entity seeking official action from, doing business with, or conducting activities regulated by the employee's agency, or whose interests may be substantially affected by the performance or nonperformance of the employee's duties.

e. Employees shall put forth honest effort in the performance of their duties.

f. Employees shall make no unauthorized commitments or promises of any kind purporting to bind the Government.

g. Employees shall not use public office for private gain.

h. Employees shall act impartially and not give preferential treatment to any private organization or individual.

i. Employees shall protect and conserve Federal property and shall not use it for other than authorized activities.

j. Employees shall not engage in outside employment or activities, including seeking or negotiating for employment, that conflict with official Government duties and responsibilities.

k. Employees shall disclose waste, fraud, abuse, and corruption to appropriate authorities.

l. Employees shall satisfy in good faith their obligations as citizens, including all just financial obligations, especially those—such as Federal, State, or local taxes—that are imposed by law.

m. Employees shall adhere to all laws and regulations that provide equal opportunity for all Americans regardless of race, color, religion, sex, national origin, age, or handicap.

n. Employees shall endeavor to avoid any actions creating the appearance that they are violating the law or the ethical standards promulgated pursuant to this order.

EXHIBIT 49-2 Department of Justice Outline of the Procurement Integrity Act

I. Disclosing and Obtaining Contractor Bid or Proposal Information or Source Selection Information

A. A present or former employee of, or person acting on behalf of or advising, the U.S. on a procurement, who has or had access to such information shall not disclose it before the award of the contract to which the information relates. (48 CFR 3.104-4(a))

B. No person shall knowingly obtain such information before the award of the contract to which the information relates. (48 CFR 3.104-4(b))

II. Offers of Non-Federal Employment

An official participating personally and substantially in a procurement for a contract in excess of the simplified acquisition threshold ($100,000) who is contacted by a bidder regarding non-federal employment during the conduct of the procurement shall:

A. Report the contact to his supervisor and the [Designated Agency Ethics Official] DAEO in writing; and

B. Reject the offer; or

C. Disqualify himself in writing to the Head of the Contracting Activity in accordance with 18 U.S.C. § 208 until authorized to resume on grounds that:

   1. the offeror is no longer a bidder; or

   2. all discussions have terminated without an agreement for employment. (48 CFR 3.104-4(c))

D. This requirement does not apply after the award of the contract or after the procurement has been canceled, although 18 U.S.C. § 208 would still require disqualification on the part of an employee who is administering a contract.

III. Accepting Compensation from a Contractor

A. A former official may not accept compensation from a contractor within a year after he served as the procuring contracting officer, the source selection authority, a member of the source selection evaluation board or the chief of a financial or technical evaluation team for a procurement for a contract in excess of $10 million awarded to that contractor.

B. The above restriction also applies to a former official who served as program manager, deputy program manager or administrative contracting officer for a contract over $10 million.

C. It applies to a former official who made a decision to:

   1. award a contract, modification, subcontract, task order or delivery order, in excess of $10 million;

   2. establish overhead or other rates applicable to a contract in excess of $10 million; or

   3. approve issuance of a contract payment or payments in excess of $10 million, or pay or settle a claim in excess of $10 million. (48 CFR 3.104-4(d))

D. Note that this restriction can apply to decisions made after the award of the contract which need not be competitively awarded. The restriction does not apply to accepting compensation from a division or affiliate of the contractor that does not produce the same or similar product or service.

E. The one-year prohibition on accepting compensation begins:

1. on the date of selection of the contractor for a former official who served in a position listed in paragraph A at that time, but not on the date of the award of the contract;

2. on the date of the award of the contract for [an] official who served in a position listed in paragraph A at that time whether or not he was serving at the time of selection;

3. on the last date an official served in a position listed in paragraph B; or

4. on the date a decision listed in paragraph C was made.

IV. Definitions

A. Contractor bid or proposal information means information not made available to the public and includes:

1. cost or pricing data;

2. indirect costs and direct labor rates;

3. proprietary information about manufacturing processes, operations or techniques; and

4. information marked by the contractor as "contractor bid or proposal information."

B. Source selection information means information not made available to the public and includes:

1. bid prices;

2. proposed costs or prices from bidders;

3. source selection and technical evaluation plans;

4. technical evaluations, cost or price evaluations, competitive range determinations, rankings of bids, reports of source selection panels; and

5. other information marked as "source selection" based on a determination that its disclosure would jeopardize the procurement.

Notes

1. Office of Government Ethics, "Principles of Ethical Conduct for Government Officers and Employees." Executive Order 12731 of October 17, 1990. Online at http://www.usoge.gov/laws_regs/exec_orders/eo12731.pdf (accessed October 22, 2010).

2. Department of Justice, Departmental Ethics Office, "Procurement Integrity Outline." Online at http://www.justice.gov/jmd/ethics/procureb.htm (accessed October 22, 2010).

Appendix I

EXAMPLES OF RATING METHODOLOGIES

This appendix offers examples of five types of rating methodologies:

1. Adjectival rating
2. Color coding
3. Small business participation rating
4. Past performance rating
5. Numerical scoring.

ADJECTIVAL RATING

This section offers two examples of adjectival rating.[1] The first example is a rating scale for technical and management factors, and the second is a scale for past performance.

The following adjectival rating scale could be used to evaluate technical and management factors and significant subfactors. A proposal need not have all the characteristics listed in an adjectival category to receive that adjectival rating. The evaluators must use judgment to rate the proposal using these characteristics.

Outstanding: An outstanding proposal is characterized as follows:

- The proposed approach indicates an exceptionally thorough and comprehensive understanding of the program goals, resources, schedules, and other aspects essential to performance of the program.
- In terms of the specific factor (or significant subfactor), the proposal contains major strengths, exceptional features, or innovations that should substantially benefit the program.
- There are no weaknesses or deficiencies.
- The risk of unsuccessful contract performance is extremely low.

Good: A good proposal is characterized as follows:

- The proposed approach indicates a thorough understanding of the program goals and the methods, resources, schedules, and other aspects essential to the performance of the program.
- The proposal has major strengths and/or minor strengths that indicate the proposed approach will benefit the program.
- Weaknesses, if any, are minor and are more than offset by strengths.
- The risk of unsuccessful performance is very low.

Satisfactory: A satisfactory proposal is characterized as follows:

- The proposed approach indicates an adequate understanding of the program goals and the methods, resources, schedules, and other aspects essential to the performance of the program.
- There are few, if any, exceptional features to benefit the program.
- The risk of unsuccessful performance is low.
- Weaknesses are generally offset by strengths.

Marginal: A marginal proposal is characterized as follows:

- The proposed approach indicates a superficial or vague understanding of the program goals and the methods, resources, schedules, and other aspects essential to the performance of the program.
- The proposal has weaknesses that are not offset by strengths.
- The risk of unsuccessful contract performance is moderate.

Unsatisfactory: An unsatisfactory proposal is characterized as follows:

- The proposed approach indicates a lack of understanding of the program goals and the methods, resources, schedules, and other aspects essential to the performance of the program.
- Numerous weaknesses and deficiencies exist.
- The risk of unsuccessful performance is high.

The next example adjectival rating scale could be used to evaluate past performance factors and subfactors.

Outstanding: The offeror's performance of previously awarded relevant contract(s) met contractual requirements and exceeded many to the Government's benefit. The prior performance being assessed was accomplished with very few or very minor problems[,] for which corrective actions taken by or proposed to be taken by the offeror were, or are expected to be[,] highly effective. Performance of completed contracts either was consistently of the highest quality or exhibited a trend [toward] becoming so. The offeror's past performance record leads to an extremely strong expectation of successful performance.

Good: The offeror's performance of previously awarded relevant contract(s) met contractual requirements and exceeded some to the Government's benefit. The prior performance being assessed was accomplished with some minor problems for which corrective actions taken by or proposed to be taken by the offeror, were, or are expected to be[,] effective. Performance over completed contracts either was consistently of high quality or exhibited a trend [toward] becoming so. The offeror's past performance record leads to a strong expectation of successful performance.

Satisfactory: The offeror's performance of previously awarded relevant contract(s) met contractual requirements. The prior performance being assessed was accomplished with some problems for which corrective actions taken by, or proposed to be taken by, the contractor were, or are expected to be, for the most part, effective. Performance over completed contracts was consistently of adequate or better quality or exhibited a trend [toward] becoming so. The offeror's past performance record leads to an expectation of successful performance.

Neutral: The offeror lacks a record of relevant or available past performance history. There is no expectation of either successful or unsuccessful performance based on the offeror's past performance record.

Marginal: The offeror's performance of previously awarded relevant contracts did not meet some contractual requirements. The prior performance being assessed reflected some serious problems, for which the contractor either failed to identify or implement corrective actions in a timely manner, or for which the corrective actions implemented or proposed to be implemented were, or are expected to be, only partially effective. Performance over completed contracts was consistently of mediocre quality or exhibited a trend [toward] becoming so. The offeror's past performance record leads to an expectation that successful performance might be difficult to achieve or that it can occur only with increased levels of Government management and oversight.

Unsatisfactory: The offeror's performance of previously awarded relevant contract(s) did not meet most contractual requirements and recovery did not occur [within] the period of performance. The prior performance being assessed reflected serious problem(s) for which the offeror either failed to identify or implement corrective actions or for which corrective actions, implemented or proposed to be implemented, were, or are expected to be, mostly ineffective. Performance over completed contracts was consistently of poor quality or exhibited a trend [toward] becoming so. The offeror's past performance record leads to a strong expectation that successful performance will not be achieved or that it can occur only with greatly increased levels of Government management and oversight.

COLOR CODING

The *Naval Sea Systems Command Source Selection Guide* describes color coding as follows: "This system uses colors to indicate the degree to which the offeror's proposal has met the standard for each factor evaluated. For instance, the colors blue, green, yellow, orange, and red may indicate excellent, good, satisfactory, marginal, or unsatisfactory degrees of merit, respectively."[2]

The following example of a color coding scale comes from a U.S. Army request for proposal.

Color	Technical Capability	Strengths	Weaknesses	Past Performance
Blue	The proposal exceeds requirements and clearly demonstrates the offeror's capability to deliver exceptional performance.	There are numerous strengths that are of direct benefit to the Government.	Weaknesses are considered insignificant and have no apparent impact to the program.	Highly relevant/very recent past performance in all identified past performance efforts; excellent performance ratings.

Green	The proposal is satisfactory; the offeror is capable of meeting performance requirements.	Some strengths exist that are of benefit to the Government; the strengths clearly offset weaknesses.	A few weaknesses exist; they are correctable with minimal Government oversight or direction.	Relevant/ somewhat recent past performance in all identified past performance efforts; acceptable performance ratings.
Yellow	The proposal is minimally adequate; the offeror is most likely able to meet performance requirements.	Few strengths exist that are of benefit to the Government; the strengths do not offset the weaknesses.	Substantial weaknesses exist that may impact the program; they are correctable with some Government oversight and direction.	Somewhat relevant/ not very recent past performance; mostly acceptable performance ratings.
Orange	The proposal is inadequate; it is doubtful whether the offeror can meet performance requirements.	[Few], if any, strengths exist that are of benefit to the Government; the weaknesses clearly offset the strengths.	Weaknesses exist that adversely impact the program; they are correctable with significant Government oversight and direction.	Little relevant past performance identified; mostly unacceptable performance ratings.

Red	The proposal is highly inadequate; the offeror cannot meet performance requirements.	There are no beneficial strengths.	Numerous weaknesses exist that are so significant that a proposal rewrite is not feasible within a suitable timeframe.	Little relevant past performance identified; almost all unacceptable performance ratings.
White	Not used	Not used	Not used	Completely lacks relevant performance history or past performance is unavailable due to offeror's failure to provide information.

SMALL BUSINESS PARTICIPATION RATING

The following small business participation evaluation methodology was adapted from the *Army Source Selection Manual,* an appendix to the *Army Federal Acquisition Regulation Supplement.*[3]

EVALUATION CRITERIA
Small Business Participation (SBP)

	Extent of Achievement of RFP Small Business Participation Objectives	Extent to which SBP Goal Rationale Supports Achievement of Successful Overall Contract Performance	Extent to which Corporate/ Division SBP Goals Satisfy RFP Objectives	Realism of Proposed SBP Goals Based on Proposal and Performance Risk	Strengths and Weaknesses
Outstanding	Proposed goals achieve or nearly achieve almost all RFP objectives	Extensive and compelling rationale for all proposed goals	Goals achieve or nearly achieve almost all RFP objectives	Highly realistic	Strengths far outweigh weaknesses
Acceptable	Meaningful goals proposed against almost all RFP objectives	Reasonable rationale for the majority of proposed goals	Meaningful goals against almost all RFP objectives	Somewhat realistic	Strengths and weaknesses are offsetting

Marginal	Meaningful goals proposed against only several RFP objectives	Limited rationale for the majority of proposed goals	Meaningful goals against only several RFP objectives	May not be realistic	Weaknesses outweigh strengths
Susceptible to Being Made Acceptable	An approach which, as initially proposed, cannot be rated marginal because of a minor error(s), omission(s), or deficiency(ies), which is/are capable of being corrected without a major rewrite or revision of the proposal. Note: A susceptible rating can be applied only prior to establishing a competitive range. It cannot be a final rating. The final rating will either increase to a rating of marginal or better, or decrease to a rating of unacceptable.				
Unacceptable	Failed to propose meaningful goals against almost all RFP objectives	Little or no meaningful rationale provided for proposed goals	Goals fail to satisfy almost all RFP objectives	Not realistic	Weaknesses far outweigh strengths

EVALUATING PAST PERFORMANCE

The following past performance rating methodology appears in the *NASA Source Selection Guide.*[4]

(a)(2) Past performance evaluation.

(A) The Past Performance evaluation assesses the contractor's performance under previously awarded contracts. The past performance evaluation shall be in accordance with FAR 15.305(a)(2) and this section. When applying the definitions below to arrive at a confidence rating, the SEB's evaluation shall clearly document each offeror's relevant past performance (e.g. currency/recency, size, content, and complexity) to assess the offeror's overall confidence rating assigned. The past performance evaluation is an assessment of the Government's confidence in the offeror's ability to perform the solicitation requirements. Past Performance shall be evaluated for each offeror using the following levels of confidence ratings:

Very High Level of Confidence

The offeror's relevant past performance is of exceptional merit and is very highly pertinent to this acquisition; indicating exemplary performance in a timely, efficient, and economical manner; very minor (if any) problems with no adverse effect on overall performance. Based on the offeror's performance record, there is a very high level of confidence that the offeror will successfully perform the required effort.

**(One or more significant strengths exist. No significant weaknesses exist.)

High Level of Confidence

The offeror's relevant past performance is highly pertinent to this acquisition; demonstrating very effective performance that would be fully responsive to contract requirements with contract requirements accomplished in a timely, efficient, and economical manner for the most part with only minor problems with little identifiable effect on overall performance. Based on the offeror's performance record, there is a high level of confidence that the offeror will successfully perform the required effort.

**(One or more significant strengths exist. Strengths outbalance any weakness.)

Moderate Level of Confidence

The offeror's relevant past performance is pertinent to this acquisition, and it demonstrates effective performance; fully responsive to contract requirements; reportable problems, but with little identifiable effect on overall performance. Based on the offeror's performance record, there is a moderate level of confidence that the offeror will successfully perform the required effort.

**(There may be strengths, weaknesses, or both.)

Low Level of Confidence

The offeror's relevant past performance is at least somewhat pertinent to this acquisition, and it meets or slightly exceeds minimum acceptable standards; adequate results; reportable problems with identifiable, but not substantial, effects on overall performance. Based on the offeror's performance record, there is a low level of confidence that the offeror will successfully perform the required effort. Changes to the offeror's existing processes may be necessary in order to achieve contract requirements.

**(One or more weaknesses exist. Weaknesses outbalance strengths.)

Very Low Level of Confidence

The offeror's relevant past performance does not meet minimum acceptable standards in one or more areas; remedial action required in one or more areas; problems in one or more areas which adversely affect overall performance. Based on the offeror's performance record, there is a very low level of confidence that the offeror will successfully perform the required effort.

**(One or more deficiencies or significant weaknesses exist.)

Neutral

In the case of an offeror without a record of relevant past performance or for which information on past performance is not available, the offeror may not be evaluated favorably or unfavorably on past performance [see FAR 15.305(a)(2)(ii) and (iv)].

NUMERICAL SCORING

In a 2008 solicitation, the National Institute for Literacy (NIFL) used the following numerical scoring methodology.[5]

Proposal Evaluation Criteria

All proposals will be evaluated in accordance with the following evaluation factors and the respective point values assigned. An award will be made to the responsible offeror whose proposal conforms to the solicitation and is most advantageous to the Government and based on availability of funds. For this solicitation, price will be a substantial factor in source selection, but technical factors are significantly more important than cost. The NIFL Contracting Officer will determine whether the difference in technical quality is worth the difference in cost or price.

EVALUATION CRITERIA	POINTS
1. QUALITY OF TECHNICAL PROPOSAL	**40**
A. The technical proposal demonstrates the offeror's clear understanding of the tasks outlined in the Statement of Work and shows how the offeror's partners, if any, will contribute to the tasks.	15
B. The technical proposal shows the offeror's application of expert knowledge of publication development, quality assurance, and peer review management. If the offeror lacks expert knowledge in one or more of the areas, the technical proposal will show that the offeror has established partnerships with other individuals or organizations to supply the missing expertise.	20
C. The technical proposal includes a statement describing how the contractor will address organizational and other conflicts of interest for persons who are consultants or who work for organizations with potential conflicts.	5
2. QUALITY OF KEY PERSONNEL	**35**
A. The technical proposal clearly shows that the key personnel have the technical knowledge and experience required for the functions, activities, and tasks described in the Statement of Work.	15
B. The technical proposal adequately describes the staff hours needed for each task and that the offeror has dedicated adequate staff hours sufficient to complete the requirement according to the established timeline.	20
3. QUALITY OF MANAGEMENT PLAN	**5**
The technical proposal will provide clear, logical, and specific plans, with provisions for identifying and correcting deficiencies, and a process for ensuring quality and timeliness of the final product.	5

4. REQUIRED CORPORATE EXPERIENCE AND CAPABILITY	20
The technical proposal describes the offeror's relevant past and current experience in projects of comparable size, complexity, and similarity to the objectives of this requirement.	20
TOTAL POSSIBLE SCORE	100

Notes

1. *Naval Sea Systems Command Source Selection Guide,* January 24, 2001. Available online at https://acc.dau.mil/Community Browser.aspx?id=30899 (accessed January 7, 2011). This material has been adapted slightly for clarity.
2. Ibid., p. 17.
3. *AFARS Appendix AA—Army Source Selection Manual,* February 26, 2009. Available online at http://farsite.hill.af.mil/reghtml/regs/other/afars/ASSM_final022609.pdf (accessed January 7, 2011). Adapted slightly for clarity.
4. National Aeronautics and Space Administration, *Procurement Notice: Source Selection Changes* (PN 04-34), May 29, 2008, pp. 6–7. Available online at www.hq.nasa.gov/office/procurement/regs/pn04-34.doc (accessed January 7, 2011). Adapted slightly for clarity.
5. National Institute for Literacy, RFP ED-08-R-0110, 2008. Adapted slightly for clarity.

Appendix II

Sample Sections L and M from a Solicitation

The following solicitation sample is adapted from a U.S. Army Research, Development and Engineering Command Contracting Center request for proposal (RFP 911SR-09-R-0031).

SECTION L: INSTRUCTIONS, CONDITIONS, AND NOTICES TO OFFERORS

L.1 Proposal Submission Instructions.

NOTICE TO OFFERORS: Offerors shall certify in their proposal that they possess at least a Secret Facility Clearance or have access through a sponsoring company. Offerors shall also propose on all Evaluation Tasks. Offerors will receive either a PASS or FAIL for these two criteria (Secret Facility Clearance and proposing on all Evaluation Tasks) in order to be considered responsive to this solicitation. Offerors' proposals that receive a FAIL will not be evaluated.

L.1.1 Each Offeror's proposal shall consist of the following:

VOLUME	FACTOR	PAGE LIMIT	COPIES
I	Technical		Original and five (5) copies
	Evaluation Task 1	50	
	Evaluation Task 2	50	
	Evaluation Task 3	35	
II	Management and Related Corporate Experience	35	Original and five (5) copies
III	Past Performance	No limit	Original and three (3) copies
IV	Cost/Price	No limit	Original and three (3) copies
	Transmittal Data*		Original and one (1) copy
*Include signed copy of Standard Form 33 and continuation sheets.			

L.1.2 The Government will not accept proposals via Federal Business Opportunities (FedBizOpps). The only method for submission of proposals is as follows:

L.1.2.1 Hand Delivery or Courier Service Address:

US Army Research, Development and Engineering Command Contracting Center

Edgewood Contracting Division

Building E4455 Lietzan Road

Aberdeen Proving Ground (Edgewood Area), MD 21010-5401

L.1.2.1.1 NOTICE FOR HANDCARRIES. During the workweek (Monday through Friday, 8:00 a.m. EST to 4:00 p.m. EST) someone will be available to receive proposals. Visitors may be required to undergo random vehicle searches. Persons hand-carrying proposals are cautioned to allow sufficient time to cover any possible delays since proposals must be at the designated place, date, and time as specified in the solicitation in order to be accepted.

L.1.2.2 Mailing address:

Director, US Army Research, Development and Engineering Command Contracting Center

Aberdeen Proving Ground, MD 21010-5401

L.2 Proposal Preparation Instructions:

L.2.1 Format: The Offeror shall submit technical, management, cost/price, past performance, and small business information in separate volumes as set forth below. All information the Offeror wishes to have considered must be submitted with the initial proposal and shall be confined to the appropriate volume. The Government will not consider any information that is not included in the appropriate volume.

Volume I—Technical Factor

Volume II—Management and Related Corporate Experience Factors

Volume III—Past Performance Factor

Volume IV—Cost/Price Factor

Transmittal data shall be submitted in a separate binder.

L.2.2 It is suggested that secure binders be used to assemble the separate volumes of the proposal for ease of evaluation. Indices to the proposal and cross-references between the proposal and the solicitation are useful for ensuring that all pertinent sections of the proposal are fully understood. The use of tabs to easily locate sections of the proposal also facilitates thorough evaluation.

L.2.3 Each volume shall be as brief as possible, yet consistent with a complete submission. Pages shall not exceed 8.5 inches in width and 11 inches in length; however, foldout pages, as appropriate, not exceeding 11x17 inches, depicting such items as charts, matrices, or schedules may be used and will count as a single page. The Offeror shall number all pages within each volume.

L.2.4 The Offeror's proposal shall be printed in a 12-point font (foldout pages or electronic spreadsheets—10-point font) with one-inch margins (top, bottom, left, and right).

L.2.5 Offerors are expected to provide sufficient detail in a clear and concise manner to completely and logically address all factors and subfactors. The Government does not desire excess verbiage, unnecessary and elaborate brochures, or lengthy, repetitious, disorganized presentations beyond that sufficient to present a complete and clear proposal. Such presentations are not desired and may be construed as an indication of the Offeror's inefficiencies and lack of cost consciousness in proposal preparation. All Offerors are reminded that unsupported promises to comply with the contractual requirements will not be sufficient. Proposals must not merely parrot back the contractual requirements, but rather must provide convincing documentary evidence in support of any conclusionary statements relating to the promised performance.

L.3 Specific Instructions

L.3.1 Volume I—Technical Factor

L.3.1.1 Technical: The Offeror is responsible for including sufficient details (without reference to contract cost) to permit a complete and accurate evaluation.

L.3.1.1.1 Format: The technical proposal shall provide a narrative discussion that addresses the three (3) Evaluation Tasks as set forth in section J. Each Section shall have an index that contains narrative titles that cross-reference the Offeror's discussion to the requirements as outlined in the SOW.

L.3.1.1.2 Content: The technical proposal shall address each Evaluation Task in a separate section and include the following elements for each Evaluation Task:

L.3.1.1.2.1 Technical Approach: The Offeror shall provide a detailed discussion of its methodology and its approach for accomplishing the requirements of each Evaluation Task, to include the planned sequence of steps to be taken, critical path, milestones, and interface and integration. The Offeror's technical approach shall be clear, logical, practical, efficient, cost effective, and complete. The Offeror shall identify potential risks with the proposed approach as well as the means to mitigate them.

L.3.1.1.2.2 Resources Required: The Offeror shall include a discussion of its understanding of all the resources required. The Offeror's discussion shall demonstrate availability of sufficient numbers of personnel having direct L3 experience to complete the requirements of each Evaluation Task. The Offeror shall include with the proposal an uncosted matrix of labor hours showing the number of hours by labor category, skill level, and grade for each phase of work in the task, identification of any subcontractor labor used, and a discussion of all work to be performed by the subcontractor in the task, a travel schedule listing number of trips and number of personnel, and a description of all assumptions used to respond to each Evaluation Task, to include assumptions used to calculate costs for labor, materials, equipment, subcontracts, and travel (actual costs shall not be included in the Technical proposal). The Offeror shall discuss all facilities (to include suitability, availability, and whether or not they are owned, leased, or sub-contracted), equipments and materials necessary to complete each Evaluation Task based upon its proposed approach. Resumes for Key Personnel shall be included as an attachment (keyed to each specific Evaluation Task) and is excluded from the page limitation. Each resume is limited to two (2) pages and shall include a description of the individual's responsibilities.

L.3.1.1.2.3 Task Order Management and Schedule: The Offeror shall identify and explain specific project management tools that shall be employed to track cost and performance for each Evaluation Task. The Offeror's discussion will include evidence of the following: adequate program visibility of each Evaluation Task at Senior Management Levels, timely reaction to problems (method of recognizing and reacting to problems), adequate schedule (method of reporting actual performance versus projected progress), and cost control (techniques for controlling expenditures). The Offeror shall identify schedule and management risks and proposed mitigation measures. The Offeror shall provide an organization plan for contract performance illustrating the interface between various elements of the organization during performance, including interface with any subcontractors and the Government. The Offeror shall explain its understanding of the sequence, complexity, and interrelationship of events in implementing the work of each Evaluation Task. The Offeror shall explain how it will schedule and track multiple task elements under each Evaluation Task and deliverables. The Offeror shall also provide a discussion of its method for managing subcontractor involvement.

L.3.2 Volume II—Management and Related Corporate Experience Factors

L.3.2.1 Management Factor: The Offeror is responsible for including sufficient details (without reference to contract cost) to permit a complete and accurate evaluation strictly from a management standpoint.

L.3.2.1.1 Format: This section shall have an index that contains narrative titles that are cross-referenced to the Offeror's discussion.

L.3.2.1.2 Content: The Management Proposal shall contain (as a minimum) the following:

L.3.2.1.2.1 Staffing Approach: The Offeror shall discuss its proposed staffing plan to demonstrate the effectiveness of its staffing retention capability and sustainment for in-house as well as subcontracted support. The plan shall include the methodology for planning and obtaining resources to support the requirements and the use of recruiting sources and the methods of obtaining them. The Offeror shall demonstrate its ability to obtain qualified personnel of diverse disciplines to meet the requirements of the solicitation. The Offeror shall demonstrate the degree to which the proposed staffing resources are highly knowledgeable in the disciplines related to requirements stated in the solicitation.

L.3.2.1.2.2 Contract Management Approach: The Offeror shall discuss their proposed approach to manage a potentially diverse effort, which may involve fragmentation of services, differences in the work requirements, the need for explicit work assignments and the ability to oversee the quality of the work to include that performed by a subcontractor. The coordination between prime and subcontractors shall be addressed. The proposal shall demonstrate how the Offeror will bring together and manage large staffs of diverse disciplines in short periods of time if orders are placed. A Contract Management Plan shall be submitted that addresses among other things how the Offeror intends to effectively manage multiple task orders in addition to its application of lessons learned to implement quality support to maximize cost effectiveness and efficiency.

L.3.2.1.2.3 Facilities: The Offeror shall include a description of all facilities (engineering, fabrication, test, and laboratory). The Offeror must identify the primary facilities at which the majority of the effort will be performed. The discussion shall demonstrate the suitability of the facilities for timely and effective completion of the work described in the solicitation. The Offeror must indicate which facilities are owned, leased, or subcontracted.

L.3.2.2 Related Corporate Experience: The Offeror is responsible for including sufficient details (without reference to contract cost) to permit a complete and accurate evaluation strictly from a corporate experience standpoint. The Offeror's discussion shall address the extent to which the contractor, or its proposed major subcontractors, has been involved as either a prime or a subcontractor on previous contracts for work similar to that required under this solicitation during the past five (5) years. The Offeror shall describe the extent to which the Offeror has corporate experience in performing engineering, research and technology, and program and integration support that are applicable to the [Chemical, Biological, Radiological, Nuclear, and Explosives] CBRNE program.

L.3.3 Volume III—Past Performance Factor: The Offeror is responsible for including sufficient details to permit a complete and accurate evaluation strictly from a past performance standpoint. The Offeror shall include an index of past performance data with each Evaluation Task where appropriate.

L.3.3.1 Format: Information contained in this section of the proposal will be used for a Performance Risk Assessment.

L.3.3.2 Content: The Past Performance Volume shall contain the following:

L.3.3.2.1 The following information shall be included for each award referenced on Government or private-sector contracts or task orders completed or at least 90 percent physically completed by the Offeror as a prime contractor or major subcontractor within the past five (5) years. (A major subcontractor is defined as one that will be providing critical services or that is responsible for efforts totaling at least 25 percent of the labor support cost.)

a. The name, address, and telephone number of the Government contracting activity and the Procuring Contracting Officer or, for subcontracts, the Administrative Contracting Officer's contact information.

b. The name and telephone number of the Government contracting activity's technical representative or Contracting Officer's Representative or, for subcontracts, the Government Contract Administration Activity.

c. Contract or subcontract number.

d. Type of contract.

e. Award price/cost.

f. Final, or projected final, price/cost.

g. Original delivery schedule.

h. Final or projected final delivery schedule.

L.3.3.2.2 A detailed narrative for each contract cited and the similarities and relevance of that work to the work required by this solicitation, objectives achieved, and cost growths or schedule delays encountered. Offerors shall provide copies of all Quality Deficiency Reports and Corrective Actions submitted by the Defense Contract Management Agency (DCMA) office within the past five (5) years. For Government contracts that did not nor do not meet original requirements with regard to either cost, schedule, or technical performance the offeror shall provide a brief explanation of the reason(s) for such factor(s) and any corrective actions taken to avoid recurrence. The Offeror shall not exceed two (2) pages for each contract cited.

L.3.3.2.3 The Offeror shall also provide the afore-mentioned information for all contracts terminated in whole or in part, for any reason during the past five (5) years, to include those currently in the process of such termination as well as those that are not for work similar to the proposed effort. The Offeror shall also provide the aforementioned information for all proposed major subcontractors.

L.3.3.2.4 In the case of an Offeror without a record of relevant past performance or for which information on past performance is not available, the Offeror may not be evaluated favorably or unfavorably on past performance.

L.3.3.2.5 The Offeror shall include in its proposal the written consent of its proposed major subcontractors to allow the Government to discuss the subcontractor's past performance evaluation with the Offeror during negotiations.

L.3.5 Volume IV—Cost/Price: Each Evaluation Task shall be priced on a cost-plus-fixed-fee basis. The cost/price proposal shall contain the following:

L.3.5.1 Content and Format.

L.3.5.1.1 The uncosted hours and labor categories contained in the technical proposal must agree with and be traceable to the costed hours and labor categories contained in the cost proposal. The Offeror shall also discuss assumptions made and its impact on the cost proposal. The cost/price proposal for each Evaluation Task shall be submitted in a separate section and shall contain (as a minimum) the following information:

L.3.5.1.2 The Offeror shall submit supporting com-putations and summaries contained in the cost proposal on CD-ROM using Excel.

L.3.5.1.3 The Offeror shall prepare a segregated cost proposal that shall include a separate breakout of cost and fee/profit for each Evaluation Task including DD Form 1861, Contract Facilities Capital Cost of Money, if applicable. Proposed costs and fee for each cost element shall be adequately broken down and explained in sufficient detail to permit a thorough analysis. Costs shall be based on an Offeror's normal workweek and predicated on the work set forth in the statements of work for each Evaluation Task. If an Offeror's proposed normal workweek is more or less than 40 hours per week, the Offeror shall so state in the proposal.

L.3.5.1.4 The Offeror shall submit verifiable cost or pricing data which will adequately support its proposal. For materials and subcontracting effort, the Offeror shall provide such data as vendor quotes, invoice prices, subcontracted services, sources, quantities, prices, degree of competition, type of subcontract, etc. These data are required to support the cost realism analysis. In the event adequate price competition does not result for this solicitation, the Government reserves the right to request a Certificate of Current Cost and Pricing Data pursuant to FAR 15.804.

L.3.5.1.5 The Offeror shall provide a summary of all direct and indirect rates (labor, overhead, general and administrative, etc.) to include the basis for estimates. Indicate how indirect costs were computed and applied, including cost breakdowns. List all other costs (e.g., travel, computer usage) and provide a basis for pricing. For travel, specify each trip, from/to, number of people, duration, airfare, per diem, rental car, local mileage amount, total cost per trip, and total cost for travel.

L.3.5.2 The Offeror shall also provide a summary sheet that incorporates each cost element for all work proposed under the solicitation (cumulative for all Evaluation Tasks).

L.3.5.3 Subcontractors are required to submit the same information required of the prime contractor. Subcontractor cost information that is proprietary may be submitted through the prime contractor in a separate sealed package. A proposal will not be accepted directly from subcontractors. It must be submitted through the prime contractor as part of the total proposal package.

L.3.5.4 The Offeror shall furnish all information that could have a bearing on cost and financial matters and that is of mutual interest in the contemplated acquisition. For example, if the proposal is to be a joint venture arrangement, explain how the financial matters are to be handled.

L.3.5.5 Cost Realism. A proposal is presumed to represent an Offeror's best efforts to respond to the solicitation. Any inconsistency, whether real or apparent, between promised performance and cost shall be explained in the proposal. For example, if the intended use of new and innovative techniques is the basis for an abnormally low estimate, the nature of these techniques and their impact on cost must be explained. Any significant inconsistency, if unexplained, that raises a fundamental issue of the Offeror's understanding of the nature and scope of the work required and of its financial ability to perform the contract may be grounds for rejection of the proposal or grounds for adjusting the proposed cost. THE BURDEN OF PROOF AS TO COST CREDIBILITY RESTS WITH THE OFFEROR.

L.3.5.6 The Offeror shall provide a compensation plan in accordance with FAR 52.222-46, setting forth salaries and fringe benefits proposed for the professional employees who will work under the contract.

CLAUSES INCORPORATED BY REFERENCE

52.215-1	Instructions to Offerors—Competitive Acquisition	JAN 2004
52.215-16	Facilities Capital Cost of Money	JUN 2003
52.215-20	Requirements for Cost or Pricing Data or Information Other Than Cost or Pricing Data	OCT 1997
52.216-1	Type of Contract	APR 1984
52.216-27	Single or Multiple Awards	OCT 1995
52.222-24	Preaward On-Site Equal Opportunity Compliance Evaluation	FEB 1999
52.222-46	Evaluation of Compensation for Professional Employees	FEB 1993
52.233-2	Service of Protest	SEP 2006
52.234-3	Notice of Earned Value Management System—Postaward IBR	JUL 2006
52.237-10	Identification of Uncompensated Overtime	OCT 1997
252.227-7017 (DFARS)	Identification and Assertion of Use, Release, or Disclosure Restrictions	JUN 1995
252.234-7001 (DFARS)	Notice of Earned Value Management System	APR 2008

SECTION M: EVALUATION FACTORS FOR AWARD

M.1 Basis for Award. The award decision will be based on the evaluation of all factors and subfactors set forth in this solicitation. Award(s) will be made to the responsible Offeror(s) whose proposal conforms to the solicitation requirements and represents the best value to the Government. The Government evaluation process will permit tradeoffs among the specific evaluation factors and will allow award(s) to other than the lowest priced Offeror(s) or other than the highest technically rated Offeror(s). The best value is the expected outcome of the acquisition that, in the Government's estimation, provides the greatest overall benefits in response to requirements.

M.1.1 The Government intends to award multiple contracts under this solicitation based upon the quantity and quality of the proposals received.

M.1.2 The Government has included Sample Evaluation Tasks 1 through 3 at Section J of the solicitation. If mission requirements dictate, the Government reserves the right to award one or more of the Evaluation Tasks as actual task order(s) under one or more of the resultant contracts. Proposals must address all three (3) Evaluation Tasks in order to be considered responsive to the solicitation.

M.2 Evaluation Approach. All proposals received pursuant to the solicitation will be evaluated in a careful and impartial manner. All factors against which proposals will be evaluated are described below and generally parallel the proposal instructions in Section L. All proposals will be evaluated by a team of individuals in accordance with the approach described below.

M.2.1 Discussions/Final Proposal Revisions: The Government intends to make an award determination without discussions. However, if discussions are deemed appropriate by the Contracting Officer, the Government will establish a Competitive Range and only those Offerors included will be allowed to enter into discussions. Offerors selected to participate in discussions shall be, as a minimum, advised of significant weaknesses and deficiencies in their proposals. They will be offered, as appropriate, a reasonable opportunity to correct or resolve them and to submit such price or cost, technical, or other revisions of their proposal that may result from discussions. At the conclusion of discussions, a final common cut-off date that allows a reasonable opportunity for the submission of written Final Proposal Revisions will be established and those selected to remain in the competitive range will be notified, as appropriate, to submit Final Proposal Revisions.

M.2.1.1 Competitive Range: The Contracting Officer will make the determination, for the SSA's approval, as to which proposals are in the Competitive Range. The Competitive Range will be determined on the basis of the merit rating, past performance, and the proposed cost (including cost realism considerations) to the Government in accordance with M.3 below and may include proposals that have a reasonable chance of being selected for award.

M.2.1.2 Final Evaluation of Proposals: Factor ratings assigned during the initial evaluation of the proposals within the Competitive Range may be revised in light of additional information/data provided during subsequent discussions and/or furnished with Final Proposal Revisions.

M.2.2 The following evaluation approach will be used:

M.2.2.1 Technical, Management, and Related Corporate Experience. The Technical Factor, Management Factor, and Related Corporate Experience Factor will receive an adjectival rating along with a narrative evaluation. This rating relates to technical, management, and corporate experience merit and reflects the degree of the Government's confidence in each Offeror's ability, as demonstrated in its proposal, to perform the requirements stated in the solicitation.

M.2.2.2 Past Performance. The Past Performance Factor will receive an adjectival rating that defines the performance risk assessment. The rating will be supported by a narrative evaluation. Performance risks are those associated with an Offeror's likelihood of success in performing the solicitation's requirements as indicated by the Offeror's record of current or past performance.

M.2.2.3 Cost/Price. The Cost/Price Factor will not receive an adjectival rating, but instead will be evaluated for realism, reasonableness, and completeness.

M.3 Evaluation Factors and Relative Order of Importance.

M.3.1 Factors/Subfactors. Each Offeror's proposal will be evaluated on the extent to which it demonstrates responsiveness to each of the evaluation factors.

M.3.1.1 Technical: Each Evaluation Task is a subfactor. The subfactors are a composite of the Technical Factor. Each subfactor will be evaluated on three (3) elements: (1) Technical Approach, (2) Resources Required, and (3) Task Order Management and Schedule.

> Evaluation Task 1—Support to the Edgewood Chemical Biological Center (ECBC) Research and Technology Directorate (R&T).

> Evaluation Task 2—Development of Spectral Library of Biological Materials.

> Evaluation Task 3—Biological Detection and Simulant Improvement Research Support.

M.3.1.2 Management: The evaluation for the Management factor includes the following three (3) elements: (1) Staffing Approach, (2) Contract Management Approach, and (3) Facilities.

M.3.1.3 Related Corporate Experience.

M.3.1.4 Past Performance.

M.3.1.5 Cost/Price.

M.3.2 Relative Order of Importance. The Technical Factor is more important than the Management Factor. The Management Factor is more important than the Related Corporate Experience Factor. The Related Corporate Experience Factor is more important than the Past Performance Factor. The Technical Subfactors, Evaluation Tasks 1–3, are considered equally important. All factors other than Cost/Price when combined are significantly more important than Cost/Price. The Government is willing to pay more if an increase in the technical merit of the proposal or past performance warrants. However, cost/price may become more significant if competing proposals are technically comparable.

M.4 Rating System, Evaluation Criteria, and Standards.

M.4.1 Technical Subfactors and Management and Related Corporate Experience Factors.

M.4.1.1 Rating System: The Technical Subfactors and the Management and Related Corporate Experience Factors will each receive one of the following adjectival ratings for technical and management merit, along with a narrative evaluation:

- Excellent—Proposal significantly exceeds the government's requirements. Numerous strengths identified that will significantly benefit the government. No deficiencies or weaknesses are identified. The proposal represents a low risk.

- Good—Proposal exceeds the government's requirements. Strengths are identified that will benefit the government. No deficiencies exist. Weaknesses may exist but they are readily correctible or capable of being resolved without substantial impact on performance, cost, or schedule. The proposal represents moderately low risk.

- Satisfactory—Proposal meets the government's requirements. No deficiencies exist. Weaknesses may exist but they are readily correctable or capable of being resolved without substantial impact on performance, cost, or schedule. The proposal represents a moderate risk.

- Unacceptable—Proposal does not meet the government's requirements. Deficiencies exist and a major proposal revision is necessary to make it acceptable. The proposal represents a high risk.

M.4.1.2 Technical Factor Rating. The following rating criteria definitions will be used to assign an overall adjectival rating to the Technical Factor based upon ratings assigned to the Technical Subfactors:

- Excellent—An "Excellent" rating will be assigned to the Technical Factor for a proposal that receives an "Excellent" rating on all subfactors.

- Good—A "Good" rating will be assigned to the Technical Factor for a proposal that receives at least a "Good" rating on a majority of the subfactors. The remaining subfactors must be rated at least "Satisfactory".

- Satisfactory—A "Satisfactory" rating will be assigned to the Technical Factor for a proposal that receives at least a "Satisfactory" rating on all the subfactors.

- Unacceptable—An "Unacceptable" rating will be assigned to a proposal that receives an "Unacceptable" rating for any factor or subfactor. A proposal with an "Unacceptable" rating will receive no further consideration for award.

M.4.1.3 Technical Factor Evaluation Criteria. Each of the Evaluation Task Subfactors will be evaluated separately and will receive its own adjectival rating. An overall rating will be assigned to the Technical Factor based upon the rating of each Evaluation Task Subfactor in accordance with M.4.1.2. The Government will evaluate the subfactors based upon the following elements:

M.4.1.3.1 Technical Approach. The Government will evaluate the Offeror's proposal to determine the degree to which the Offeror's proposed approach will meet all the requirements of the prospective Evaluation Task. The approach will also be assessed to determine the degree to which the Offeror includes the planned sequence of steps to be taken, critical path, milestones, and interface and integration in order to meet the requirements of the Evaluation Task. The evaluation of the Offeror's technical approach will also determine the degree to which the approach is clear, logical, practical, efficient, cost effective, and complete. The Offeror's proposal will also be reviewed to assess the risks associated with the proposed approach and the proposed mitigation measures.

M.4.1.3.2 Resources Required. The Government will evaluate the Offeror's proposed staffing matrix to assess the adequacy of the staff proposed in terms of quantity, technical capability, and availability. The offeror's proposed personnel matrix will be reviewed to determine its completeness in terms of labor hours, showing the number of hours by labor category, skill level, and grade for each phase of work in the task, identification of any subcontractor labor used, and a discussion of all work to be performed by the subcontractor in the task; a travel schedule listing the number of trips and the number of personnel to respond to each Evaluation Task; and costs for labor, materials, equipment, subcontracts, and travel (actual costs shall not be included in the technical proposal). The list of facilities proposed by the Offeror will be reviewed to assess their suitability and availability to complete the requirement as outlined in its proposed technical approach. The Government will also review the list of proposed equipment and materials to determine if adequate or excessive resources are proposed.

M.4.1.3.3 Task Order Management and Schedule. The Government will evaluate the extent to which the Offeror's proposed project management tools will effectively track cost and performance for each Evaluation Task, to include scheduling and tracking multiple task elements under each Evaluation Task, deliverables, and the management of subcontractor involvement. The Government will also evaluate the Offeror's proposed approach on the following: adequate program visibility of each Evaluation Task at Senior Management Levels, timely reaction to problems (method of recognizing and reacting to problems), adequate schedule (method of reporting actual performance versus projected progress), and cost control (techniques for controlling expenditures) for soundness, completeness, and efficiency. The Offeror's organization plan will be reviewed to determine the extent to which it illustrates the interface between various elements of the organization during performance, including interface with any subcontractors and the Government. The Government will evaluate the degree to which the Offeror's proposal demonstrates an understanding of the sequence, complexity, and interrelationship of events in implementing the work of each Evaluation Task. The Government will evaluate the extent to which the proposed mitigation measures adequately address management and schedule risk.

M.4.1.4 Management Factor Evaluation Criteria. The Government will evaluate this factor based on the extent to which the Offeror has addressed the following:

M.4.1.4.1 Staffing Approach. The Government will evaluate the extent to which the Offeror's approach to staffing is sound and demonstrates an effective method for staffing retention capability and sustainment for in-house as well as subcontracted support. The Government will review the Offeror's Staffing Plan to determine the degree to which it can be effectively implemented to obtain the necessary resources through its identified recruiting sources. The Offeror's plan will be evaluated to determine the degree to which it demonstrates the ability to obtain qualified personnel of diverse disciplines to meet the requirements of the solicitation, as well as the degree to which the proposed staffing resources are highly knowledgeable in the disciplines related to the requirements stated in the solicitation.

M.4.1.4.2 Contract Management Approach. The Government will evaluate the Offeror's proposed contract management approach to determine the degree to which the Offeror has demonstrated capability to manage a potential diverse effort that may involve fragmentation of services, differences in the work requirements, the need for explicit work assignments and the ability to oversee the quality of the work to include that performed by subcontractor. The approach will be assessed to determine if the proposed coordination between prime and subcontractors has been addressed and whether it will allow for efficient operations. The proposal will also be reviewed to determine the soundness of the proposed approach to assemble and manage large staffs of diverse disciplines over short durations. The proposed Contract Management Approach will be evaluated to determine the degree to which it addresses how the Offeror intends to effectively manage multiple Task Orders, in addition to its application of lessons learned to implement quality support to maximize cost effectiveness and efficiency.

M.4.1.4.3 Facilities. The Government will evaluate the extent to which the Offeror has demonstrated that it has facilities suitable for the performance of engineering, fabrication, test, and laboratory-related requirements. The Government will also evaluate the extent to which the proposal's description of all facilities (engineering, fabrication, test, and laboratory) is adequate enough to determine suitability of the facilities. The Government will also evaluate the degree to which the Offeror has access to facilities as it relates to facilities that are owned, leased, and/or subcontracted.

M.4.1.5 Related Corporate Experience Factor. The Government will evaluate the extent to which the Offeror has demonstrated that it possesses the depth and breadth of corporate experience necessary to perform efforts relevant to engineering, research and technology, and program and integration support that are applicable to the CBRNE program.

M.4.2 Past Performance Factor. The Government will evaluate the Offeror's and its major subcontractors' current and past performance through a performance risk assessment group (PRAG). The Government's evaluation will describe the degree of confidence the Government has in the Offeror's likelihood of success in performing the solicitation's requirements and may use data provided by the Offeror and data obtained from other sources. The burden of providing thorough and complete past performance information rests with the Offeror. The degree of confidence will be measured in terms of the risk associated with an Offeror's past performance by assessing how well it satisfied the following, as a minimum:

M.4.2.1. Provided a quality product or service in terms of technical performance for compliance with previous contract requirements, accuracy of reports, and technical excellence.

M.4.2.2. Performed timely work in terms of meeting milestones, reliability, responsiveness to technical guidance, completing deliverables on time, and adhering to contract schedules, including contract administration.

M.4.2.3. Controlled costs in terms of performing within or below budget, using cost efficiencies, the relationship of negotiated costs to actuals, submitting of reasonably priced change proposals, and providing timely, current, accurate, and complete billing.

M.4.2.4. Conducted business relations in terms of providing effective management; demonstrating a cooperative and proactive behavior with the Contracting Officer, Contract Specialist, and the

Contracting Officer's Technical Representative; being responsive to inquiries, resolving problems, and satisfying the customer.

M.4.2.5 Rating System. The Past Performance Factor will receive one of the following adjectival ratings, which will define performance risk:

- Low—Offeror's past performance record provides essentially no doubt that the Offeror will successfully perform the required effort.

- Moderate—Offeror's past performance record provides some doubt that the Offeror will successfully perform the required effort.

- High—Offeror's past performance record provides significant doubt that the Offeror will successfully perform the required effort.

- Unknown—The Offeror has little or no relevant performance record identifiable; equates to an unknown risk having no positive or negative … evaluation significance.

M.4.3 Cost/Price Factor. The Government will evaluate the Offeror's proposed cost/price for Evaluation Tasks 1, 2, and 3 for realism, reasonableness, and completeness.

M.4.3.1 Basis for Cost/Price Evaluation.

M.4.3.1.1 Proposals for Evaluation Tasks 1, 2, and 3, priced on a cost-plus-fixed-fee basis, will be evaluated on the probable cost of performance. The probable cost of performance will be measured based on the anticipated performance cost and the proposed fee that will be earned. The probable cost of performance is defined as the Government's best estimate of contract cost resulting from the Offeror's proposal. Cost realism may involve an adjustment of the proposed cost and fee, whenever it is determined that the proposed cost does not reflect the probable cost of performance. Any adjusted cost will represent the Government's estimate of probable cost that will be used in the final evaluation to determine best value.

M.4.3.2 Cost Realism. The Government will evaluate the realism of each Offeror's proposed cost. The cost realism analysis will determine: (1) whether the estimated proposed costs are realistic for the Offeror's technical approach, (2) whether the Offeror has a clear understanding of the Government's requirements, (3) whether the Offeror adequately addresses any unique methods of performance, and (4) whether the Offeror's materials adequately support technical performance as proposed.

M.4.3.3 Cost Reasonableness. The Government will evaluate the Offeror's cost/price proposal to determine if costs are reasonable based on cost/price analysis as set forth in FAR 15.4.

M 4.3.4 Cost Completeness. The Government will evaluate cost completeness to determine if the costs are complete in terms of adequacy of the identification, estimation, and support of all relevant costs.

M 4.3.5 Total Cost/Price. In the final analysis for source selection purposes, the Government will add together the probable cost plus fixed fee for each Evaluation Task that the Offeror has proposed to arrive at a total evaluated cost/price for each Offeror.

Appendix III

DEFINITIONS

Acquisition. Acquiring goods or services by contract. In the federal government, acquisition begins with the identification of a government requirement that is expected to be satisfied through the contracting process.

Acquisition cycle. FAR Part 7 lists "milestones for the acquisition cycle" that begin with acquisition plan approval and end with contract award. However, this term is sometimes also used to describe events that begin with identification of the government requirement and end with contract award or delivery of the product or service.

Acquisition plan. A plan established to meet the FAR Subpart 7.1 requirement that agencies perform acquisition planning for all acquisitions. Agency regulations normally establish procurement cost thresholds beyond which written plans are mandatory and assign responsibility for preparing and approving acquisition plans.

Acquisition team. FAR 1.102 defines an acquisition team as consisting of "all participants in Government acquisition including not only representatives of the technical, supply, and procurement communities but also the customers they serve, and the contractors who provide the products and services."

Advisory multistep process. A variation on conventional source selection procedures. Potential competitors are asked for preliminary information, based on which the government informs them whether it considers them to be viable competitors for a planned source selection.

Alternative dispute resolution. This originally meant an alternative way to settle disputes between the contracting officer and a contractor, usually over a matter involving a particular contract. The idea was to have some sort of arbitration, or mediation, to avoid the time and expense of going to the federal courts or the boards of contract appeals. Later this term was also applied to situations involving protests wherein alternatives to going to the Comptroller General or the courts are pursued.

Architectural and Transportation Barriers Compliance Board (Access Board). An independent entity that formulates government positions involving access to buildings, equipment, and transportation for people with disabilities. The so-called Section 508 accessibility standards for electronic and information technology (Section 508 of the Rehabilitation Act Amendments of 1998) have had a particular impact on contracting.

Architect-engineer (architectural-engineering; AE) services. Professional services of an architectural or engineering nature that include:

- Services defined by state law as being AE services, or
- Certain contract AE services associated with real property (such as research, planning, development, design, construction, alteration, or repair), or
- Other professional services of an architectural or engineering nature or incidental services that members of the architectural or engineering professions might logically or justifiably perform.

Armed Services Board of Contract Appeals. A board established by the Secretary of Defense to which contractors may appeal a contracting officer's final decisions.

Best and final offer (BAFO). A term formerly used to establish a common cutoff date for receipt of proposal revisions. All offerors still being considered for award were requested to submit a best and final offer by a particular date and time. Now instead of being asked for a best and final offer, competing contractors are asked to submit a final proposal revision by a particular date and time. Some still informally refer to the final proposal revision as the BAFO.

Best and really final offer (BARFO). A derisive term referring to the past government practice of obtaining multiple BAFOs in order to obtain price reductions.

Best value. The expected outcome of an acquisition that, in the government's estimation, provides the greatest overall benefit in response to the requirement. FAR Part 15 specifically addresses the lowest price technically acceptable (LPTA) method of source selection and the tradeoff method of source selection as ways to obtain best value. Some believe that the *best value continuum* described below may also imply that price could be the only factor to consider in obtaining best value. However, this does not appear to be a widely held view.

Best value continuum. As described in FAR 15.101:

An agency can obtain best value in negotiated acquisitions by using any one or a combination of source selection approaches. In different types of acquisitions, the relative importance of cost or price may vary. For example, in acquisitions where the requirement is clearly definable and the risk of unsuccessful contract performance is minimal, cost or price may play a dominant role in source selection. The less definitive the requirement, the more development work required, or the greater the performance risk, the more technical or past performance considerations may play a dominant role in source selection.

Bidder. This term usually refers to a competing contractor when the procurement is conducted using sealed bidding as described in FAR Part 12. It is occasionally used in a broader sense to mean any entity competing for a government contract.

Blanket purchase agreement (BPA). According to FAR Part 13, a simplified method of fulfilling repetitive needs by establishing "charge accounts" with qualified sources of supply.

Broad agency announcements. Directed toward advancing the state of the art rather than focusing on specific hardware or system solutions, this method of solicitation for basic and applied research is not as constricting as conventional source selection and affords the government wide latitude in selecting sources (contractors).

Brooks Act. A government law pertaining to the selection of architects and engineers to provide services to the government.

Bundling. Consolidating two or more supply or service requirements that had previously been procured under separate contracts into a solicitation for a single contract that is likely to be rendered unsuitable for award to a small business because of its size or other characteristics.

Case law. A term often used to describe precedent established by the Comptroller General or the federal courts in opinions issued by these bodies. In this book, it refers to established precedents related to source selection.

Catalog prices. Prices regularly published by businesses or otherwise available for inspection by customers.

Central Contractor Registration. A government database containing information about government contractors and those aspiring to become government contractors. Generally, registration is needed in order for a contractor to do business with the government.

Certificate of competency (COC). As defined in FAR 19.001, a certificate issued by the Small Business Administration stating that the holder is "responsible" for the purpose of receiving and performing a particular contract. (See the definition of responsible.)

Clarifications. An exchange with competing contractors that may take place after receipt of proposals and before contract award when award is to be made without holding discussions. Clarifications give the contractor an opportunity to clarify proposal content but not to change the content beyond the correction of minor or clerical errors.

Combined solicitation/synopsis. A streamlining procedure described in FAR Subpart 12.6 that combines notifying industry of the issuance of a solicitation and the solicitation itself in one single *governmentwide point of entry* (GPE) entry.

Commercial item. The definition for commercial "item" as set forth in FAR 2.101 encompasses a wide variety of both items and services available or, in some cases, expected to be available, in the commercial marketplace.

Communications. Exchanges that may take place after receipt of proposals but before the establishment of a competitive range. FAR 15.306 describes situations in which communications may be held and situations in which communications must be held.

Competition in Contracting Act. A law passed in 1984 that was designed to enhance competition in the awarding of contracts by federal agencies. Its many provisions include the stay provisions or stay rules, defined later in this appendix, which have had a substantial impact on the source selection process.

Competitive range. A group of top-rated proposals, considering both cost and merit. The purpose of creating a competitive range is to limit the number of offerors with which the government will hold discussions. FAR Part 15 provides that a competitive range may be further reduced by the contracting officer for "purposes of efficiency."

Comptroller General. Head of the Government Accountability Office (GAO); appointed by the president for a 15-year term. Among many other responsibilities, the Comp Gen issues opinions in response to protests submitted to the GAO by disappointed bidders/offerors.

Contract clause. A term or condition in a solicitation or contract that applies after contract award and is made a part of the contract. FAR-required clauses are found in FAR Part 52.

Contracting office. As used in this book, an office that awards contracts and furnishes contracting services and expertise leading to the award of contracts.

Contracting officer. As used in this book, a person authorized to enter into, administer, and terminate contracts.

Contract specialist. A government employee in the contracting series who normally works under the technical supervision of a contracting officer. Unless a contract specialist is also a contracting officer, he or she may not sign contracts on behalf of the government.

Contract Management. As used in this book, a monthly magazine published by the National Contract Management Association (NCMA). The primary audience are people involved in federal government acquisition.

Cost analysis. As defined in FAR 1.404, "the review and evaluation of the separate cost elements and profit in an offeror's proposal ... and the application of judgment to determine how well the proposed costs represent what the cost of the contract should be, assuming reasonable economy and efficiency."

Cost realism analysis. As defined in FAR Part 15, "the process of independently reviewing and evaluating specific elements of each offeror's proposed cost estimate to determine whether the estimated proposed cost elements are realistic for the work to be performed." Cost realism analysis must be used for cost-reimbursement source selections and may be used on fixed-price contracts.

Court of Federal Claims. A U.S. court whose many responsibilities include the hearing of both preaward and postaward protests by disappointed bidders and other interested parties.

Customer. Sometimes used by contracting personnel to mean the organization, such as a program office, that submits a procurement package requesting that a solicitation be issued and the actual acquisition begin. Also used to refer to the people or organizations that will actually use the product or service being procured.

Debriefing. When contractors are eliminated from the competition for a source selection, they are entitled to a debriefing. Depending on the point in the process at which they have been eliminated from the competition, they can request either a preaward debriefing or a postaward debriefing. The content of the debriefings is prescribed by law and regulation and is fully described in FAR 15.505 and FAR 15.506.

Defense Acquisition University. A Department of Defense educational institution that provides for and encourages training in a wide range of acquisition-related matters.

Deficiency. As defined in FAR 15.001, "a material failure of a proposal to meet a Government requirement or a combination of significant weaknesses in a proposal that increases the risk of unsuccessful performance to an unacceptable level."

Delivery order. An order for supplies placed against an established indefinite delivery contract.

Design to cost. A process wherein design or development contractors are charged with designing/developing products that not only meet government technical requirements, but also will meet not-to-exceed cost/price goals when the products that are designed/developed are ultimately procured.

Discussions. Exchanges that take place with competing contractors in the competitive range. Discussions are held in order to obtain more favorable proposals. Discussions are normally concluded when final proposal revisions are requested.

Draft request for proposal (draft RFP). A draft document in RFP format that contains the government-proposed content for the actual RFP. It is sent to prospective contractors before issuance of the actual RFP so that contractor input can be obtained in designing (some call it *building*) the actual RFP.

Earned value management system. A project management system that tracks cost, schedule, and performance accomplishments against projections.

Evaluation factors. The factors shown in the solicitation that are used to discriminate between competing contractors in a best value acquisition.

Evaluation subfactors. Factors used to subdivide evaluation factors into smaller components.

Exchange. Any intercourse between the government and the private sector regarding a planned or ongoing negotiated acquisition. Exchanges include presolicitation exchanges, clarifications, communications, and discussions.

Excluded Parties List System (EPLS). An electronic web-based system that identifies parties excluded from receiving federal contracts and certain subcontracts.

Executive agency. Any agency in the executive branch of the U.S. government.

Executive order. An order issued by the president of the United States, the head of the executive branch of the government.

Expected value. A statistical tool helpful in decision-making. As used in this book, it is also a consensus probability assessment of projected success based on multiple individual assessments of past performance achievements.

Fair and reasonable price or cost. A cost or price is normally considered to be reasonable if it does not exceed that which would be incurred by a prudent person in the conduct of a competitive business. Proposed prices or costs are determined to be fair and reasonable through price analysis or cost analysis. In some cases, probable costs and life cycle costs may be taken into consideration.

Federal Acquisition Circular. A publication used to make interim changes to the Federal Acquisition Regulation.

Federal Acquisition Regulation (FAR). The primary regulation in the Federal Acquisition Regulation System. Other parts of the system are the agency regulations that implement or supplement the FAR.

Federal Acquisition Report. A publication of Management Concepts, Inc., that addresses news, trends, and other items of interest to those involved in government acquisition.

Federal Awardee Performance and Integrity System (FAPIIS). A government-operated system for use by government personnel wherein information about contractor performance is stored. It includes information from various other government databases.

Federally funded research and development centers. R&D activities sponsored under a broad charter by a government agency.

They receive 70 percent or more of their financial support from the government.

Federal Register. Published by the Office of the Federal Register, it is an official daily publication containing rules, proposed rules, and notices from federal agencies and organizations, as well as executive orders and other presidential documents.

FedBizOpps. See governmentwide point of entry.

General Services Agency (GSA). A government organization with an extensive range of acquisition-related responsibilities, including the execution and management of a wide variety of task order contracts for governmentwide use.

Government Accountability Office (GAO). An independent, nonpartisan agency that works for Congress. Often called the "congressional watchdog," GAO investigates how the federal government spends taxpayer dollars. Among its broad range of responsibilities, it accepts protests from disappointed bidders and issues opinions.

Governmentwide commercial purchase card. A purchase card used by the government that is similar in nature to a commercial credit card.

Governmentwide point of entry (GPE). As defined in FAR Part 2, the single point at which information about government business opportunities exceeding $25,000, including synopses of proposed actions, solicitations, and associated information, can be accessed electronically by the public. It is located at www.fedbizopps.gov or www.fbo.gov.

Head of the agency. Per FAR 2.101, "the Secretary, Attorney General, Administrator, Governor, Chairperson, or other chief official of an executive agency, unless otherwise indicated, including any deputy or assistant chief official of an executive agency."

Historically black college or university. Defined in the name itself, such an institution must be so determined by the Secretary of Education.

HUBZone. Historically underutilized business zone. Businesses within these geographic areas may be entitled to preferential treatment for specific procurements.

Imprest fund. A cash fund established to permit the government to make payment in cash for relatively small amounts.

Inherently governmental function. A function that should be performed by people in government, not contracted out to the public sector. A list of these functions is found in FAR Subpart 7.5. The list is not all-inclusive.

Integrated product team (IPT). A term used by some agencies to describe the team concept used in acquisition planning and execution. The Defense Acquisition University defines an integrated product team as "a multidisciplinary group of people who are collectively responsible for delivering a defined product or process."[1]

Interested party. As used in determining eligibility to submit a protest, this is an actual or prospective offeror whose direct economic interest would be affected by the award of a contract or failure to award a contract. In private-public competitions (see the definition for *outsourcing*), an interested party may be the party submitting an offer on behalf of the government. In the past, some organizations that were not competing contractors were occasionally determined to be interested parties under the "economic interest" protest criteria. For example, a trade association might have been determined to be an interested party if a significant part of its membership would have been affected by the award or nonaward of a contract.

Invitation for bid (IFB). The solicitation used in the sealed bidding method of procurement. In sealed bidding, only a price is submitted (unless bid samples are required), and award is made to the lowest bid price from a responsive and responsible bidder, provided that the price is determined to be fair and reasonable.

Item for negotiation (IFN). A proposal evaluation form used by some agencies to identify the need for exchanges with competing contractors.

Lowest-price technically acceptable (LPTA). One method of obtaining best value in source selection. Award is made to the competing contractor offering the lowest price among those with acceptable proposals.

Make or buy program. A contractor's plan for a contract wherein the contractor identifies the effort to be performed in-house and the supplies or services to be obtained through subcontracting or other purchase.

Market prices. Current prices in the open market that can be substantiated by competition or from sources independent of a particular offeror.

Market research. As defined in FAR Part 2, "collecting and analyzing information about capabilities within the market to satisfy agency needs."

Merit factors. A term often used to describe the non-cost factors in a source selection, Some prefer this term to *technical factors* because it encompasses both technical and management factors.

National Contract Management Association. An association of acquisition professionals from government and the private sector.

Negotiation. A method of procurement that differs from sealed bidding in that discussions are permitted and the award decision may be made based on factors other than price or cost alone. Also used in the FAR to describe "discussions" in a noncompetitive environment.

Non-cost factors. Proposal evaluation factors that are not cost or price factors.

Nondevelopmental item (NDI). Any previously developed item used or planned for use exclusively for governmental purposes by a federal agency, a state or local government, or a foreign government with which the United States has a mutual defense agreement. An NDI may also be any of those items with minor modifications of a type customarily available in the commercial marketplace.

North American Industry Classification System (NAICS). Used for classifying North American businesses for statistical purposes, the NAICS manual is used by the Small Business Administration and contracting agencies in defining what constitutes a small business for any particular acquisition of a supply or service.

Offeror. An entity that makes an offer to the government that may be accepted by the government, thus creating a contract. The term is most often used in connection with negotiated procurements, but in some cases it is used to refer to an entity submitting a bid under sealed bid procedures.

Office of Federal Procurement Policy. Part of the Office of Management and Budget, it provides overall direction for government procurement policies. Among many other pursuits, it issues best-practices guides and chairs the Federal Acquisition Regulation Council.

Office of Government Ethics (OGE). A separate agency within the executive branch of the federal government that is responsible for establishing executive branch policies regarding conflicts of interest and other related ethical matters.

Office of Management and Budget (OMB). A cabinet-level office within the Executive Office of the President that was formerly known as the Bureau of the Budget. It assists in preparing the federal budget and oversees the manner in which budgeted funds are expended. It issues circulars and policy letters to federal agencies with a broad range of management guidance, such as OMB Circular A-76, which discusses those functions that are inherently governmental.

Oral presentation. A presentation given to government evaluators in a manner directed by the provisions of a solicitation. Oral presentations may substitute for or augment written information from competing contractors.

Outsourcing. As used in this book, a term that describes competitions held between the government and private contractors to determine if work that is not of an inherently governmental nature should be done by government employees or by the private sector.

Past performance. A FAR-required proposal evaluation factor that addresses how well competing contractors have performed on past contracts. The contracting officer may waive the use of this factor if he or she appropriately documents the contract file to explain why past performance is not being considered.

Past Performance Information Retrieval System (PPIRS). An electronic database of contractor past performance information.

Past performance questionnaire. An agency-prescribed form used by evaluators in obtaining past performance information from contractor-furnished points of contact or from other sources.

Performance risk assessment group (PRAG). A group established to evaluate the past performance of competing contractors and to perform a risk assessment of probable future performance based on the record of past performance.

Performance work statement. A performance-based require-ments document used in solicitations and contracts. See the defi-nition for *statement of work.*

Postaward notification. A notification to all competing contractors (except those that have already received a preaward notification) that had a proposal in the competitive range but were not selected for award. FAR 15.503 prescribes the content of the notification.

Preaward notification. The contracting officer notifies competing contractors when their proposals are excluded from the competitive range or otherwise eliminated from the competition. Preaward notification of all competing offerors is also required prior to the award of contracts that have been set aside for certain socioeconomic purposes or where a certain segment of the private sector receives a benefit for socioeconomic purposes. FAR 15.503 prescribes the content of these notifications.

Precedent. As used in this book, guidance established when the Comptroller General or the federal courts issue opinions that interpret the meaning of source selection laws and regulations and judge the appropriateness of the manner in which these laws and regulations were applied.

Preproposal conference. A conference for competing contractors that is conducted by the government after a solicitation has been issued but before proposals are due. The government reviews the requirements of the solicitation and answers any questions com-peting contractors may have. Some agencies also use this term to describe a conference held after a draft RFP has been issued but before the actual RFP is made available.

Presolicitation conference. A conference for potential offerors that is held by the government before a solicitation is issued to obtain input from the private sector. Where appropriate, this feed-back may be reflected in the solicitation.

Presolicitation exchange. Any communication that is held with prospective contractors before a solicitation is issued.

Procuring contracting officer (PCO). A duly appointed contracting officer whose duties include soliciting offers and awarding contracts. Sometimes this individual may be referred to as the principal contracting officer.

Proposal evaluation board. A term used by some agencies to describe those who evaluate proposals from competing contractors.

Proposal revision. A revision of a contractor-submitted proposal. Once the closing date for receipt of proposals has passed, proposals may be revised only when permitted or directed by the contracting officer.

Price analysis. The process of examining and evaluating a proposed price without evaluating the separate cost elements and profit that are reflected in the price. It is used to determine if prices received are fair and reasonable. The government compares a proposed price with such things as other prices paid for the same or similar products or services in the past, prices offered or bid by competitors, catalog prices, government estimates, or other benchmarks.

Probable cost. A projected cost determined by cost realism analysis and used to adjust contractor-proposed costs to reflect what evaluators believe the actual costs will be. Probable costs are used instead of proposed costs to determine the best value when the government is contemplating a cost-reimbursement contract. Probable costs may also be used when conducting risk assessments and responsibility determinations for fixed-price contracts.

Procurement administrative lead time (PALT). Generally, the time from receipt of an acceptable procurement request at the government contracting office until the time a contract award is made.

Program office. As used in this publication, the government office responsible for a program requirement that will be met through the use of a contract.

Program officer. As used in this publication, the individual that has been assigned primary responsibility for a program requirement that will be met through the use of a contract.

Proposals. Contractor submissions in response to a request for proposal.

Proposal evaluation board (PEB). A term used by some agencies to describe a group established to evaluate the proposals of competing contractors.

Proposal revision. A change to a proposal made by a competing contractor. The contracting officer may request or allow competing contractors to submit changes/revisions to their proposals during the discussion phase of source selection. All competing contractors still being considered at the conclusion of discussions must be given an opportunity to submit final proposal revisions.

Protest. As defined in FAR Part 33, a written objection by an interested party to any of the following:

- A solicitation or other request by an agency for offers for a contract for the procurement of property or services
- The cancellation of the solicitation or other request
- An award or proposed award of the contract
- A termination or cancellation of an award of the contract, if the written objection contains an allegation that the termination or cancellation is based in whole or in part on improprieties concerning the award of the contract.

Purchase card. See *Governmentwide purchase card.*

Purchase Order. FAR Part 2 defines a government purchase order as an offer by the government to buy a supply or service under specified terms and conditions.

Quality. An attribute that can be determined through factors such as an offeror's past performance, compliance with solicitation requirements, technical excellence, management capability, personnel qualifications, and prior experience. According to FAR 15.304, quality must be addressed in every source selection.

Quote. A submission from a contractor in response to a request for quotation (RFQ).

Quoter. An entity that submits a quote to the government, rather than submitting an offer. This means that the government must subsequently make an offer to buy that is accepted by the quoter, either by signature or by performance.

Rating methodology. The manner in which the evaluation factors and subfactors in proposals are scored or rated. The most common rating methods are numerical scores, adjectival ratings, and color ratings.

Rating proposals. Categorizing the relative quality of proposals to help determine best value. For example, one or more proposals could be categorized as "outstanding," while others might be deemed "acceptable" or "marginal."

Responsible/responsibility. To obtain a contract, a contractor must be found to be responsible by the contracting officer. This determination of responsibility is based upon an assessment of the contractor's ability to perform and an assessment of the contractor's will to perform, as demonstrated by past performance.

Responsive/responsiveness. To obtain a contract, a contractor must be deemed to be responsive. This means that the contractor must comply with solicitation instructions and must not take exception to the government's requirements as described in the solicitation.

Representations and certifications. Solicitation provisions require that the contractor certify or represent various matters that may pertain to its eligibility to receive an award or that assist the government in obtaining business-related statistics. For example, a contractor could represent whether it is a woman-owned small business. FAR 4.1201 requires contractors to complete electronic annual certifications and representations in conjunction with registration in the Central Contractor Registration (CCR) database.

Request for information (RFI). A document that is used to obtain private-sector input for planning purposes. Unless specified by individual agencies, there is no required format for RFIs.

Request for proposal (RFP). The solicitation normally used for negotiated procurements under FAR Part 15, including best value source selections.

Request for quotation (RFQ). The solicitation often used for simplified acquisitions (as described in FAR Part 13) and sometimes used for competition between task order contract holders.

Requirements document. The document that tells contractors what the government will require them to do under the contract. The various types of requirements documents include purchase descriptions, statements of work, and statements of objectives.

Reverse auctioning. A procurement technique whereby bidders' prices are disclosed to other bidders, who may then offer a lower price. Reverse auctioning is most typically used in government for information-technology–related procurements such as those involving personal computers and monitors.

Sample-itis. A term used in this book to refer to the practice of preparing new solicitations by copying from previous solicitations rather than tailoring the solicitation to the requirement at hand.

Scoring proposals. See the definition for *rating proposals*. These terms are generally synonymous.

Service-disabled veteran-owned small business concern. A small business for which at least 51 percent of the ownership is held by one or more veterans with a disability that is service-connected, and the daily operations are controlled by those veterans. If the veteran(s) have permanent and severe disability, daily business operations can be controlled by a spouse or permanent caregiver.

Should cost. A method of cost analysis in which the government evaluates the economy and efficiency of the contractor's operations, rather than assuming that its actual or historical costs reflect efficient and economical operation.

Significant weakness. As defined in FAR 15.001, a proposal flaw that appreciably increases the risk of unsuccessful performance.

Simplified acquisition. A procurement executed using the provisions of FAR Part 12.

Simplified acquisition thresholds. The dollar limitations for use of FAR Part 12 procedures. FAR 2.101 currently gives the following definition:

> 'Simplified acquisition threshold' means $150,000, except for acquisitions of supplies or services that, as determined by the head of the agency, are to be used to support a contingency operation or to facilitate defense against or recovery from nuclear, biological, chemical, or radiological attack (41 U.S.C. 428a), the term means—

(1) $300,000 for any contract to be awarded and performed, or purchase to be made, inside the United States; and

(2) $1 million for any contract to be awarded and performed, or purchase to be made, outside the United States.

Additionally there are test programs establishing higher thresholds for certain commercial items.

Site visit. When work under a contemplated contract is to be performed at a location other than contractor or subcontractor locations (for example, if work is to be performed at a government location), competing contractors may be invited to visit the site before submitting proposals.

Small business. A business concern that is independently owned and operated, is not dominant in the field of operation in which it is bidding on a government contract, and meets size standards established by the Small Business Administration (SBA). The SBA publishes these standards in the *North American Industry Classification System Manual (NAICS Manual).*

Small Business Administration (SBA). According to FAR 19.210, the SBA counsels and assists small business concerns and helps contracting personnel ensure that small business concerns, including small disadvantaged businesses, veteran-owned businesses, businesses located in HUBZones, and others, receive a a fair proportion of contracts for supplies and services.

Small business size standards. Standards established by the Small Business Administration and published in the *NAICS Manual.* Different standards exist for different segments of industry.

Small disadvantaged business. A small business concern that is owned by one or more "disadvantaged individuals."

A disadvantaged individual is a person who is socially or economically disadvantaged by virtue of his or her identification with a particular group. For example, some Asian Americans, African Americans, or Native Americans can be found to be disadvantaged. Normally, small disadvantaged business concerns seek certification from the Small Business Administration to receive preferential treatment. See FAR 2.101 for more details.

Solicitation. Any request inviting potential contractors to submit a bid, offer, or quotation. Solicitations under sealed bid procedures are called invitations for bid (IFBs). Solicitations under negotiated procedures are normally requests for proposals (RFPs). Solicitations under simplified acquisition procedures require the submission of either a quote or an offer. Often, a request for quotation (RFQ) is used for simplified acquisitions.

Solicitation provision. A provision of a solicitation that pertains to the solicitation and not to any resultant contract. One example is the Instructions to Offerors—Competitive Acquisitions provision that is found in FAR Part 52 and used in competitive negotiated procurements.

Source selection advisory council (SSAC). A group established to oversee the operations of proposal evaluation groups (such as the SSEB) and to advise the source selection authority on matters such as establishing the competitive range and selecting a source.

Source selection authority (SSA). A government employee given the responsibility to select the source or sources whose proposal(s) represents the best value for the government and to perform other functions specified in FAR Part 15. The contracting officer acts as the SSA unless the agency head appoints another person for a specific acquisition or group of acquisitions

Source selection decision. An independent decision made by the source selection authority as to which contractor(s) will receive a contract as a result of conducting a particular source selection process. The rationale for the decision must be clearly documented.

Source selection evaluation board (SSEB). A board established to evaluate proposals from competing contractors.

Source selection information. Information that must be protected under the Procurement Integrity Act.

Source selection official (SSO). Sometimes used as a synonym for the source selection authority. It may also be used to refer to any official involved in the source selection process.

Source selection plan (SSP). A term used by many agencies to describe the document that contains particulars about the planned process to obtain best value, including the overall source selection strategy. Agency regulations normally assign responsibility for plan preparation and plan approval.

Statement of objectives (SOO). A government-prepared requirements document incorporated into the solicitation that states overall performance objectives. It is used in solicitations in which the government intends to provide the maximum flexibility for each offeror to propose an innovative approach to meeting the government's requirements.

Statement of work (SOW). A requirements document that addresses what a contractor is supposed to accomplish under the contract. It may be design-based—the government tells the contractor how to do the work—or performance based—the government simply explains the performance required rather than giving how-to instructions. When the requirements document (statement of work) is performance-based, it is normally referred to as a *performance work statement* rather than a statement of work.

Stay provisions/stay rules. Portions of the Competition in Contracting Act (CICA) that provide that an agency must (except under very limited circumstances) delay award if it receives a protest before award or must suspend contract performance if it receives a protest after award. In the latter case, the stay provisions apply only if the protest was received within 10 days after the contract was awarded or within five days after a debriefing date offered to the protestor.

Streamlined solicitation for commercial items. A procedure that allows for combining the synopsis and the solicitation into one entry at the GPE. See FAR Subpart 12.6 for instructions for using the procedure.

Subfactors. Evaluation factors in a government solicitation may be divided into subfactors to emphasize certain aspects of the factors or to facilitate proposal preparation and evaluation.

Synopsis. A brief description of a proposed contract action or award. With some exceptions, the government is required to publicize proposed contract actions of $25,000 or more by synopsizing them in the GPE. With certain exceptions, awards of $25,000 or more also must be synopsized in the GPE.

Task order. A delivery order under a task order contract.

Task order contract. An indefinite delivery contract for services. Often task order contracts are indefinite delivery/indefinite quantity contracts with a minimum and a maximum amount.

Technical analysis. An analysis of proposal costs by people with specialized engineering, science, or management skills to determine if the labor hours, categories of labor, material, scrap rates, and other such elements in cost proposals are reasonable.

Technical evaluation team (TET) or technical evaluation panel (TEP). A group established to evaluate the non-cost aspects of proposals.

Technical factors. A term sometimes used to refer to the non-cost factors in a best value source selection. Some agencies make a distinction between technical factors and management factors when using this term; others do not.

Technical personnel. A term generally used in the FAR to describe individuals on the acquisition team who are not contracting personnel, users, supply personnel, or customers. The term is most often used to describe scientific, engineering and other personnel whose occupations deal with the sciences.

Third-party draft. An agency bank draft, similar to a private individual's check, that is used to pay for supplies or services.

Total quality management (TQM). A holistic management approach that seeks to continually improve processes. W. Edwards Deming, considered a leading proponent of TQM, advocated that businesses "end the practice of awarding business on the basis of price tag." Instead, he urged buyers and sellers to build long-term relationships, something that is difficult to maintain in government contracting.

Tradeoff. One method of obtaining best value in source selection. In a tradeoff acquisition, cost or price and non-cost factors are considered in an integrated assessment, and the government may accept other than the lowest-priced proposal.

Value analysis. A technique used as a part of price or cost analysis to determine the value of a cost or service that may include factors other than just the proposed cost or price—for example, life cycle costs such as the costs of operation and disposal.

Veteran-owned small business. A small business that is majority owned (51 percent or more) by veterans and whose management and daily operations are controlled by one or more veterans.

Weakness. As defined in FAR 15.001, a flaw in a proposal that increases the risk of unsuccessful contract performance.

Where in Federal Contracting? (WIFCON). A privately run website offering a wide variety of information of interest to the acquisition professional.

Woman-owned small business. A small business that is majority owned (51 percent or more) by one or more women and whose management and daily operations are controlled by one or more women.

Note

1. Defense Acquisition University, Acquisition Community Connection, "Integrated Program Teams." Online at https://acc.dau.mil/Community-Browser.aspx?id=24675&eid=24691&lang=en-US (accessed October 22, 2010).

Appendix IV

ADDITIONAL RESOURCES

A number of additional acquisition resources, including education and training resources, publications, and websites are listed below, The list is not all-inclusive and is not intended as an endorsement of the resources.

EDUCATION AND TRAINING

In addition to the education and training resources listed here, many junior colleges and other academic institutions located near major government contracting offices offer a variety of acquisition training. Many government agencies also offer in-house training.

Acquisition Solutions
Arlington, Virginia
www.acqsolinc.com

American Graduate University
Covina, California
www.agu.edu

Atlantic Management Center Inc.
Falls Church, Virginia
www.amciweb.com

Bellevue University
Bellevue, Nebraska
www.bellevue.com/acquistion

Bottomline Concepts LLC
Madison, Alabama
www.bottomlineconcepts.com

Centre Consulting
Vienna, Virginia
www.centreconsult.com

Certified Contracting Solutions
Louisville, Colorado
www.certifiedsolutions.com

Comprehensive Language Center
Arlington, Virginia
www.comprehensivelc.com

Defense Acquisition University
Fort Belvoir, Virginia
www.dau.mil

ESI International
Arlington, Virginia
www.esi-intl.com

FedBid, Inc.
Vienna, Virginia
www.fedbid.com

Federal Acquisition Institute
Fort Belvoir, Virginia
www.fai.gov

Federal Contracts Training Center
Riverwoods, Illinois
www.FCTCenter.com

Federal Market Group
Warrenton, Virginia
www.gbs-llc.com

Federal Publications Seminars
Washington, DC
www.fedpubseminars.com

Florida Institute of Technology
Melbourne, Florida
www.fit.edu

General Services Administration
Washington, DC
www.gsa.gov

George Washington University
Washington, DC
www.gwu.edu

Graduate School
Washington, DC
www.graduateschool.edu

Management Concepts, Inc.
Vienna, Virginia
www.managementconcepts.com

National Contract Management Association
Ashburn, Virginia
www.ncmahq.org

Next Level Purchasing
Moon Township, Pennsylvania
www.nextlevelpurchasing.com

Northwest Procurement Institute, Inc.
Edmonds, Washington
www.npi-training.com

Saint Louis University
Saint Louis, Missouri
www.slu.edu

University of California—Irvine Extension
Irvine, California
http://extension.uci.edu/ncma

University of Tennessee—Knoxville
Knoxville, Tennessee
http://thecenter.utk.edu

University of Virginia
Charlottesville, Virginia
www.scps.virginia.edu/

VA Acquisition Academy
Frederick, Maryland
www.acquisitionacademy.va/gov

Villanova University Online
Tampa, Florida
www.villanovaU.com/ncma

PUBLICATIONS

A number of publications contain news items, legal precedents, and analyses pertinent to the source selection process. (Many of these publications require a paid subscription.)

AT&L Magazine
www.dau.mil

Bid Protest Weekly
www.generalcounsellaw.com

Briefing Papers
http://west.thomson.com

Contract Management
www.ncmahq.org

Federal Acquisition Report
www.managmentconcepts.com

Federal Computer Week
www.fcw.com/

Federal Times
www.federaltimes.com

Government Computer News
www.gcn.com

The Government Contractor
http://west.thomson.com

Government Executive
www.govexec.com

The Nash and Cibinic Report
http://west.thomson.com

WEBSITES

A number of websites can help keep contracting professionals up to date on the rules and precedents relating to source selection. In addition to the valuable content they provide, some websites offer links to more specialized source selection information—for example, links to agency source selection manuals.

ACQUipedia
https://acquipedia.dau.mil

Acquisition Central
www.acquisition.gov

Bid Protest Weekly
www.generalcounsellaw.com

Court of Federal Claims (Decisions)
http://www.uscfc.uscourts.gov/opinions_decisions_general/
Published

Defense Acquisition Guidebook
https://dag.dau.mil

Electronic Guide to NIH Acquisition
http://acq-map.od.nih.gov

Federal Acquisition Institute
www.fai.gov

Government Executive
www.govexec.com

Government Accountability Office (Protest Opinions/Reports)
www.gao.gov

National Contract Management Association
www.ncma.org

Office of Federal Procurement Policy
www.whitehouse.gov/omb/procurement

Sell2USGov
www.canadainternational.gc.ca/sell2usgov

USA.gov
www.usa.gov

Where In Federal Contracting (WIFCON)
www.wifcon.com

INDEX

The COR/COTR Answer Book, Second Edition

Bob Boyd

Today, many CORs, COTRs, and other members of the acquisition team are taking on additional responsibilities from their contracting officers—including overseeing and monitoring contracts. If you are facing these new challenges, your knowledge of contracting issues is critical to your success. *The COR/COTR Answer Book, Second Edition,* provides the practical guidance you need to ensure each contract's successful completion. Written in an easy-to-use Q&A style, this comprehensive guide includes answers to 460 common questions on how to monitor and oversee contracts.

ISBN 978-1-56726-215-5 ■ Product Code B155 ■ 405 pages

Federal Acquisition ActionPacks

Federal Acquisition ActionPacks are designed for busy professionals who need to get a working knowledge of government contracting quickly—without a lot of extraneous detail. This ten-book set covers all phases of the acquisition process, grounds you firmly in each topic area, and outlines practical methods for success, from contracting basics to the latest techniques for improving performance.

Each spiral-bound book contains approximately 160 pages of quick-reading information—simple statements, bulleted lists, questions and answers, charts and graphs, and more. Each topic's most important information is distilled to its essence, arranged graphically for easy comprehension and retention, and presented in a user-friendly format designed for quick look-up.

Or order the single titles that are most important to your role in the contracting process. Either way, this is the most effective, affordable way for both buyers and sellers to get a broad-based understanding of government contracting—and proven tools for success.

Earned Value Management	**Best-Value Source Selection**
Gregory A. Garrett	Philip E. Salmeri
ISBN 978-1-56726-188-2 ■ Product Code B882	ISBN 978-1-56726-193-6 ■ Product Code B936
173 Pages	178 Pages
Performance-Based Contracting	**Government Contract Law Basics**
Gregory A. Garrett	Thomas G. Reid
ISBN 978-1-56726-189-9 ■ Product Code B899	ISBN 978-1-56726-194-3 ■ Product Code B943
153 Pages	175 Pages
Cost Estimating and Pricing	**Government Contract Basics**
Gregory A. Garrett	Rene G. Rendon
ISBN 978-1-56726-190-5 ■ Product Code B905	ISBN 978-1-56726-195-0 ■ Product Code B950
161 Pages	176 Pages
Contract Administration and Closeout	**Performance Work Statements**
Gregory A. Garrett	Philip E. Salmeri
ISBN 978-1-56726-191-2 ■ Product Code B912	ISBN 978-1-56726-196-7 ■ Product Code B967
153 Pages	151 Pages
Contract Formation	**Contract Terminations**
Gregory A. Garrett and William C. Pursch	Thomas G. Reid
ISBN 978-1-56726-192-9 ■ Product Code B929	ISBN 978-1-56726-197-4 ■ Product Code B974
163 Pages	166 Pages